NATIONAL SELF-IMAGES AND REGIONAL IDENTITIES IN RUSSIA

*In memory of my Grandmother
The wisest person I have ever known*

National Self-Images and Regional Identities in Russia

BO PETERSSON
Lund University

LONDON AND NEW YORK

First published 2001 by Ashgate Publishing

Reissued 2018 by Routledge
2 Park Square, Milton Park, Abingdon, Oxon OX14 4RN
711 Third Avenue, New York, NY 10017, USA

Routledge is an imprint of the Taylor & Francis Group, an informa business

Copyright © Bo Petersson 2001

All rights reserved. No part of this book may be reprinted or reproduced or utilised in any form or by any electronic, mechanical, or other means, now known or hereafter invented, including photocopying and recording, or in any information storage or retrieval system, without permission in writing from the publishers.

Notice:
Product or corporate names may be trademarks or registered trademarks, and are used only for identification and explanation without intent to infringe.

Publisher's Note
The publisher has gone to great lengths to ensure the quality of this reprint but points out that some imperfections in the original copies may be apparent.

Disclaimer
The publisher has made every effort to trace copyright holders and welcomes correspondence from those they have been unable to contact.

A Library of Congress record exists under LC control number: 2001086246

ISBN 13: 978-1-138-73323-7 (hbk)
ISBN 13: 978-1-138-73321-3 (pbk)
ISBN 13: 978-1-315-18776-1 (ebk)

Contents

List of Tables vi
List of Abbreviations and Acronyms vii
Acknowledgements viii

Introduction 1

1 Points of Departure 6

2 Setting the Scene 45

3 The Past Dimension 59

4 The External Dimension 93

5 The External/Internal Dimension 120

6 The Internal Dimension 140

7 Concluding Remarks 186

Bibliography 197
Interviewee Profiles 206
Appendix A: List of Questions 209
Index 210

List of Tables

Table 3.1	Pride of the national past by region	62
Table 3.2	Pride of the national past by political affiliation	66
Table 3.3	Pride of the national past by age group	67
Table 3.4	Shameful aspects of the national past by region	82
Table 3.5	Shameful aspects of the national past by political affiliation	86
Table 3.6	Shameful aspects of the national past by age group	88
Table 4.1	Overall assessments of the prevalence of external threats	94
Table 4.2	Overall assessments of the prevalence of internal threats	94
Table 4.3	Overall assessments of most desired international partners	104
Table 4.4	Most desired international partners by region	105
Table 5.1	Overall assessments of Russia's right to influence foreign countries	127
Table 5.2	Assessment of CIS integration projects by region	130
Table 5.3	**Assessment of CIS integration projects by political affiliation**	131
Table 5.4	Assessment of the existence of a specific Russian mission in world politics	136
Table 6.1	Comparison between the concepts 'Russia' and 'the Russian Federation'	142
Table 6.2	Assessments of democracy in Russia	146
Table 6.3	Assessments of democracy in Russia by age groups	148
Table 6.4	Assessments of democracy in Russia by political affiliation	148
Table 6.5	Assessments of democracy in Russia by region	150
Table 6.6	Overall assessments of most prevalent domestic threats	162
Table 6.7	Assessment of the risks of disintegration of Russia	164
Table 6.8	Assessments of most prevalent domestic threats (KPRF)	169

List of Abbreviations and Acronyms

CIS	Commonwealth of Independent States
DVR	Democratic Choice of Russia
EU	European Union
Gulag	Head Administration of Camps
KGB	Committee of State Security
Kh	Khabarovsk
KPRF	Communist Party of the Russian Federation
KPSS	Communist Party of the Soviet Union
LDPR	Liberal Democratic Party of Russia
Nato	North Atlantic Treaty Organisation
NDR	Our Home is Russia
NIS	Newly Independent States
OSCE	Organisation of Security and Cooperation in Europe
P	Perm
RR	Russian Regions
SD	State Duma
Spb	St. Petersburg
UN	United Nations
US	United States
V	Volgograd
VR	Russia's Choice

Acknowledgements

To write an academic book is quite different from experiencing the loneliness of a long distance runner. Of course, the writer is the one who has to do the actual pressing of the keys on a keyboard, but there is so much more to authorship than the admittedly lonely hours spent in front of a computer. Had I not had the benefit of intellectually rewarding exchanges of views, discussions and get-togethers, had I not been unselfishly assisted when abroad, and had I not been able to enjoy the hospitality of old and newly-found friends, what a pathetic book this would have been! Numerous friends, colleagues and acquaintances have contributed to improving and enriching this monograph. I wish to thank them all, even though but a few can be mentioned below.

The Swedish Council for Research in the Humanities and Social Sciences (HSFR) has been the main financial benefactor of the three-year project – 'Russian Self-Images and Foreign Policy Orientations in a Time of Change' – which underlies this book. In this enterprise, Lotta Wagnsson has been a principal intellectual sparring partner. We have been working together on the HSFR project, and I have greatly enjoyed our meeting of minds. Likewise, it has been a pleasure to have Johan Matz onboard the HSFR project, and he, too, has provided valuable input to my work.

My inner circle has furthermore consisted of Björn Badersten, Christian Fernández, Catarina Kinnvall and Barbara Törnquist-Plewa, all at Lund University. They have all read and commented drafts at different stages of completion, for which I am truly grateful. I am also indebted to those dear friends and colleagues who agreed to read the next-to-final version of the manuscript, even though it certainly meant using summer days that could have been used for better purposes. Theirs were fresh pairs of eyes and they all made immensely important suggestions for improvements to the manuscript. So, great words of thanks go to Farid Abbaszadegan, Christina Danielsson, Klas-Göran Karlsson, Per Månson, Inger Sjunnesson, Lars Göran Stenelo and Carolina Vendil.

Moreover, I benefited greatly from comments on early drafts offered by Tom Bryder, Kristian Gerner, Ulf Hedetoft, Magnus Jerneck, Christer Jönsson, Kerstin Nyström, Alexa Robertson and Ingvar Svanberg. Also,

Ekströmer, Viktor Mokhov, Oksana Oracheva, Ludmila Popkova, Helena Rytövuori-Apunen, and Elena Vinogradova all guided me on to useful texts previously unknown to me. I would also like to express my appreciation to Olga Filippova, Jan Leijonhielm and Ray Taras for their general support and encouragement. And Annika Hughes has, besides offering useful comments to the text, made valiant efforts to disentangle the somewhat unorthodox linguistic structures I have at times tried to apply.

Without the support of a great number of people in the field, the book would not have been feasible. Most of all, I would like to express my gratitude to those 110 Russian men and women who selflessly set aside time to allow themselves to be interviewed. Furthermore, the cooperation with Oksana Oracheva was tremendously important in the opening stages. Not only did she make the practical arrangements for my visit to Perm, but she was also a much needed intellectual sounding board for the make-up of the pilot study and the final construction of the questionnaire. I would also like to thank Viktor Mokhov, Oleg Podvintsev and his family, as well as Ljuba Fadeeva, for their great hospitality during my stay in Perm. Similarly, invaluable practical arrangements were made on my behalf in the other regional centres visited during my work. For this I would like to thank Natalya Akkusina, Elina Demenkova, Vladimir Gel'man and Vladimir Ugryumov regarding St. Petersburg; Aleksandr Maksimov, Andrei Rogozhin and Anna Zeleznova in Volgograd; and Tatyana Tolkacheva and Svetlana Zamanskaya in Khabarovsk. Natalya Akkusina provided me with welcome linguistic back-up in connection with my interviews in St. Petersburg, as did Alyona Efimova in Volgograd.

Most of the interviews with State Duma deputies were conducted on my behalf in Moscow by Maria Tisell, and by Sofia and Martin Uggla. I am greatly appreciative of this. Maria Tisell also wrote the transcripts of her interviews, while Askar Sarsenov with great efficiency and precision took care of the interviews conducted by Sofia and Martin. I made a number of interviews with State Duma deputies in connection with a seminar arranged by SIPU International in Stockholm. I would like to express my appreciation to Bo Synnerholm and Hans Norgren at SIPU International for allowing me to use this opportunity, as well as to Katarina Salén and Jocke Emthén for, through their practical arrangements, greatly facilitating the interviews. Also, heart-warming hospitality was extended to me by my dear friends Anila and Anders Blixt in connection with the interviews in Stockholm.

Apart from the all-important financial backing I received from the HSFR, generous contributions were also given by the Swedish Defence Research Establishment (FOA); the International Office at Lund University; the Wenner-Gren Foundation; and Rector Nils Stjernquist's Research Fund. All this support is hereby gratefully acknowledged.

Bo Petersson,
Lund,
August 2000

Introduction

This book deals with the question of what, to the minds of Russian politicians of the late 1990s, the country they live in is, and what it ought to be. In other words, it is a study of national self-images in Russia. These images pertain to the Russian state polity and encompass cognitive and affective strands regarding Russia's past, its friends and foes externally and internally, and Russia's role in the international arena, as well as key issues related to internal developments. Altogether, this provides for a picture of the political climate of a turbulent period in recent Russian history. The study will also suggest likely internal courses of development within this vast state.

National self-images could be described as partial representations of national identity. Indeed, this book serves to assess to what extent a new sense of national identity emerged in Russia during the decade after the dissolution of the Soviet Union. I argue in this book that the development of a civic national identity, centred around the belonging to the state polity and not to an ethnic community, is the only viable option to try to prevent further disintegration and bring about much needed internal stability and cohesion in the country. As I will venture to show, however, there are formidable obstacles to be overcome. For instance, it is quite clear that certain ethnically related lines of division, as well as tensions between the regions and the Moscow centre, may hamper the development of the sense of community that is so badly needed for the evolvement of a national identity defined within more inclusionary parameters.

Within the project, interviews have been undertaken with parliamentarians in Moscow, as well as with regional politicians, primarily parliamentarians, in St. Petersburg, Volgograd, Khabarovsk and Perm. In such a manner, insights were gained about similarities and differences between central and regional levels of political life and, to some extent, between different age groups and representatives of various political affiliations. All in all, 110 interviews were conducted between September 1997 and April 1999. The findings which have emerged from these interviews provide a symptom of sorts regarding prevailing tensions and sources of friction between the federal centre and the regions in Yeltsin's Russia. They testify to the widespread phenomenon of scapegoating and finger-pointing towards perceived internal enemies which is so familiar in countries undergoing turbulent political and economic upheaval. And finally, they constitute indices of what seemed to be lacking by way of intra-state cohesion and community of feeling within the Russian Federation at the time the interviews took place. To put it somewhat differently, the basic rationale of this book has been to assess prevailing national self-images among regional parliamentarians in Russia, in order to gauge the strength of any existing intra-federational glue. Also, my attention has been devoted to the endeavour of identifying the nature and quality of such a glue.

As I undertake the final amendments and corrections to this volume, we have reached the end of the first half of the year 2000. Thus, the Russian Federation is at this point in time drawing closer to the first full decade of its post-Soviet statehood. Furthermore, during the time I have been working on this book, the period of incumbency of the Federation's first president, Boris Yeltsin, has reached its end. The empirical findings presented in the book all concern the final three years of his presidency. Those were indeed tumultuous and uncertain years, even though they were so to a lesser extent than the years of Yeltsin's first tenure as president. To refresh the memories of my readers, Boris Yeltsin was elected president of the Russian Federative Republic in June 1991, at a time when the Soviet Union still was in existence and Mikhail Gorbachev tried to cling on to the reins of presidential power at the union level. August 1991 saw Yeltsin's finest political hour, as he courageously led a successful opposition against the ring-leaders of the failed coup which took place that very month. The intention of the plotters had been to strengthen Soviet power, prevent a far-reaching power-sharing treaty between the political centre and the union republics which was in the offing, and do away with some of the most crucial advances towards democracy and decentralisation that had been made during the *perestroika* period. We know the result; the coup ended in total failure and disgrace for its leaders, and only hastened the final demise of the Soviet Union. In the aftermath of the coup, the Communist Party of the Soviet Union was banished and an intense power struggle developed between Yeltsin and Gorbachev, during which it soon became obvious that the former was on the rise and that the time of the latter as a politically relevant actor was running out. The Belovezha accords between the Russian Federative Republic, Ukraine, and Belorussia in early December 1991 dealt the final death blow to the Soviet Union, which was formally dissolved only three weeks later.

The years immediately after the dissolution of the Soviet Union turned out to be no less dramatic, however. The latter part of 1992 and the first nine months of 1993 were characterised by an intense power struggle between the President and the parliamentary structure inherited from Soviet times. The parliament may partly have had dubious democratic credentials, but in claiming a substantial share of rights in the state division of labour it was faithful to the constitutional framework existing at the time. In late September 1993, Yeltsin had had enough of parliamentary intransigence. He issued a decree that the parliament be dissolved and new elections be held for a new parliamentary body. As the parliament refused to comply, Yeltsin ultimately chose to break their resistance through the use of force. Lives were lost in the battle over the White House in Moscow on 2-3 October 1993. After the violent resolution of the conflict, Yeltsin could stay on in power uncontested. However, his legitimacy had been tainted, and the almost saintly halo he had acquired as a defender of democratic values during the failed coup two years earlier had undeniably started to lose its brightness. Even so, a new constitution, which was more or less tailor-made to suit Yeltsin's desires for a strong executive, was adopted through a popular referendum in December 1993, and simultaneously, a new bicameral parliament was elected. It would seem, therefore, that there were some preconditions for political developments being put on a more orderly track.

That was not to be, however. Instead of the tug-of-war between the executive and the legislative, the clash of interests between the centre and the regions came to the fore. Nowhere was this more visible than in the case of the secessionist strivings of the Republic of Chechnya, situated in the northern Caucasus. The final years of Yeltsin's first tenure were tainted by the disastrous first war with the breakaway republic, between December 1994 and August 1996. Not only did the intense war effort fail to bring the republic to heel, but it also claimed an appalling tribute by way of the loss of tens of thousands of lives, civilians as well as soldiers, Russians and Chechens alike. Against all odds and predictions, however, Yeltsin managed to secure his re-election for a second presidential tenure in June and July 1996.

Luckily, the period between September 1997 and April 1999, when this investigation was undertaken, could not match the years of the first tenure by way of political drama. Nevertheless, they were undoubtedly eventful and uncertain. A persistent social, economic and political crisis prevailed, most of all, perhaps, symbolised by an increasingly ailing president. Whereas Yeltsin only a few years before had seemed vigorous, immensely powerful and almost invincible, he now seemed feeble, erratic and increasingly beset by ill health. As if trying to retain his reputation as a man of action and the indisputable boss, he sacked four prime ministers in the course of 16 months between May 1998 and September 1999. During this period the rouble collapsed, the regions of the Russian Federation successively increased their leeway and independence at the expense of the federal centre, and the state defaulted in its payments of wages and pensions, as a result of which a series of politically motivated strikes took place. In the international arena, while Russia still tried to uphold its image of being some form of great power, tensions soared with the United States, which had grown increasingly assertive in its global policies.

In March 2000, Vladimir Putin was elected president, and thus a new era was inaugurated in Russian politics. The first decade in the political life of post-Soviet Russia was dominated by Boris Yeltsin, and the second decade may well be equally dominated by Putin. Since I am an academic author, and as such essentially egoistic, I have from time to time asked myself whether this study, which focuses on some aspects of political and societal developments under Yeltsin, might be relevant even outside the time frame of the Yeltsin era. I believe that it certainly can. Not only do I trust that this book will offer some documentary insights into the actual political climate during the latter part of the Yeltsin period, but I also believe it can help to shed some additional light on the sentiments and societal milieu that brought Putin to power. He clearly did not arise from out of the blue.

Furthermore, even though the political situation has seemingly changed with the coming into power of Putin, the basic dynamics remain the same. At the time of the Russian parliamentary elections in December 1999, the electoral bloc Unity/The Bear, which was backed by Putin in his capacity 'as a citizen' and which in turn backed him for the presidential elections in March 2000, gathered considerable following among the Russian regions. This would indeed seem to be paradoxical, since Putin and his party had, if anything, argued in favour of a strong and able federal centre which, without question, would be superior to the regions. The matter was probably one of simple bandwagoning behaviour, however. If Putin's popularity finally were to wane, and in the event that no constitutional amendments had been undertaken up to that point, I believe that the old dynamics would rather quickly reassert themselves. So, in that sense, studying what took place during the latter years of Yeltsin's presidency will simultaneously tell us something about what is going on, at least under the surface, in Putin's Russia.

In fact, I would even argue that Russia has yet to enter a stage where it would be pertinent to stop applying the label 'post-Soviet'. My contention is rather that the Soviet Union lives on, one way or the other, in the minds and mentalities of, at the very least, those politicians who were born in the 1950s or earlier. Mental structures are sticky, and notions regarding what Russia is, was, and should be that were nurtured by these generations towards the latter part of the Yeltsin era, will continue to be valid for quite some time to come. This is why I firmly believe that the findings presented in this book will provide some useful insights into the political sentiments and societal dynamics in, not only Yeltsin's, but also Putin's Russia.

On yet another level, I trust that this book will be valuable for the reader who takes an interest in the general study of collective identities, and more particularly, national self-images. I believe that this book can increase the understanding of how politically active individuals depict their states in times of crisis, upheaval, and partial stabilisation. And I believe it can shed some light on the processes that favour internal cohesion in a polity beset by crisis, as well as on those that aggravate that crisis by stigmatising groups and actors not deemed worthy of partaking in united national efforts.

After having named all these reasons why this book deserves to be read, I guess it is time for the reader to judge for him-/herself. My theoretical and methodological points of departure are laid out in Chapter 1. This is where I introduce and discuss the concept of national self-images as understood and used by me. In Chapter 2, some background data are provided about my respondents and their regions. The empirical findings emanating from my interviews are presented in Chapters 3-6, which deal with, in turn, the past, external, external/internal and internal dimension of the national self-images encountered among my respondents. In Chapter 7, finally, I offer some concluding remarks, and discuss the relevance of my findings for the interpretation of the situation in Putin's Russia. As for now, let me only say that for my part, the world which my interviews uncovered proved to be a most exciting one. I invite my readers to share it with me.

1 Points of Departure

Defining and Discussing the Concepts[1]

National identities, like other varieties of collective identities, are elusive phenomena that are notoriously difficult to define. I would venture to propose that one point of access is through the images that come to expression in texts and statements encountered in the public as well as in the private realm. From a theoretical point of view this book deals with individuals' images of what their own state polity is and ought to be, or to use a more precise term, what will henceforth be referred to as national self-images. It is my contention that the study of national self-images also offers a comparatively practicable way of getting closer to national identities.

In my view, national self-images are partial representations of national identity that simultaneously provide cognitive and affective structures which, in turn, inform that identity. I am not, however, arguing that the two concepts are necessarily synonymous.[2] Whereas identity in general provides an answer to the questions 'Who am I? Who am I not' (set 1), and national identity like other collective identities addresses the questions 'Who are we? Who are we not?' (set 2), the national self-image will provide, as it were, a Polaroid-like representation providing an answer to the questions 'What is our country? What is it not?'[3] (set 3). By way of inference, the last-named set of questions provide partial answers to the first two sets of questions, and they may under optimum conditions match the second set completely. When national identity is weak or non-existent, the second pair of questions will be largely irrelevant on this level, since no sense of community will be generated by the state polity, but there will still have to be a, albeit negative and/or indifferent, response to the third set of questions. There is admittedly substantial overlap here, but on the whole I take national identity to be a more general and all-encompassing concept (cf. Parekh 1995:257), whereas the national self-image is more of an itemised, if yet abstract, depiction.[4]

National self-images relate not only to what the holders of them know, but also to what they like and do not like (cf. Boynton and Lodge

1994:186). Therefore, it is imperative to recognise that there is a significant affective component to the national self-images, and that affective and cognitive elements coexist in comprising them (Depkat 1997:111). In essence, the affective component could be regarded as the glue that holds collective identifications together (Rouhana 1997:15). Without the affective component, the identification with the state polity would be nothing more than 'the descriptive, objectivist, extraneous sense of "being a passport-holder" of a particular country' (Hedetoft 1995:11). Furthermore, if for instance sentiments of shame outweigh those of pride, collective identifications will, in the longer run, be hard to sustain. Feelings of pride and shame are closely 'associated with the urge to belong' (Scheff 1994:277), and therefore it would not be appropriate to disregard them in the context of national self-images. Rather, I would hold them to constitute a centrepiece of any national self-image. Consequently, the concepts of pride and shame both loom large in my study.

Cottam (1992:3) assumes 'images' to be 'cognitive organising devices and information filters'. Her influential definition is not quite satisfactory in my opinion, precisely since it does not take into account the affective component. Also, I would like to enrich the definition by adding the lens notion (Miller and Gronbeck 1994:8; Fiebig-von Hase 1997:7-8), since organising devices and information filters per se have rather passive connotations. They may admittedly only let through a limited amount of any incoming information, to make it fit with existing and prevalent beliefs, but the information that does get through would still be unaltered as such. However, if we also think in terms of the lens conception, this allows us to see the possibility of the incoming information being affected in other ways besides being screened. For instance, if one envisages a contact lens, it might be coloured a rosy red or a deep blue, and may thus change the quality of the holder's perceptions. Depending on the inherent traits of the lens, it could rectify a myopia or, for that matter, aggravate it. These are also the functions that national self-images, as a sub-species of images, would be expected to perform. Taking all of this into account, I would like to suggest the following definition: *National self-images are cognitive and affective conceptual lenses, organising devices and information filters which partly represent, and partly inform national identity.*

National self-images have a bearing on the past and the future (Kelman 1965:24), and they may have substantial durability over time. They draw upon memories and myths of a glorified past, and may contain notions of a future mission (Lebow 1981:197, cf. van Evera 1994:26-30). The present tense is, of course, of the most obvious importance in our day-to-day activities, and therefore there is a highly salient present dimension as well, even if it is debatable whether it could be dissociated from the past. This issue will be dealt with at some length below.

As argued by Hirshberg (1993:78), the maintenance of a positive national self-image is crucial for continued public acquiescence and support for government. Such a self-image has an integrative function and helps transform an aggregate of human beings into a collective, experiencing a common sense of purpose (Hirshberg 1993:78, Lebow 1981:197). National self-images normally contain idealised stereotypes of the in-group, which serves to reinforce this tendency (Hirshberg 1993:78).

Internal cohesion will to a considerable extent increase collective self-assurance in dealings with the outside world. But there are also other implications that national self-images may have on relations with collective actors outside of one's own community. Self-images organise and simplify information about others, especially in cases when information is scant or time is scarce (Blanton 1996). No doubt, the national self-images and the images of main partners, adversaries, and enemies in the surrounding world are to a significant extent defined in relation to each other (Gerndt 1988, Hedetoft 1995, Herrmann and Fischerkeller 1995, Neumann 1996, Blanton 1996, Sikevich 1996, Hönicke 1997). They evolve in a 'dialectical flux' (Milojkovic-Djuric 1994:iii). Or, in the words of one analyst, they 'mutually define each other in an imaginary demarcation of difference within a normative and evaluative continuum' (Hedetoft 1995:77). This is in conformity with the basic premise of all constructions of identity, namely that the constitution of an in-group is fundamentally dependent on the distancing from a more or less alien out-group. By stating what 'we' are, it is also made quite clear what 'we' are not and do not want to be, i.e. what 'they' are (Billig 1995:66, Christie 1998:3, Sikevich 1996:69).

There is an impressive body of literature which indicates the implications of collective identity on action. For example, one author finds a nexus between 'new definitions of self' and 'core changes in foreign policy' (Prizel 1998:2). Likewise, several scholars have underlined the link between collective identifications, on the one hand, and actions towards the out-group, on the other (Waever *et al* 1993, Prizel 1998, Kellas 1998). Bloom (1990) argues that it is a natural and compelling drive of individuals to come together and to share with others collective identifications and, when the symbols of the group identifications are threatened, act together to ward off such threats. Again, such actions will typically be directed towards the out-group. Even though there has been some preoccupation within the social sciences with enemy images as the most prevalent construction of Other (cf. Fiebig-von Hase/Lehmkuhl 1997), it should be noted that this is the most extreme variant, albeit a highly important one. The full spectrum is discrete, and there are several less drastic variants of Other-images that are conceivable, besides those depicting an enemy (Herrmann and Fischerkeller 1995, Hedetoft 1995:77-79, 103-105). The unifying factor that connects these images and epitomises the Other, however, is that he/she is not deemed to be part of Us.

Regarding the key theoretical concept of this study, the term '*national self-image*' is the one most frequently used in the theoretical literature. There are, however, several drawbacks connected with the use of this particular adjective. First and foremost, one will often find that nation and state are conflated, for instance through the indiscriminate use of the adjective 'national'. The main problem in this regard is that the noun 'state' lacks a satisfactory adjectival counterpart, and even in academic discourse 'national' refers to 'state' as well as to 'nation' (cf. Brubaker 1996:16, fn. 6). Frequently one comes across substantial confusion and a lack of conceptual clarity (Oommen 1997, Barrington 1997). Therefore, so as to signal my own bearings, I would like to make it clear that the term 'national', when used in conjunction with the term 'national self-image', will denote a reference to the political community, the state polity (cf. Parekh 1994:501, fn 14). But it does not relate to the state apparatus only, since for the state not to be an empty shell, and for it to have some durability and viability, there will have to be some sense of loyalty and some emotional bonds to it among its citizens (Brown 1999:283, Buzan 1983:36-53, Avraamova 1998, Kymlicka 1995:13), i.e. making exempt totalitarian rule by brute force, and maybe also daily and costly transactions whereby the state caters for the self-interests of vast, if not all, segments of the population (cf. Hurd 1999).

Behind my choice of the adjective lies the fact that I am referring to a notion of civic nationhood (Smith 1991:9-14, Kellas 1998), which is built upon citizenship, territorial residence, shared social ties and adherence to a common civic culture, but not on common descent. Above all, this makes it stand out in contrast with ethnic nationhood which is primarily defined from the vantage point of ethnic parameters and common descent, but it also means something more than the official nationhood referred to by some authors (Anderson 1983, Kellas 1998, Holmes 1997). This last-named variety builds upon patriotism related to the state apparatus and its paraphernalia but it is, the way I see it, basically devoid of any emotional attachments, like those based on a shared civic culture or shared social ties (Kellas 1998:65, cf. Miller 1995:188-189). More than widespread popular identifications, it denotes top-down indoctrination attempts undertaken by the governing elites. The citizen turns out to be the aforementioned passport holder of his/her state. There has to be something more to the picture than that.

My subscription to the notion of civic nationhood does not exclude cultural aspects from the study (cf. Robertson 1998), even if culture is frequently and perhaps predominantly associated with the paradigm of ethnic national identity (Hedetoft 1995:182, Pearson 2000:93). Quite on the contrary, as suggested above, civic nationhood is indeed often based on a shared civic culture and shared social ties (Kellas 1998:65, cf. Avraamova 1998:221, Tempelman 1999:18). As pointed out by Hedetoft (1995:182), 'culture may be ethnic – or ethnic in part – but could also draw on a number of other life spheres and ontological imaginings'. And as Kymlicka (1995:24) reminds us, '[w]hat distinguishes "civic" nations from "ethnic" nations ... is not the absence of any cultural component to national identity, but rather the fact that anyone can integrate into the common culture'.

At this juncture, it should also be pointed out that a sense of a common past, as well as common historical experiences and memories, will certainly go together with the notion of civic nationhood. Thus, for example, memories or myths of a 'golden age' with regards to literature and art would, without doubt, be elements of pride that are also inherent in a civic nation. It would be an aberration to think that this is the exclusive property of ethnically based nations.

These concepts, then, are my theoretical working tools in brief, and I have, alas, been all too aware, already from the outset, that the social realities as mediated through my respondents would sooner or later intervene. It has not been possible to maintain a clinical divide and screen out ethnic modes of identification from the study. Nor is it indeed desirable to do so, since an appreciation of the extent to which ethnic factors of identification enter the picture will help to gauge the strength and the quality of the affective glue that serves to keep the Russian state polity together. And certainly, the concept of national self-images, focused as it is on civic modes of national identification, will be instrumental in identifying cases where more ethnically defined conceptions of the nation come to the surface.

At this point I should also hasten to add that I depict both 'ethnic' and 'civic' nations as ideal types that will never be encountered in their pure form. In actual fact, all viable state polities display combinations of the two basic modes of identification (Smith 1991). Also, I do not necessarily see the gain of civic identifications as tantamount to the loss of ethnic identifications, or vice versa. Rather, my main point concerns what appears to be the most dynamic driving force with regard to collective identifications within a certain state polity, and whether it is ethnic or civic patterns of identification that tend to be predominant for defining patterns of popular identification within a certain national frame (cf. Rouhana 1997).

Specifics of the Russian Case

Given also the specific case at hand, concentrating primarily on civic aspects instead of ethnic ones makes sense, since the state itself has traditionally been vital for Russian nationhood (Prizel 1998). Even though recent research has suggested that the centrality of this particular identification may be receding (Avraamova 1998:198), the state itself is, alongside language and ways of life, most often mentioned by inhabitants of Russia as a ground for common identifications (Sikevich 1996:75). This may not be very surprising when considering that about 150 nationalities coexist in the territory of the Russian Federation. Indeed, this is the very problem that is illustrated by the Russian lexical dichotomy between the concepts *russkie* and *rossiyane* (Sakwa 1996:182, Tishkov 1997; McAuley 1997:28, fn. 27, Avraamova 1998:201-208). The latter term denotes all citizens of the Russian Federation, whether Russians, Tatars, German, Bashkirs, Kalmyks or whichever group, whereas the former refers solely to Russians. This is a case where the English language – or, for that matter the Swedish language – is prone to mislead us, since both words are translated as 'Russians', whereby this crucial nuance is not conveyed.

Purporting that the state has been vital for Russian nationhood through the centuries is certainly not tantamount to holding that Russia at other points in history has been close to the attainment of civic national identity. Rather, it is fair to say that this kind of identity never took proper root in Russia (Greenfeld 1992:230). Despite strenuous efforts by Russian rulers, by tsars and red commissars, to instil feelings of loyalty and emotional attachment among the population at large, societal stability relied largely on the foundations of submission to the rulers and their governing apparatus. Civic national identity is carried by citizens, not by subjects, which historically has made it difficult for Russia to develop towards this ideal (cf. Barner-Barry and Hody 1995:32-58). In the period spanning from the 18th to the 20th century, there was indisputably widespread popular pride of being subjects of a strong state and thus having some part in its achievements (Greenfeld 1992:197), but these sentiments were never quite separated from the fear of the ultimate capability of the state to inflict harm on, and indeed destroy, its subjects by forceful and repressive means. Surely, intimidation has never been a solid basis for welding together and inspiring organic feelings of commonality within a certain population, or between it and the state polity which is using such means. Hence, in the past, endeavours to nurture national identity in Russia have largely ended up as official nationhood being put into practice (cf. Prizel 1998).

In Western Europe the development of national identity occurred from the late 18th and early 19th centuries onwards (Anderson 1983, Smith 1991, Hall 1999). In the prototypical case of France, national identity evolved dynamically in a state polity defined within relatively restricted geographical parameters. When France started its quest for trans-ocean and trans-Mediterranean colonies, there was already a well entrenched sense of national identity in the core of the colonial realm. By supplying certain in-group/out-group dichotomies, the existence of suppressed and patronised colonies helped to reinforce national identity dynamics at the home base even further. The Russian Empire had nothing of this, even if Russia was clearly a colonial power (Kommisrud 1996). From the lifting of the Mongol yoke in the late 15th century, Russia continually expanded outwards, and the subjugation of non-Russian[5] peoples and tribes was surely that of self-perceived betters claiming their right to dominate inferior peoples. The perhaps clearest case of this was the Russian foray into Central Asia in the second half of the 19th century. However, since no ocean separated the metropolis from its colonies, it was in many cases far from clear what constituted the core and what made up the periphery (Shaw 1999). Also, and further compounding the matter, colonial expansion took place at a time when the social construction of Russian national identity was marred by the clash between the so-called Slavophiles and Westernisers who dissented on what cultural belongings and primary political orientations were desirable for Russia.

Therefore, the development of national identity in Russia was intertwined with the expansion of empire, making it hard to tell the two phenomena apart (cf. Sakwa 1996:368). The true nature of Russian national identity came to be a vexing issue and, indeed, an 'accursed question' (Prizel 1998). The simultaneous processes of cultivating collective identifications pertaining to the state polity, on the one hand, and the increasing physical extension of the empire, on the other, blurred already in the 19th century the distinction between *russkie* and *rossiyane*. The chief defining characteristics of the imperious *russkie* amounted to allegiance to the Russian crown, belonging to the Russian-Orthodox faith, and use of the Russian national tongue. Therefore, at least, the dividing line between the *russkie* and those *rossiyane* who were fellow Slavs was rather thin.

The Slavophile movement exemplified this problematique. While thus defined in opposition to the Westernisers, who adamantly tried to bring Russia closer to Western Europe, the Slavophiles propounded the basic community and common destiny of the Slavs. Thereby, this creed partly served to Other the European fringes of the Russian Empire, such as Finland, Poland, Estonia, Latvia, and Lithuania, where nationalist strivings were conspicuous in the second part of the century. Also, Slavophilism in essence amounted to the exclusion of adherents of other major religions, for example Muslims and Jews, from the major in-group of Orthodox Slavs. Hence, the tenets of the influential Slavophile movement were quite removed from the ideals of civic national identity.

Indeed the same could be said about the practitioners of Russian official nationalism, at least towards the close of the 19th century. Due to their inherent will to expand the external borders, they were opposed to Slavophile ideas of grooming the ties solely within a rather closely-knit cultural community. However, they agreed on the desirability to strengthen the position of, for example, the Russian language and Russian cultural practices to solidify the Empire (Karlsson 1995:100). Consequently, there was a forceful drive towards Russification throughout the imperial realm at the close of the 19th century. Official nationalism in Imperial Russia was consequently not unused to trying to impose certain markers of ethnic Russians across the board.

Nor did the Soviet period make the picture any different in this respect. The at times rampant official Soviet nationalism was certainly not devoid of ethnically Russian emphases. While the authorities tirelessly chanted that the Soviet people knew of no ethnic characteristics, reality was, at least from the early 1930s onwards, quite different (Kommisrud 1996). The denomination of the Soviet Union as such was, admittedly, without any geographically or ethnically restricting specifications, but with the passing of time, 'Soviet' and 'Russian' increasingly developed into synonyms.[6] The horrific Stalin-time deportations of whole peoples from their homelands, such as the Crimean Tatars, Chechens, Volga Germans and others in the wake of World War II, bore glaring witness to how dismally little tolerance was at times granted non-Russian Others.

The Preferability of Civic Modes of Identification

All told, there is thus reason to venture the assessment that the evolution of something approaching a civic national identity would be quite a novel achievement for Russia. Even so, it should be made very clear from the outset that I personally regard the success of the endeavour to nurture this kind of identification as pivotal for the future stability of the Russian Federation. This new kind of construction enterprise has to dissociate itself fully from the false pretences of the Soviet-man period, where the dominance of Russians (*russkie*) was introduced and imposed, as it were, through the kitchen door (Kommisrud 1996). Instead, it has to build on the basic disregard of ethnic factors and must upgrade the emphasis on territorial and constitutional commonality.

As it is pointed out by Neumann (1999:37), 'if active othering is proposed as the price of achieving integration, that price seems to be too high to pay'. Pitting ethnic groups against each other can hardly be the solution to Russia's perennial economic and political problems, and the tragic developments in Chechnya in 1994-96, and again since the autumn of 1999, have vividly demonstrated what havoc such a practice can bring. It would seem as though civic national identity generally entails less drastic outlooks on adversaries and antagonists, at least as far as the internal arena is concerned.[7] There seems to be a fair chance that internal Others might be depicted as being less hostile and less abominable. In other words, where civic national identity tends to predominate, sheer enemy images regarding the inside do not seem to be that prevalent.

Given that belonging to a territorially and constitutionally defined entity seems to be an experience that is less focused on being part of an essentialised, everlasting project than is the case with an ethnically defined commonality, images held of the Other tend indeed to be more nuanced and gradualist in the case of civic national identity (cf. Hedetoft 1995:49). Here, the commonality is to a greater extent defined in inclusionary terms. To use Brown's analogy (1999), ethnic nationhood can be compared with belonging to the family that one is born into, whereas membership in the civic nation is somewhat easier for the individual to affect, since it can be likened best to becoming part of the family that one marries into. In neither case is belonging to the national community an easy thing to achieve, but in the latter case there are at least greater chances for the individual's free choice and his/her concomitant actions to make a difference. Even so, a brother- or sister-in-law is seldom to be found in the very core of the family, but will often, instead, be relegated to the wings or to the relative emotional periphery for quite a period of time. Admittedly, however, in theory at least, no resident is excluded a priori from being part of a nation defined on the basis of a sense of civic togetherness. Even though one is far away from the best of all possible worlds, and it would be more than naive to believe in the emergence of virtuous circles in the case of a successfully fostered civic nationhood in Russia, it might at least improve the chances of steering away from the development of vicious circles of ethnic discord and internal strife. So in this sense I take a clearly normative stance.

In other words, this study deals with national self-images of *rossiyane*, even though the vast majority of them happens to be *russkie*. As one of my respondents remarked, '*rossiyane* is not a nationality, it is belonging to a state which is not ethnic' (SD 2). The term *rossiyane* denotes 'the officially sanctioned macro identity called upon to consolidate the modernising society' (Avraamova 1998:201). The question is, then, whether this identity as a *rossiyan*, being officially sanctioned, has acquired or may acquire the characteristics of a civic national identity (cf. Zdravomyslov 1996), or whether it will be tantamount to the aforementioned empty shell. The latter would be highly portentous for the future development of the Russian Federation. As it is somewhat drastically put by Kymlicka

(1995:13), 'multination states cannot survive unless the various groups have an allegiance to the larger political community they cohabit'.

In any case, the bulk of the *rossiyane* have to relate to their state polity somehow. They simply have to relate to the state, the Russian Federation, of which they are citizens. It affects their daily lives in numerous ways, they live and work there, and they will presumably have *some* kind of emotional attachment to it (cf. Avraamova 1998). It is of course conceivable that this presumed emotional attachment turns out to be nothing more than of the dubious quality awarded to one's tax collector. Had there only been this kind of hollow official nationalism, however, it seems to me as if processes of disintegration would have come to the fore to a much larger extent. In this study, the application of the theoretical concept of national self-images will serve to fathom the extent and quality of the thus presumed emotional bonds.

Why Discuss National Self-Images in Russia?

The state-centred paradigm has, in recent years, been increasingly questioned and challenged within international relations theory (Walker 1993; Lapid and Kratochwil 1996; Krause and Renwick 1996). The criticism levelled against state-centrism is justified on many accounts. One might wonder why, then, one should bother to study national self-images of the current Russian state polity (cf. Robertson 1998). I would venture to say that the fact that the Russian Federation remains a regional great power, with a huge arsenal of nuclear weapons and numerous other significant capabilities, is reason enough. It constitutes one of the largest states in the world, and its impact is still considerable in several arenas. Even allowing for marginal alterations in its set-up, it is likely to stay that way for the foreseeable future, and developments in a country of such vastness are important for its inhabitants as well as for the surrounding world. And finally, despite internal rumblings during the recent decade, the regions have, with the notable exception of Chechnya, so far largely stayed put. In sum, I posit that it is of considerable interest to try to establish whether or not there seems to be any chances of attaining a viable sense of civic nationhood in this extensive country, just as it is of interest to try to see whether centrifugal tendencies and regionally based identity structures seem to be reinforced, at the expense of the centre-based polity. Collective self-images among Russian politicians are likely to have some impact on the policy choices being made. This is most obvious for the domestic arena, but it is conceivable that they have at least some indirect effect on outward behaviour as well.

Thus, to investigate prevalent national self-images in Russia is, at least in my opinion, a worthwhile undertaking, and the whole issue of current representations of Russia has 'a sweeping contemporary salience' (Neumann 1999:65). However, and this is to yield somewhat to the criticism against state-centrism, it is of course conceivable that other collective self-images, apart from national ones, might exert an influence on internal unity, such as those that are related more to regional belonging or religious affiliation. Considering the size of the Russian Federation and the turbulence of the last decade, this would seem more than likely. At this point, I should also add that I do not consider identities and collective self-images to be all-important and the only factor impinging on internal cohesion. For instance, bare economic necessities have most certainly hampered the drive of the early 1990s towards accelerating sovereignisation of the Russian regions. Even though economic performance and social standards are, according to most indicators, disappointingly low in the Russian Federation as a whole,[8] few factors indicate that individual regions would be better off alone. Be that as it may, common unifying identities and self-images throughout Russia are certainly prone to foster greater cohesion among the in-groups, and thus also contribute to increasing the legitimacy of political elites working in the interest of these in-groups (cf. Hall 1999). In other words, the existence of common frames of reference, as far as national self-images are concerned, would at the very least seem to facilitate joint problem-solving activities.

How to Study National Self-Images in Russia

Having said this, it is vital to point out that I will not attempt to isolate and describe *one* single image of Russia, shared by all of the inhabitants of the Federation. Usage of the singular would, apart from conveying a false sense of uniformity, also lack the necessary dynamism (cf. Nederveen Pieterse 1991:198). Instead, I have expected from the outset to come across strands of several varieties of national self-images. I will thus not reify any particular national self-image to be a notion, present and omnipresent, in the minds of all citizens (cf. Mavratsas 1999:94, Parekh 1995:267, Neumann 1999:27). To be sure, every individual will have his/her national self-image, and he/she will, consciously or unconsciously, form a part of collectives having basically similar cognitive and affective frameworks related to the state polity. Consequently, there will be several broad varieties of the national self-image, some of which may diverge rather substantially. 'Foundations are contradictory, and objectives are divergent', stresses Avraamova with regard to national identifications (1998:215). Some prevalent manifestations of these broad varieties will, as they have appeared to me, be displayed through the findings of this book.

In other words, we will be encountering national self-images that are shared by several groups and maybe even broad categories of people, but they will not be shared by all of the vast population of the Russian Federation (cf. Kowert and Legro 1996:475). As it has been aptly put by Hellberg Hirn (1998:178), 'there are rural and urban, male and female ways of being Russian, and Russianness does not look quite the same in the centre as it does on the periphery'. When comparing different self-images we will unquestionably find that there are certain tensions between them. In the end, therefore, it may even prove to be more adequate to refer to regionally held self-images than nationally held ones. However, the images are still national in the respect that they *pertain* to the civic nation, even though they are not *shared* nation-wide. What I am after, then, is to try to uncover existing tensions within and between the national self-images encountered in the regions that figure in the investigation. Indeed, as I have suggested, I am interested in my respondents' images of the state polity of which they are a part. If it transpires that my respondents merely profess to being targets of the official nationalism of the Russian Federation, this would indeed be indicative of a lack of internal cohesion within the state.

As put by Ringmar (1996:83), '...questions regarding identities are not always at stake, but are only raised at certain – rather unique – periods in the life of an individual or a society. In what we could call "normal times" identities are simply "there" to be used and relied on rather than analysed and worried about'. Only in pointed and rather exceptional situations, in times of trouble, will collective identity be put into question, broken down and/or re-constructed, he maintains. As argued by other authors in the field, it is only in times of crisis that social scientists, through for example the technique of asking questions in interviews, can expect to get closer to the salient identities of their respondents. This is so since it is only in such times of turbulence and trouble that identities surface in the minds of the individual bearers, and make these individuals aware of having them in the first place (Waever and Kelstrup 1993:81-82). Without doubt, if accepted, this line of argumentation has certain methodological implications for studies such as this.

I would, however, argue that it is possible to study identities under less drastic circumstances, even though methodological challenges are formidable. Even so, it can be argued that the contemporary Russian citizen finds him-/herself exactly in the kind of situation where identifications most certainly are in flux. The dissolution of the Soviet Union in 1991 brought about a need for collective re-orientations for elites and the public alike. Among those aspects that had to be assessed anew was Russia's role in the international arena, as well as the main domestic trends of development and state of affairs, to mention but a few (cf. Tumarkin 1994:199). The prevailing contemporary pattern of identifications could, in fact, be labelled as critical in the sense that the state polity continues to find itself at a turning point, as extended and prolonged as it may seem (Avraamova 1998:215). To illustrate this, every general election held in the Russian Federation since the dissolution of the Soviet Union has, by foreign and domestic analysts alike, been depicted as *the* fateful election, which will fundamentally determine the future path of Russia. This was true for the parliamentary elections and the referendum on the constitution in 1993, as well as the parliamentary elections in 1995 and the presidential polls in the summer of 1996. And certainly, the same tune was sung at the time of the parliamentary elections in December 1999, and even more so in connection with the presidential elections in March 2000. In a similar vein, it seems to be justified to claim that Russia is still at a crossroads, and the process of constructing more durable identities is yet to be completed. This should indeed add to the relevance of this study, even though the author is well aware of the problems involved when aiming at a moving target.

Making the Theoretical Concept Operational

National self-image is a most solemn-sounding concept, and there is a risk that, if left unspecified, it may take on an almost metaphysical existence.[9]

If this is allowed, the concept loses its scientific value. Even though attempts at making abstract concepts operational may turn out to be more or less blunt, it is nevertheless necessary to undertake them. Kaplowitz (1990:47) has tentatively offered some valuable specification regarding 'the most salient aspects of national self-imagery'. The components singled out by him are 'what a people likes and dislikes about itself, how it views its history, the resultant "lessons" it has learned, its aspirations and desires, the ways in which it may want to change, its conceptions of national purpose and interest, and its perceptions of its powers and limits'. After having tried to specify and elaborate on the elements listed by Kaplowitz, thereby excluding some and adding others (Petersson 1998a, 1998b, 1999), I have reached the conclusion that nothing is really gained by employing too compartmentalised a scheme of the make-up of national self-images. Such an amendment could certainly be done, but it proved difficult to make a meaningful application of it to the empirical subject-matter. What was gained in specificity and depth was lost in universal applicability and width. A less specific scheme certainly gives less guidance through the subject-matter, but on the other hand, it is better for the purposes of supplying frames that are flexible enough to contribute to a more thorough understanding of the case at hand.

Instead of giving a more detailed catalogue of what comprises the national self-images, I will therefore suggest a simple scheme of analysis, where two basic dimensions and six sub-dimensions are discerned, namely:

A. Temporal dimension
A1. Past dimension
A2. Present dimension
A3. Future dimension
B. Spatial dimension
B1. External dimension
B2. External/internal dimension
B3. Internal dimension

These broadly formulated dimensions will allow for an interpretative approach. The dimensions and the sub-dimensions provide a general framework within which single items can be analysed and discussed. Identities are, as was pointed out above, elusive phenomena that certainly do not count among tangibles. Hence, they cannot be squeezed into narrow boxes and compartments. Yet, if identities and collective self-images are to be analysed at all by social scientists, they have to be approached somehow. I feel that the broad dimensions enumerated above constitute a viable middle way between width and depth, and that they can be exploited fruitfully through the employment of in-depth interview methodology. The dimensions might strike some readers as being too broad and too general to provide guidance throughout the analysis, but it has to be the task of the individual researcher to fill them with a more solid substantive content in the course of his/her study.

The Temporal Dimension

Basically, then, I envisage national self-images to be grounded in time and space. The past is highly important for any national self-image, and perhaps even more so in states that, like Russia, have traditionally played a significant role in the global or regional arena. Cognitive and affective views of the past are of tremendous importance in forming the self-images, even though most of the facets comprising them may seem to concern the present. Of the temporal sub-dimensions, the one concerning the past is the most significant by far and, indeed, its predominance is so vast that it is even justified to use the term 'past dimension' throughout when referring to the temporal dimension. The reasons for adhering to this practice will be elaborated further below. By offering accounts on the nature of common heritage and routes to the future, as well as by offering yardsticks by which the present may be measured (Preston 1997:72), the past dimension provides the foundation for the spatially oriented sub-dimensions which will also be dealt with below. In other words, 'history is the centerpiece of identity' (Cohen 1999:28).

In this respect, one may venture to make a comparison between individual and collective levels of identity, even if one, under most circumstances, is ill advised to do so. In both cases, the past dimension is absolutely crucial, providing points of departure and guidance for the future, as well as feasible explanations regarding whence we came and perhaps even predictions, by way of extrapolation, concerning where we are heading (cf. Hedetoft 1995:11). At both levels, recollections of a 'golden age' constitute a source of strength and inspiration, and may be said to comprise the very glue of the affective dimension of identity.

Furthermore, it should be recalled by way of analogy with the individual level of identification, that to try to answer the question 'Who am I?' without referring back to past experiences is a hopeless and vain exercise. After having gone through traumatic periods of one's life, one may even try to burn photographs and get rid of personal documentation in similar drastic ways, but this is a futile endeavour, since, sooner or later, flashbacks are bound to occur.

This is not to say that the process of trying to delve into the past dimension is devoid of problems. It certainly is not. Fundamental as it may be, the question that I asked my respondents on aspects or periods in the Russian past of which they felt proud or ashamed, turned out to touch upon most intricate and vexing issues. One of my interviewees, a deputy of the St. Petersburg City Duma, mused:

> This is a most complicated question, since we do not know the real history of Russia. In our country, history has been rewritten every fifteenth or twentieth year. Therefore, we do not know our history adequately.
>
> (Spb 12)

So, he aptly asked me, which particular history did I have in mind? One of his colleagues almost echoed his assessment, saying:

> I went to the Soviet school and was taught history the Soviet way. There history was filtered, some traits were stressed, whereas yet others were distorted.
>
> (Spb 8)

Similarly, another respondent, from the Volgograd Oblast Duma, was careful to point out that Russian history had always been manipulated, so who could actually trust it now? (V 11, cf. SD 32, P 12).

This crucial problem has been adroitly discussed by scholars who have undertaken research on Russian national identities similar to that presented in this study (Sikevich 1996:92).[10] For instance, in her essay on the official Soviet-time cult of the Great Patriotic War, Tumarkin (1994:50-51) observes that '[d]eliberate distortions of history for political reasons ... were the trademark of Soviet historical writing almost since its inception'. Moreover, the practice of filtering history in school curricula, in order to make it fit with prevalent political beliefs (Karlsson 1987), was adhered to prior even to the Soviet period. Given these facts, it is clear that the problems we face here abound. On the other hand, these days the academic community at large has to a significant degree turned away from the notion that there is one single course of events called history, just waiting out there to be uncovered and reconstructed by latter-day historians. The past is, in all countries and in all societies, an intrinsic part of the present and vice versa. Thus, the present perennially 'recreates the past' (Baucom 1999:5), but readings of the past also affect the views taken regarding the present. There are no objective givens, but a chain of events and processes that are eternally subject to interpretations and reinterpretations on the part of current generations. So, in this sense, Russia is not a case apart, but rather a case which bears out this general state of affairs with exceptional clarity.

It is indeed justified to ask which particular history we are discussing, and certainly, the individual's own preferred reading of history is highly crucial to his/her sense of collective belonging, i.e. identity. Drawing largely upon a typology developed by the Swedish historian Klas-Göran Karlsson (1999), I would argue that there are several conceivable uses of history that are available for those individuals encountered in the study. The quest for a 'usable' past (Maier 1988, Sakwa 1996:201, Prizel 1998:9) is highly salient in the kind of situation in which the Russian public and Russian political elites found themselves at the time of the dissolution of the Soviet Union, and it continues to be highly relevant in the contemporary situation. A usable past would be one that could aptly be used for the purposes of the present and the future. What, then, are these purposes, and whose are they?

The first relevant use of history is what Karlsson (1999) labels to be of the existential kind. Clearly, the individual has a need to be part of a larger something. This kind of belonging makes life easier in a number of ways, it gives strength, resilience, and a feeling of physical and mental well-being and security, it facilitates social relationships with the in-group, and it simplifies otherwise insecurity-ridden choices of appropriate courses of action. And, if one can hark back to a golden age in the collective's past, it becomes easier to bear less glamorous or even miserable aspects of one's own day-to-day existence. These are, indeed, 'therapeutic effects of national pride' (Greenfeld 1992:220). So, there is certainly an existential aspect of history involved here, but the individual need not be aware of the fact that he/she is using the past in such a manner. However, in my view, the noun 'use' can, in this context, carry with it some undesired connotations, since it may be associated with full, deliberate and instrumental control or even manipulation. And yet, the very point here is that individuals enjoying the benefits of this historically grounded commonality may not at all times be aware thereof. Individual acts of recollection of the collective past may lean towards the subconscious and axiomatic. This aspect should be kept in mind.

Furthermore, there is a legitimising use of history, which is certainly not administered without the practitioner knowing it (Karlsson 1999). In George Orwell's satirical masterpiece, *Animal Farm*, one of the leaders of the rebellion against human rule, the pig Napoleon, consistently legitimises his increasingly totalitarian practices by rhetorically enquiring whether his subjects really want to return to the bad old days of human leadership: 'Surely none of you wishes to see Jones back?' (Orwell 1986). This is the well-known technique of negative legitimation, the tactics of claiming that even though things might not be ideal at the given point in time, they were far worse before (Vendil 2000:16). *Animal Farm* was, of course, modelled on developments in the Soviet Union and the fact that Bolshevik rule, to a great extent, was legitimised by references to the alleged ruthlessness of Tsarist Russia. Somewhat later in the course of history, Vladimir Lenin became, in person, the principal beacon and lightning rod in the Soviet system. Prior to Yosif Stalin's ascendancy to absolute power, that soon-to-be dictator legitimised his quest for prominence by contending that he was the most loyal heir to Lenin. Nikita Khrushchev, in his day, argued that Stalin's brutal government had been a deplorable aberration, and that he was the one who would be able to bring the Party back to its true, Leninist roots. He would resurrect the squandered heritage. Similar tactics were, in the early years of *perestroika*, employed by Mikhail Gorbachev, who added that Leonid Brezhnev's ineffective rule had contributed to the distancing of the Party from the path once indicated by the founder of the Soviet state. In this last-named case the tactics misfired, however, as it became increasingly evident that Lenin's name could no longer be invoked for the sake of gaining legitimacy among the bulk of the politically aware Soviet population, as for example more and more archival sources indicated that Lenin, too, had favoured mass terror as a means to attain political ends.

Finally, one should mention the non-use of history (Karlsson 1999), the possible exercise of which is quite relevant to bear in mind when trying to see how members of Russian political elites deal with their national pasts. According to a legend, a Chinese Emperor once decreed that all books be burnt so that history started with him. The Soviet past offers a plethora of examples of a very real non-use of history, and is replete with examples of obliteration of once-prominent political leaders from history books, such as Leon Trotsky, Nikolai Bukharin and Khrushchev himself. This is certainly a highly instrumental use, but even here there may be more deep-seated and axiomatic sub-varieties at work. The non-use may therefore be employed both as part of the existential use, as well as part of the legitimising one. During most of the post-war Soviet period, it was impossible to refer openly to the Stalin-time repression. The subject was not broached, even though most Russians had lost family, friends or acquaintances to the purges and the Gulag archipelago. Just like the proverbial elephant in the living room, it was there all the time and was highly conspicuous in a number of ways, but it is too painful and too embarrassing to talk about (Hochschild 1994:22, in Karlsson 1999:159). This, and the fact that the legitimising use was so widespread during the Soviet period, frequently on rather dubious grounds, may very well make it tempting for members of current Russian political elites to revert to the non-use of history. In any case, the need for a Russian equivalent to the German *Vergangenheitsbewältigung*, especially in the light of the atrocities of the Stalin era, seems to be obvious enough.

From a more general perspective, the above lines of reasoning certainly support the established view that recollections of national pasts are selective, and that what has been dubbed collective amnesia is often as important for the viability of national identifications as are acts of collective remembrance (Baucom 1999:7, Smith 1991, Cohen 1999). This observation was made with admirable clarity by Renan (1882/1994) more than 100 years ago.

As should have become clear by now, it is not by accident that questions pertaining to the Russian past figure prominently in my investigation. This brings me back to the simple scheme I have proposed for the study of national self-images. Accordingly, the past sub-dimension is the most prominent one within the temporary dimension at large. The spatial sub-dimensions are relevant in a present tense and therefore, evidently, overlap the temporal dimension (cf. Baucom 1999:5). I have, however, chosen to deal with aspects relating to the present under the heading of the spatial dimension. Furthermore, as was briefly indicated above, predictions of a future common goal or common mission might form part of the national self-image, even though the salience of these traits are most likely to be subordinate to the aspects pertaining to a perceived common past. For no other reason than that of a straightforward disposition of the text, it has proved to be natural to deal with these future aspects when studying the spatial dimensions, or more specifically, together with the topic of Russia's great power status. This is why, as suggested above, I will henceforth cling to the label 'past dimension'. The employment of the term of this specific sub-dimension simply conveys more precise information about what is to be dealt with.

Without a perceived glorious past or golden age providing some kind of guidance, the lodestars for reaching distant goals pertaining to a future mission will, most likely, not seem illuminating enough. So, in this sense, I would tend to disagree with Brown (1999) who holds that, for adherents to a civic nation, prospects for the future are more important for collective identifications than are recollections of their perceived common past. The reason for this, he goes on to argue, is that common descent is not a factor that is relevant to civic national identity, making it stand out in stark contrast to the ethnically based national identity, where myths of common origin constitute a centrepiece. This line of reasoning is of course a valid one. However, I would argue that there is more to the past dimension than beliefs and myths relating to a common ethnic descent. There will be shared historical memories, regardless of whether or not a people inhabiting a state polity is united by a common ethnic descent and 'common blood'.

As mentioned above, Russian nationhood has tended to focus on Russian statehood itself, and emotional attachments to the Russian state polity will certainly, to quite a considerable extent, be tied to historical recollections. The Russian case is not unique in this. British national identity can hardly be said to be constructed around common ethnic descent. Britishness is rather an overarching, overlapping kind of identification, partly contending with ethnically centred identities like Englishness, Scottishness, and Welshness (Langlands 1999:60-64). Still, the past glory of the Empire has been highly important for twentieth-century conceptions of what constitutes Britishness (cf. Hedetoft 1995:133), whereas endeavours to construct a brighter and better future, if no doubt important, would rather seem to gather citizens around ideologically defined platforms than around nationally defined ones.

It is my contention, then, that the past dimension most often will be of vital importance for the maintenance and further development of civic national identities. However, in post-colonial settings, for instance in states where external borders have been drawn in a markedly arbitrary manner, it is quite conceivable that there will be precious little by way of common historical recollections on which to build any civic nationhood. For political elites wishing to keep such a polity together, working towards common, unifying goals in the near future would certainly be a natural strategy to follow. This is the kind of situation in which the leaders of the post-Soviet Central Asian states would seem to find themselves at the current point in time. Similarly, where a country has been torn apart by devastating internal strife, and where the population has to cope with an economically or otherwise difficult situation, the immediate past will have very little to offer. Thus, in my opinion, the only justifiable and viable way of garnering internal cohesion would seem to be to appeal to a better common future. The eventual fruitfulness of such a strategy is, however, quite another matter.

The Spatial Dimension

As the above discussion has shown, there is quite obviously a temporal dimension to national self-images, which is fundamental and underlies the interpretations of the present. In order to situate and orient him-/herself properly in this present, the individual also needs to have some kind of relationship to ongoing events and processes. As argued by Preston (1997), there are three cornerstones to the make-up of collective identities, namely history, locale and networks. Locale comprises not solely territorial aspects (Preston 1997:43-47), but territory undoubtedly constitutes a centrepiece.

Even though the imminent demise of national identities has for quite some time been predicted by many insightful social scientists, those very identities have proven to be remarkably sticky and resilient, not least so in the context of the European Union during the 1990s. For instance, the Danish 'no' and the French 'near-no' in the national referenda on the accession to the Maastricht Treaty are evident cases in point. Admittedly, there are several other important collective identifications that suggest the opposite, but even so it would seem to me that the potentially most formidable challenges to the hegemony of national identities in today's world emerge from other spatially constructed collective identities, such as regional identities on a micro (such as Quebec, Catalonia, Abkhazia) or macro level (cf. Herb and Kaplan 1999). The most significant example of the latter remains the European Union. Territorially grounded identities might also emerge at regional levels which defy classification according to our conventional micro-meso-macro scale, since they exist in an area of the globe where the nation-state level has never, in the first place, been a very adequate yardstick. One example of this would be Central Asia, where, for instance, Tajikistan is delimited according to internal borders that were drawn up in the Soviet period, seemingly arbitrarily at the whim and/or following the divide-and-rule strategies of Stalin and his henchmen during the late 1920s and early 1930s. To this day, developments in this region remain volatile and unpredictable, at least to most Western analysts, and this is, no doubt, to a large extent due to the prevalence of cross-cutting, family- or clan-based, yet regionally grounded loyalties (Ertürk 1999). These affinities do not recognise the primacy of state borders, rather they seem to disregard them altogether. Even so, they are constructed to match a territorially defined togetherness, so that they too turn out to be, in essence, spatially constructed.

Thus, territory, place and space remain crucial to collective identifications in today's world, even though many arguments could be made in favour of viable collective identities centred around non-spatial categories such as gender, class, or race (Dijkink 1996, Herb and Kaplan 1999, Scholte 1996). As maintained by Herb (1999:17), 'there is something about the territory itself that adds an essential component to national identity (...) The space itself helps to weld together fragmented individual and group experiences into a common nation story. The territory creates a collective consciousness by reinventing itself as a homeland'. Says another author: 'Defining *who* "we" are has simultaneously in large part been a question of where persons are in the world' (Scholte 1996:43). And it goes almost without saying that when assessing identities that are centred around an existing state polity, such as the Russian Federation, the spatial dimension is, if not absolutely essential, at least very difficult to get around. Indeed, we seem to be stuck with a somewhat circular argument: the inhabitants of the Russian Federation feel a certain togetherness because they are all inhabitants of the Russian Federation.

In a seminal book, R. B. J. Walker (1993) has demonstrated the faults and shortcomings of the application of the state-centred paradigm to the analysis of ongoing processes and events in today's world. According to his convincing line of argumentation, this traditional mode of analysis is even morally and ethically defunct, since it, among other things, legitimises the perspective that whereas rule of law should be the unconditional yardstick inside the state proper, one need not really bother about the destinies of those Others left outside the state borders. Inside is Order, outside is Anarchy, and one should mind one's own business and take care of one's own citizens. This way of perceiving the world, he holds, might well pave the way for violent clashes between Us and Them, engendered in the name of national identities that have to be defended at all costs. And to the social scientist, Walker goes on to argue, this way of viewing the world inhibits the proper analysis of political processes, since politics should be regarded as politics, no matter whether it goes on inside or outside of artificial state borders. The basic driving forces remain the same in both cases, and should be analysed through the use of the same theoretical and methodological instruments. Differentiating between domestic politics and international relations simply does not make sense, and this fallacy impels political scientists to do away with professional instruments of analysis that it otherwise would be perfectly natural to employ.

Walker's argument is as persuasive as it is cogent, and is one for which I have deep professional sympathy. Even so, in this study I shall do exactly what he warns against, namely analyse regionally prevalent national self-images among Russian politicians, departing from the inside-outside scheme. And I shall do so since 145 million inhabitants still live inside that spatial container entitled the Russian Federation, and the developments of that vast state body still, to a significant degree, affect the political climate of the world. This does not mean that I do not concur with Walker's normative argument. I most certainly do. It is precisely because of the tendency of the inside-outside thinking to engender and consolidate forceful and negative mental depictions of the Others that I have chosen this point of departure. In cases where such processes of Othering seem to be prominent, they should be borne out and analysed, with a view to discuss the consequences they might have. In other words, given the compelling nature of the inside-outside categorisation, I shall be using it throughout the text when discussing the spatial facets of national self-images. There is also an added bonus, since this will simultaneously help me to demonstrate that the boundary between what is inside and what is outside in today's Russia is highly fuzzy and indeterminate.

Many authors have testified to the tremendous importance attributed to territorial aspects for Russian national identifications (Hellberg Hirn 1998:126-127, Dijkink 1996:95-108, Prizel 1998:230, Tumarkin 1994:218). The Motherland (*Rodina*), is understood and defined as a deeply physical entity, with its vast expanses of territory, its mountains and hills, forests, and rivers. This has added to the problem-ridden nature of today's Russian national identifications with their profound difficulties of establishing what is inside and what is outside. To give what may be the most striking example, the city of Kiev has traditionally been defined as the historical cradle of Russia, or to use the formulation of an old proverb 'Novgorod is our father, Kiev is our mother, Moscow is our heart, Petersburg is our head' (Hellberg Hirn 1998:35). Since the dissolution of the Soviet Union in 1991, this very mother of Russia is no longer part of the state polity denominated the Russian Federation. According to the political demarcation lines that signify state borders, Kiev is to be found outside of the Russian Federation, in the sovereign state of Ukraine. 'Kiev was the mother of all Russian cities, and yet Kiev is in another country today. It cannot be like that. I cannot imagine Stockholm without Sweden, but that is the way it is here', lamented one of my respondents from the St. Petersburg City Duma (Spb 13). Equally colourfully, another interviewee argued that losing Ukraine 'was like having an arm chopped off' (V 2).

In all, one quarter of the previous land mass of the Soviet Union is no longer defined as Russian soil (Shaw 1999:58). Not since the late 17th century, before the reign of Tsar Peter I (also known as Peter the Great), has the physical extent of Russia been as restricted as it is today. Seemingly, linguistic inventions, such as the political sub-division of the outside world into the less-than-clear categories of the Near Abroad (i.e. the former Soviet Union except for, most likely Estonia, Latvia and Lithuania) and the Far Abroad (the rest of the world), might help to alleviate some of the emotional stress caused by the changing political landscape and the ensuing consequences of these changes for national identifications. A third term, namely the Not-Abroad, has been suggested by some analysts, above all when discussing the recalcitrant republic of Chechnya. This indicates that to define what comprises contemporary Russia is no easy matter. I shall have reason to return to this problematique in subsequent chapters.

Selecting the Interviewees

This study pinpoints sentiments shared by members of intermediate political elites, mostly parliamentarians at regional levels. Individuals are not important in their individual capacities, but only as bearers of such sentiments. Consequently, when quotes are given or personal views are referred to, individuals will not be identifiable by name.[11]

The choices of the different cities are attributable to several factors. The State Duma interviews are there to provide a centre perspective. Originally, I had hoped to be able to conduct interviews with the deputies of the Moscow City Duma, so as to add a geographically defined centre perspective that would be provided by politicians on the same level as the regional deputies. Unfortunately, however, the deputies of the Moscow City Duma, or rather their gatekeeper, the Deputy Speaker of the City Duma, one Alexander N. Krutov, chose not to participate in the study. Mr. Krutov told me, in no uncertain terms, that neither he nor his fellow members of the City Duma could muster the time, strength, or indeed the interest to participate in the study. And incidentally, being an educated natural scientist himself, he confessed to harbouring a certain disbelief in the validity of the theories and methods of 'soft' social sciences.

This stood out in stark contrast with the response provided at the various regional locations involved in the study. Hence, the reaction of Mr. Krutov served, in my view, to give at least some credence to the multitude of regional allegations, encountered in the interviews, concerning a certain Moscow arrogance. By way of substitution, and in order to include a control group where the members would seem likely to lean towards a centre perspective, I decided to include members of the State Duma, and thereby especially try to get hold of those who were residents of the city of Moscow. However, the account of the results will mostly be structured around the findings of the regions.

Concerning these regions, St. Petersburg was chosen due to its relatively liberal sentiments. Volgograd, on the other hand, was included because it, at the time of the study, was centrally located in the communist party landscape, often denominated as the Red Belt. Khabarovsk is there to provide a Far Eastern perspective, so as to balance the otherwise unchallenged European slant. Perm, finally, was the subject of a pilot study during which my list of questions attained its final shape.[12] It is not a bearer of such characteristic traits as are the other cities, and it enjoys a comparatively calm and dispassionate political climate. For this reason, it is a valuable point of reference.

It should be pointed out that I have deliberately abstained from including any of the national republics of the Russian Federation in the study. There is a reason for this. Collective self-images in the national republics pertaining to the Russian Federation might be expected to diverge substantially from those encountered in the regions belonging to what, for the lack of a better term, may be described as the Russian heartland, i.e. the Russian Federation minus the national republics. This has been demonstrated through studies performed by Russian scholars in the field (Ivanov 1999).[13] My contention is that if noticeable differences in national self-images seem to be borne out by interviews with political elites in the Russian (*russkie*), territorially defined regions of the Federation, this will be quite indicative of potential rifts in the body politic at large. The conclusion could then be drawn that, if brought into the picture, sentiments in the national republics would tend to accentuate such cleavages even more.

Furthermore, there are several reasons for my letting regional politicians form the bulk of the respondents. The pivotal one is the need to discern and discuss differences and similarities between the regions and the centre, as well as between regions. In such a manner, the study throws some light upon domestic cohesion in the Russian Federation. For the sake of adding some somewhat subordinated, yet supplementary perspectives, I will also deal with the impact of political party affiliations and age group belonging, even if these perspectives will be given less space within the analysis. The singling out of the party factor makes it at least rudimentarily possible to gauge the effects of the slowly emerging Russian party system on the national self-images adhered to by the respondents.

The focus on legislators should, however, in no way be interpreted as though I hold this particular category of politicians to be pre-eminent by way of power and influence in the Russian regions. This would be far from the truth since in the regions, as well as in the centre, the executive branch definitely has the upper hand (cf. Stoner-Weiss 1997:7). Rather, they constitute a middle-of-the-road category between the most influential political elites and the general public, and precisely therefore, they form an interesting stratum for the study of prevalent national self-images and dynamics of national identification. Presumably, they display a blend of political awareness, relative accessibility and proclivity to uncover some elements of their non-instrumental collective identifications, which sets them aside from members of the executive, as well as the general public. Hitherto, they have also constituted a somewhat neglected category in research on Russian national identities.[14]

The regional samples, the way they were encountered and understood by me, are deemed representative for the sentiments adhered to among parliamentarians at that particular location at that particular point in time.[15] Thus, I offer my readers an account of interviews with primarily regionally based politicians in Russia, conducted during the period extending between the autumn of 1997 and the spring of 1999. The study provides some documentary evidence of the Russian political climate in various regions within the time span in which the interviews were undertaken.

Selecting What to Analyse

The analysis of public opinion is indispensable for a thorough understanding of politics and the bottom-up processes it entails, not least of course in democracies and countries undergoing a process of democratisation. The fact that my study does not include this perspective, therefore, does not mean that I find this particular dimension unworthy of consideration, since nothing could be further from the truth. However, quite a frequent strand of criticism often levelled at an author of a scholarly piece of work is fittingly subsumed under the heading of 'why did you not write a different book'. Certainly, every author is painfully aware that he/she will have to make strategic choices and delimitations, and in this volume I have chosen to assess national self-images and regional identities among a stratum of Russian political elites, predominantly at intermediate levels of power.

Concerning the co-variation between elite level policy choices and popular collective identifications at large in the Russian Federation, Wagnsson (2000) has found there to be partial convergence between the two strata during the 1990s. Whereas there was commonality of views between the elites and the populace regarding, for example, the desirability of drawing closer to the developed world, there was huge dissension on other crucial issues. Regarding the question of Nato extension to the east, which it will be recalled was a theme raised persistently by Russian politicians throughout the period between 1994 and 1999, the public, it seemed, hardly subscribed at all to attempts by the elites to 'securitise' the issue (cf. Buzan *et al* 1998) and invoke the spectre of renewed cold-war-like antagonisms. The endeavours of the Russian politicians to present scenarios in identity-related terms met with almost no success whatsoever, not least since, stunningly enough, the knowledge of what Nato actually comprised seemed to be close to non-existent among a significant number of the public (Wagnsson 2000). Similarly, as argued by other authors, the Russian public was largely indifferent about the fate of their Russian compatriots living abroad in the CIS after the dissolution of the Soviet Union, even though this item was very high on the political agenda during the first part of the 1990s (Shlapentokh *et al* 1997:160-161).

On the other hand, in connection with the acute phases of the first war over Chechnya in the period between 1994 and 1996, the populace was more prone to respond in a sympathetic manner to the politicians' calls for the need to safeguard the wholeness and integrity of the Russian Federation (Wagnsson 2000). However, even though the public partly held some greatly negative and sombre images of Chechens, as it did of other peoples originating from the Caucasus (cf. Petersson and Wagnsson 1998), it was not convinced of the pertinence of launching a protracted war for the sake of safeguarding those values. So, in this case as well, despite the attempts of the government to dress the presumed need for a certain policy in an identity-related garb, it did not manage to latch onto corresponding perceptions among the public.

By way of contrast, and this concerns a period which was not covered in Wagnsson's study, the second Chechen war (starting in September of 1999 under the premiership of the subsequent President, Vladimir Putin), seems to indicate that on this occasion, politicians and the public mood were largely congruent. In an opinion poll measuring the popularity of prospective candidates for the presidency in late January 2000, Putin collected the stunning rating of 62 per cent (*Sydsvenska Dagbladet*, 25 January 2000). The renewed campaign against Chechnya was clad in a verbal costume depicting the need to come to terms with an evil and vicious Other, comprised by Chechen ardent followers of Islamic fundamentalism, who allegedly were terrorists and hostage-takers. According to the official line of argument, the threat emanating from the Chechens was directed against the very heart of Russia and the territorial sanctity of the Russian state, as well as against the physical well-being of individual Russians. This will be developed further in subsequent chapters.

On the whole, the seeming popularity[16] of the aggressive official rhetoric bore sad witness to the compelling nature of simple in-grouping and out-grouping schemes, which appear to be able to attract considerable following, even among the educated public (Kovalev 2000).

The findings of the Nato part of Wagnsson's study might, indeed, indicate that the study of responses related to identities and self-images emanating even from intermediate elite levels of politicians may say little, if anything, about the prevailing moods within Russian society at large. This might well be true, but it is my contention that my choice of respondents will prove to be interesting and relevant in and of itself. As I said, this is precisely why I chose to write this particular book and no other. This aside, I would like to underline the need for carrying out studies of the interplay between the elite and popular levels in contemporary Russian politics. Wagnsson's study is one example of fruitful attempts to address such a need, and elsewhere I myself have been involved in making preliminary contributions to such efforts (Petersson and Wagnsson 1998). And I also believe that my choice of an intermediate category of analysis might actually facilitate the bringing together of the two perspectives.

Methodological Considerations

When studying identities and identity-related phenomena, personal interviews constitute, in my view, an indispensable method of social science research. Save perhaps the study of personal diaries and focus groups, there is no other method which permits the scholar to get equally close to the individual respondents. This is not to say that it is a perfect instrument. To be sure, there are far too many components engendered by the social interaction with the interviewer to allow us to infer that the interviewees' responses accurately reflect their mental depictions and 'inner worlds' (Alvesson and Deetz 2000:83).

According to Patton (1987:115), 'the fundamental principle of interviewing is to provide a framework within which respondents can express their own understandings in their own terms'. How, then, should this aim be realised? Putnam (1973:18) argues caustically that 'interviewing elites requires a strategy quite different from that familiar in most survey research. Closed-ended questions are efficient for researchers and allow respondents the convenient option of not taking the exercise seriously. But they are fatally flawed as instruments for understanding basic beliefs and values'. Thus, elites are often considered less receptive to closed questions (Heradstveit 1979:39). The open-ended interview is by definition more flexible and it is definitely more suitable for extracting nuances of opinion (Magomedov 1997:43). On the other hand, Heradstveit (1979:35) cautions that the informal interview technique is fraught with its own dangers, like the risks of posing leading questions and coming up with distorted perceptions of what has been said.

Therefore, a middle way is to rely on a semi-structured interviewing method, where the central questions are formulated beforehand, but where there also is a readiness to follow up on relevant issues raised by the interviewee (Stenelo 1984:30, Yin 1984:83-84, Patton 1987:111-112, Möller 1996:56-66). This is neither a free-floating conversation, nor a strictly structured questionnaire (Kvale 1997:32). Therefore, it is still possible, in Merton's (1990:12-13) terms, to 'uncover a diversity of relevant responses, whether or not these have been anticipated by the interviewer'. This is the route chosen in this study.

Thus, certain themes have been obligatory in each interview, but if the respondents have dealt with these topics spontaneously, the corresponding questions have not been asked. The internal order of the questions has been determined by the course the conversation has taken, and there has at all times been a preparedness to ask follow-up questions so as to make it possible to dwell upon subjects seemingly deemed to be vital by the interviewee, as well as of relevance for the study. The flexibility thus displayed is conducive to the shaping of a more conversation-like interview, and helps to bring about a better inter-personal relationship between interviewer and interviewee, since the interviewer thereby demonstrates that he or she is paying attention to what has been said (cf. Möller 1996:56-66, Holme and Solvang 1996:105). There is admittedly a downside to this flexibility since it is almost inevitable that specific questions be dropped in certain cases. Moreover, alterations in the exact formulations of the questions have been permitted so as to make it possible to counter-respond adequately to the responses given by the interviewee (cf. Kvale 1997:117). A similar methodological approach has been used by Magomedov (1997:43), who, like myself, held it to be 'a reliable mechanism for eliciting sincere evaluations and statements from the respondents'.

Out of the 110 interviews, 83 were undertaken by myself, and the remaining 27[17] were conducted by Swedish collaborators of mine, operating under my instructions. The subsequent stage of going through the transcripts and extracting the response patterns has in all cases been undertaken by myself. Therefore, I have been on top of the process and have also familiarised myself well with the interviews not conducted by me personally.

The rank-and-file regional parliamentarians might be expected to respond more candidly than their colleagues at the central level, not to mention, say, key members of the presidential administrations. For the last-named, as well as for another feasible category of respondents, namely the governors of the regions of the Federation, every statement given in an interview situation would have tended to be, as it were, a political statement, and would thus have been heavily slanted towards instrumental aims. By concentrating my efforts on parliamentarians at regional levels, I hope to have been able to reduce this degree of instrumentality. This raises another intricate question, that is whether instrumentally motivated answers in an interview situation should not be said to reflect collective identifications, but something else. There is no ready and clear-cut answer to this problem, which is reminiscent of the controversy in international relations theory as to whether interests or identity generate action (cf. Ringmar 1996, Katzenstein *et al* 1996). An in-between view would have it that action can be generated by both, and that identity is central in defining interests, that in turn prompt action (Jepperson *et al* 1996:53). In a similar vein, reflexive, as well as instrumental uses of language (cf. Petersson 1990), can be expected to underlie answers in an interview situation supposed by the researcher to sketch the make-up of national self-images among the respondents.

It is therefore my contention that even answers which seem to be given for instrumental reasons are likely to indicate identity-related lines of reasoning, since these will most often have contributed to the formulation of the instrumental interests in the first place. However, it would still seem more preferable to try to get at the more axiomatic strands of the national self-image, which would appear to be less affected by concerns other than those informed by identity. To supply a down-to-earth example of the latter mechanism: let us imagine a respondent who has a heavy working schedule and very limited time. He (and in the Russian regional political context it would most likely be a he) may have granted the interviewer one hour of his time and is really set on answering his/her questions in a forthcoming manner. However, in supplying his thoughtful answers, he finds that the allotted time is rapidly running out. Still, he takes an interest in the project and would like to give his answers to the full set of questions. Then, all of a sudden, he is confronted with the question of whether there are any aspects of the Russian past of which he feels personally ashamed. His immediate reaction is that there certainly are such aspects, but, on afterthought, he thinks that he should really start to prepare for a press conference that is taking place thirty minutes later. And he knows that if he starts to elaborate on why he feels personally ashamed of what took place at the time of Stalin's purges back in the 1930s, time will be slipping away fast. Therefore, he chooses to hold back on his initial impulse, and instead he replies that there are no such aspects in the Russian past. Thus, he has saved what might be five precious minutes, and he has done so, not because collective identities that he adheres to prompted him to do it, but since he had the highly instrumental interest of saving time, in order to make better preparations for his next commitment of the day. To be sure, such sources of distortion can never be fully eliminated. They may, however, be reduced by approaching a category of respondents that can be assumed to be less pressed by other instrumental considerations, while of course still being a relevant target group for studying phenomena such as national self-images among political elites.

Another problem, familiar to all experienced interviewers, is the one that concerns the disparity between what was actually said and conveyed at the time of the interview, and what is recorded and registered on the tape. Obviously, the tape can only retell part of the story, and is greatly flawed when it comes to conveying irony, mimicry, gestures, and the like. I believe there is no optimal solution to this problem. However, if one makes sure that there is not too much of a time lag between the interview and the writing of the transcript, one will be able to retrieve considerable portions of the setting of the interview from memory. And then, one will be able to add notes about recollected and significant non-audible details to the transcript itself. Certainly, what constitutes a reasonable time lag is subject to individual variations, but my own experience is that after two weeks my recollections definitely started to recede.

Moreover, some specific methodological problems associated with the study itself should be touched upon at this point. Firstly, there is a rather limited personal set-up in most regional *dumy*. When interviews are carried out with as much as a third of the deputies in the course of one week, it is quite natural for the respondents to discuss their experiences with those who have still not been interviewed. This problem is further accentuated by the fact that in locations such as Perm, Volgograd and Khabarovsk, visits to the assemblies by foreign scholars do still not constitute that frequent a phenomenon. (In Moscow and St. Petersburg they have certainly lost their aura, if indeed they ever had one.) For these reasons, one cannot rule out the possibility that deputies discuss suitable responses between them. Thus, the responses may not carry quite the individual brand striven for. They may, however, as was discussed above, still indicate collective identifications, albeit with more than a tinge of instrumental considerations.

Secondly, the experience of the Soviet period is not all that distant, and the older generation at least may still feel somewhat uncomfortable in an interview situation. They may, therefore, deliberately choose to hold back their inner opinions, for instrumental reasons of a different type from those encountered by our hypothetical time-pressed politician above. This problem was not, however, something I sensed to be of major consequence in these particular interviews.

Thirdly, 19 months lapsed between the interviews in Perm and the final ones undertaken in Moscow. Quite obviously, this reduces the comparability of questions regarding aspects of the current political situation. However, it also paves the way for constructing an illuminating analysis of change and continuity in political moods and sentiments during the period at hand.

Finally, regarding some of the questions that were put to the respondents, one cannot rule out the prospect that a certain 'politeness effect' has been at work, serving to accentuate the point made earlier that interviews by no means constitute accurate reflections of the interviewees' inner worlds. To be more specific, this concerns above all two topics raised by me in the course of the interviews, namely those dealing with the possible existence of foreign models for Russia to follow in its future development, as well as the question of which countries should be the main international partners of Russia. In the answers to both of these questions, Sweden, and indeed Scandinavia as a whole, was ranked highly. This may have been at least partly due to the fact that the interviewer was Swedish.[18] Even though several respondents gave spontaneous assurances that there was no such connection, the interviewer's origin may at least have made them think along these lines.

Somewhat related to this is another, more fundamental trait. All of the 110 interviews have been conducted in Russian. In some but not all cases there has been linguistic back-up assistance by Russian colleagues or local auxiliary staff. This raises the question whether the same responses would have been elicited by Russian colleagues, if they had asked the same questions of the same respondents, using the same methodology. As one of my Russian assistants put it: if she had put the very same questions to my respondents, she would probably have received somewhat different results. The interviewees would presumably, in both cases, have been quite sincere, maybe even frank, in speaking their mind. Even so, and this was her point, precisely because they were, in the one case, speaking to a foreign scholar, and in the other addressing a young fellow Russian who also happened to be a woman (cf. Svedberg 2000), they would express themselves differently, depending on the extent to which they sensed the existence of common frames of reference.

I certainly believe that my Russian collaborator had a most valid point, which is in conjunction with the familiar insider/outsider problem of fieldwork methodology, so often encountered by anthropologists and ethnologists (Geertz 1988, Marcus and Fischer 1986). And it is probably fair to say that in this sense, even though the basic results would be the same for insider and outsider scholars using the same questions and the same methodology when dealing with the same respondents, nuances would differ to an extent that is not insignificant.

It is, therefore, with a certain sense of humility that I posit that the results presented below will lay out the picture of Russian self-images as encountered by a scholar having an outsider's perspective. And I do not believe that there exists a safe, untainted, objective way, totally devoid of all biases, of painting that picture. As a scholar with an outsider's perspective, I cannot dissociate myself from the object that I am researching. Neither would, of course, a Russian scholar be able to do so. I am at all times interacting with my research object, in other words with my respondents, and the results of this interaction are to be found in this book. My part of the interaction is evident in several ways, since I have developed and applied the theoretical framework, supplied my interpretations all along, and not least, made the translations of the lengthy quotes encountered in the following chapters. This is the way it should be.

There is no objective reality to be uncovered 'out there', and neither should we pretend this to be the case.

The Slightly Salted Pickle

In a review of an early report emanating from this project (Petersson 1998a), my Danish colleague, Peter Ulf Möller (1999), harboured some misgivings, lest the method of posing next-to fixed questions to the respondents be too rigid a way to elicit responses that would serve as indicators of national identities. And certainly, as has been stated above, identity is a notoriously elusive concept. How does the social scientist know that he/she is studying identity in the first place? Of course, the researcher could always choose to argue that identities are like elephants, hard to define but prone to be recognisable once they are encountered. Or he/she could argue that, since all aspects of human actions and interactions involve the study of identities anyway, all social science research will, at all times, take matters of identity into account. By letting everything be encapsulated by the operational definition, nothing is actually left out – and so the definition is rendered worthless.[19]

Neither of the above constitutes a satisfactory way to treat the most serious question of how the social scientist is supposed to know that he/she is actually studying identities. Actually the crux of this matter was what prompted me to deal with national self-images in the first place, instead of tackling national identities head-on. Still, this is admittedly a rather roundabout way of addressing the problem, and so, consequently, I shall spell out my way of looking at this crucial and complicated matter.

Möller's main concern was that I, through my semi-structured, next-to-fixed question approach, would beg the question and more or less impose pre-defined identities on my respondents. In his view, there was a risk that, while uncovering some traits of my respondents' collective identities, I would also leave other aspects unexplored, precisely because they were not covered by my questionnaire. My pilot study approach made him think of the old anecdote about KGB specialists, who had devised a brain scanner, making it possible to fathom the national identities of the respondents, provided the KGB team asked the proper questions. When electrodes were thus applied to the forehead of an American, a Cadillac was promptly shown on the screen, and when the experiment was performed on a

Frenchman, the image of a half-clad Brigitte Bardot appeared before the researchers. However, when a Russian was put in the respondent's booth, the screen was blank for a long time. Not until the Russian was given a shot of vodka did something materialise, namely a slightly salted pickle. And so, the valid argument of Möller went, did I not run the risk of being unable to catch the image of the salted pickle, even though it certainly, somehow, formed part of Russian identity?

Möller's point is well taken, and I do believe that, had I confined myself to presenting the numerical quantifications of the response patterns below, I would certainly have run the risk of applying an overly rigid research methodology. This is why I wish to stress the semi-structured quality of my interviews. With few exceptions, all of the interviews lasted 45 to 100 minutes. Indeed, one can argue that 'even a 30-minute interview generates a rich, vast body of evidence' (Scheff 1996:294). The interviews were taped, with two minor exceptions, after which they were thoroughly transcribed into texts that were attentively read and re-read on numerous occasions. As previously mentioned, the semi-structured quality of the interviews permitted the respondents to elaborate on proximate themes that they deemed to be of relevance for the discussed topic. Altogether, the tapes and the transcripts constitute a wealth of information that most surely serve to represent if not all the salted pickles in the can, at least a significant number of them. Hence the multitude of rather lengthy quotes to be found in the following chapters. Quite simply, I found it to be of the utmost importance to convey the impression that my respondents, real people of flesh and blood, took an active part in the arguments developed in this book. Altogether, I would certainly venture to say that the screen will not remain blank.

There is one more aspect that I would like to underline here. Möller's criticism somehow seems to denote a belief in some kind of objective reality 'out there' that can be uncovered, provided that the researcher is patient and empathetic enough. I do not concur. It is the results of my interaction with the interviewees that will be recounted in the following chapters, and it is my interpretation of the answers that will guide the readers along. By the same token, my questionnaire did not contain any formulations explicitly asking for identity or national self-images, but rather used other questions to infer how identities and national self-images, to my mind, emerged in the given responses (cf. Alvesson and Deetz 2000:141).[20] The method of direct naming struck me as being far too simplistic and unidimensional. I believe one can make an analogy with birds caught in their natural habitat. If one grasps them too lightly, they will fly away, but if one grasps them too tightly, they will simply die.

To revert to the previous metaphor, other social scientists, deploying other modes and methods of investigation, will certainly be able to produce kinds and varieties of pickles from the can that in several respects differ from the ones I have found. No social scientist will ever be able to reveal the entire contents of that can, a fact which may be frustrating to some. To make matters worse for those prone to feel this sense of frustration, the can itself is constantly in the process of being socially reconstructed and reshaped, with regards to both its form and contents. However, it is my belief that if brought together, the findings of all those scholars who disclose some part of these ever changing contents of this ever changing can, will produce valuable insights into those elusive phenomena called Russian national self-images and, by extension, Russian national identity. It is also my firm belief that this applies for insiders as well as outsiders.

Notes

1. Early versions of the theoretical framework have been published in Petersson (1998a), (1998b). and (1999) and in Petersson and Wagnsson (1998).
2. For an opposing view, see Sucharov (1999:10).
3. It has been suggested to me that the most appropriate question relating to the third set would be 'What is the country I/we live in...?' et cetera. It is a good point. Still, I have decided to disagree on the grounds that you need not be a resident of the country of which you retain a national self-image.
4. Again for a different view, see van Alphen (1991:15) who argues that 'Identity and alterity ... are ... changeable products of the ongoing process of constituting a self-image'. Thus, he holds that the construction of the self-image actually determines identity. See also Gerndt (1988:12) for similar lines of reasoning.
5. i.e. not *russkie*.
6. Be it noted, though, that the notion of what was truly Russian (*russkii*) was thereby also watered down (Sakwa 1996:31, 198).
7. See, however, the cautions offered by Smith (1995:101) and Pearson (2000:106).
8. According to fresh statistics, 40 percent of the Russian population were estimated to be on the wrong side of the minimal level of subsistence, and thus earn less than 40 dollars a month (*Sydsvenska Dagbladet*, 14 June 2000).
9. See Kolikov (1997) for a case in point.
10. Cohen (1999:39) makes analogous observations in her study of the case of Slovakia.
11. See, however, the list of interviewee profiles provided after the list of references.

12. The main questions were chiselled out halfway through the pilot study. The subsequent amendments to the questions used for the interviews were modest and the lion's share were later put to all respondents.
13. In Ivanov's study there was, for instance, an indication of remarkable and worrisome ethnic animosities among the people of the national republic of North Ossetia where 84 percent of the Ossetian and 70 percent of the Russian respondents found it conceivable that they might take active part in a violent conflict to defend the interests of their own national group (Ivanov 1999:11).
14. See, however, McAuley (1997) who in her interesting, but chiefly empirical, study certainly takes this category into account.
15. This applies to a lesser degree to the pilot study in Perm. There, the main objective was to refine the questions to be asked in subsequent rounds, and the majority of the interviewees were, in fact, party leaders, and not deputies of the regional assembly.
16. One should, however, also point out that it had become increasingly difficult for mass media so inclined to try to convey more nuanced pictures of the second Chechen War. The relative absence of independent-minded media outlets in this regard certainly also had an impact when it comes to moulding the public view.
17. These were all interviews with State Duma representatives, undertaken in Moscow.
18. My collaborators, who conducted the bulk of the interviews with the State Duma members, were also Swedish.
19. This, in my view, is the net effect of Kymlicka's (1995:18) argument that nation is synonymous with culture which, in turn, is synonymous with people. Presto! In other words, by studying one of these phenomena, we are simultaneously studying the other two as well - to the same extent.
20. The full list of questions is provided in Appendix A.

2 Setting the Scene

Centre-Periphery Relations: A Background

This background is provided for the benefit of those readers who are not thoroughly familiarised with the constitutional make-up of the Russian Federation. Readers who are acquainted with the Russian political scene may want to skip the following pages and proceed directly to the next chapter, where I start to introduce the empirical findings emanating from my study.

The present administrative organisation of the Russian Federation comprises a rather confusing jig-saw puzzle, basically counting its origins from the territorial sub-divisions used in the days of the Soviet Union. Under the terms of the 1993 Constitution, the Russian Federation consists of 89 constituent elements, *sub'ekty*, or regions,[1] of different denomination. Of these, 21 are national republics. The remaining regions are primarily populated by Russians (*russkie*), and defined through territorial criteria as opposed to ethnic ones. 6 of these territories (*krai*), 49 are provinces (oblasti), 2 are cities of federal significance (Moscow and St. Petersburg), 1 is an autonomous province (*oblast*), and 10 are autonomous districts (*okrugi*). All regions are named explicitly in the Constitution, and any revision of the set-up would necessitate a complicated legal procedure, in accordance with the practice for changing a federal constitutional law. Any amendments to the paragraph in question, no. 65, have to be accepted by 3/4 of the deputies of the Federation Council and 2/3 of the members of the State Duma (Nilsson 1998:19).

According to the Constitution, these different constituent elements are equal in rights. In essence, however, the 21 national republics are somewhat different in kind. The only constitutional clause giving them preferential treatment is paragraph 68, where it is spelled out that they retain the right of having their national tongue as an official language alongside Russian. In the 1992 Federation Treaty, however, things stood somewhat differently. This Treaty was concluded between the centre and 19 of the republics (Chechnya and Tatarstan chose to abstain from acceding), at a time when Yeltsin was trying to woo the republics in his struggle with the then parliamentary structure, the Congress of People's Deputies, led by its speaker, Ruslan Khasbulatov. The timing of the Treaty contributes to the understanding of why the republics were granted rather far-reaching rights in this document. Among other things, they were given the privilege to retain revenue from the extraction of natural riches in their territories, as well as the right to conclude treaties with foreign powers. However, at the time of the referendum on the Constitution in December 1993, the support of the republican leaders was not as badly needed by the President as it had been at the time of the showdown with the parliament, meaning that these rights were not reiterated in the Constitution. Nor was there any reference to the Federation Treaty therein.

The Constitution itself is not terribly clear as regards the allocation of rights and duties between the centre and the regions. According to its paragraph 72, there is to be shared jurisdiction between the centre and the regions in a number of vital issues. These areas are certainly not marginal ones. They concern, for instance, the use of land and water resources, the disposal of subterranean riches, environmental protection, basic principles of the collection of tax revenue, as well as the establishment of common principles regarding local self-government. Hence, there are substantial grey zones as regards the delimitation of rights and duties, and this less-than-clear legal foundation paves the way for a tug-of-war between the centre and the regions. The situation is further compounded by the fact that, in addition to what is said in the Constitution, there is an unwieldy array of bilateral treaties that, from 1994, were concluded between the centre and individual regions. These were certainly called for, since there was a need for reaching more precise agreements on the division of labour within the areas of shared jurisdiction. However, they were often not made public, which further added to the opacity of the division of labour. Even though the national republics were first to sign such agreements, most territorially defined units had, towards the late 1990s, reached similar understandings with the Centre.

All in all, the individual regions' room for manoeuvre has, to a significant degree, been determined by the bargaining skills of their negotiators, as well as by the region's political weight and the personal relations between regional and federal leaders (Shlapentokh *et al* 1997:169). Here, the Republic of Tatarstan is a case in point. The republic was widely acclaimed for having reached almost optimum results when hammering out its relations with the federal centre in the power-sharing treaty that the Tatarstani team negotiated with Russia in 1994. Above all, the Tatarstani were successful in acquiring their rights to withhold fiscal revenue for their own benefit, instead of channelling it all on to Moscow to await reimbursements and subsidies. As was pointed out above, Tatarstan chose not to be party to the 1992 Federation Treaty. The fact that the republic, even against this background, managed to strike such an advantageous deal with Moscow contributed, no doubt, to the envy experienced in several of the territorially defined Russian regions, where it was argued with remorse that the treatment awarded the national republics was unduly preferential (Shlapentokh *et al* 1997). Undoubtedly, the question of finances and taxes constituted the sorest point in the relations between the centre and the periphery during the 1990s. In 1997 it was for example estimated that only two thirds of the expected tax revenue reached the federal till (Shevtsova 1999:205). Moreover, since the average levels of material well-being vary across the Federation, some regions, such as Moscow, St. Petersburg and Perm, have come to be net contributors to the federal budget, whereas the bulk of the regions constitute net beneficiaries. This is an obvious ground for resentment among the better-off.

The position of the regions vis-à-vis the centre was greatly enhanced as the regional heads of executives started to be popularly elected, from 1995-1996 onwards. This practice gave them a strong position of legitimacy in their regions, and they could no longer be removed by the federal president (Shevtsova 1999:204). More than any existing constitutional provision this meant a tremendous boost to the regions at the expense of the federal centre.

During the period when the Yeltsin administration turned a blind eye towards the rather bold endeavours of the regions to strengthen their hands, several regions, and above all the national republics, undertook some legislative acts which, subsequently, have come to be clearly at odds with the 1993 Constitution. The most well-known case in point was when, following a regional referendum in 1992, a constitutional clause was inserted into the Basic Law of Tatarstan, stating that the republic be regarded as an independent subject according to international law with a special relationship to the Russian Federation (Shevtsova 1999:41). In the Republic of Bashkortostan, also, several legislative acts were adopted that would seem to be in contradiction with the Constitution or federal law.

When Vladimir Putin assumed his presidential powers in the spring of 2000, he issued, after only a couple of months, a decree in which he instructed the legislators of Bashkortostan to bring certain republican laws and constitutional clauses in line with federal and constitutional regulations. This concerned, for instance, the stipulations that the president of the republic be a speaker of Bashkir, the laws concerning the vast delimitations of the powers of the republican president, as well as passages mandating the republic to accede to international organisations and to exchange diplomatic representatives with foreign powers (*Russian Regional Report*, 17 May 2000*)*. Also, in July 2000 Putin secured parliamentary acceptance for the reinstatement of the federal president's prerogative to fire regional heads of the executive, in cases where they had contravened the federal Constitution or federal law (*RFE/RL Newsline*, 19 July 2000). Thus, already in the first months of Putin's presidency, it seemed as though the most conspicuous aspects of this War of the Laws might soon be over. During the last years of Yeltsin's presidential tenure, however, the disarray defined a substantial part of day-to-day political realities in the Russian Federation.

When I undertook my interviews, there was a temporary lull in the armed hostilities between the federal centre and the national Republic of Chechnya. Following the devastating war of 1994-96, when the federal centre had to acknowledge a humiliating defeat at the hands of the vastly outnumbered Chechen rebel forces, Chechnya enjoyed, for a couple of years, *de facto* independence. On the basis of the Khasavyurt agreement of August 1996, which had been hammered out by the then Russian representative and security advisor of President Yeltsin, Alexander Lebed, and the Chechen President-to-be, Aslan Maskhadov, the final settlement of the *de jure* status of Chechnya was to be postponed for five years. However, during this period, Chechnya declined to send their representatives to the proceedings of the Federation Council, and had practically all appearances of a sovereign state. At the time of my interviews, most Russian politicians seemed to have resigned themselves to this state of affairs. This was soon to change, however, and already in September 1999 the second Chechen War was launched by the centre. I shall have ample reason to return to this matter later.

About the Cities

Khabarovsk was, as mentioned above, included in the study to provide a correction of an otherwise non-rectified European slant. It is a city situated on the nexus between the rivers Amur and Ussuri in the Russian Far East. The city was founded back in 1858 and gained its city rights in 1880. According to the last Soviet-time census in 1989, the city was inhabited by 600 000 people, and in the Khabarovsk Krai there are today an estimated 1.6 million inhabitants. However, it is fair to assume that outward-bound migration has been considerable after the dissolution of the Soviet Union. Khabarovsk was hit hard by the revised transportation and energy tariffs of the post-Soviet period, and many entrepreneurs discovered that terms of trade were not very favourable in this remote corner of the Russian Federation. Khabarovsk is, however, situated only some 40 kilometres from the borders of the Peoples' Republic of China. There is a budding border-region trade, but also some local concern about an unregulated influx of cheap Chinese labour.

Although it has some crude-refinery capacity, Khabarovsk retains no major energy sources of its own. Hence its problems with contemporary energy tariffs. The region shares the basic dilemma of the rest of the Far East, in that it has to face the legacy of a colony-like status in the Russian Empire, as well as in the Soviet Union. The region was, and still is, rich in natural resources, and main traits of its economy have for a long time been resource extraction and, given its strategic location, maintenance of defence capabilities. In sum, a lop-sided, almost monocultured economy developed, something which is very hard to come to grips with today (Shaw 1999:212). Therefore, it is natural that, in contrast to St. Petersburg and Perm, Khabarovsk is among the net recipients of subsidies from the federal budget.[2]

Historically, Khabarovsk has been able to benefit from its key geographical position astride several crucial routes of communication, by riverways and along the Trans-Siberian railway. Today, this advantage has largely abated. Still, the Krai's port facilities on the Pacific, such as Nikolaevsk-na-Amure, Vanino, and Sovetskaya Gavan', gained in importance as the Soviet Union dissolved and several hitherto important ports on the Baltics and the Black Sea were lost to the Russian navy and merchant fleet. These ports are today in dire need of investment, but are nonetheless also bases for the fishing fleet in the area, and the processing of fish and crabfish is a highly important source of revenue for the Krai. The produce is increasingly being sold in Japan and Korea, but it is uncertain how much of this trade is being registered in the official statistics.

My sample of interviews from Khabarovsk contains also 3 interviews with deputies of the Duma of the Jewish Autonomous Oblast (JAO). The JAO does not possess the status of being one of the 89 regions of Russia, and belongs administratively to the Khabarovsk Krai. The JAO, with its oblast centre Birobidzhan, is sparsely populated, and in 1995 there were 210 000 inhabitants, with some 80 000 living in the city. Despite its name, the Jews do not amount to more than about 4% of the population of the JAO. Rather, the reason for its establishment in 1928 (it acquired its status as an autonomous oblast in 1934) was ostensibly that Stalin had planned to make it a national home for the diaspora Jewry, thus acquiring financial funding from the western world, which had not yet settled to give the Jews a national home in Palestine. Later on, in connection with his anti-Jewish campaign of the early 1950s, Stalin may have had other, more sombre plans for Soviet Jews, namely to deport them on a mass scale to the faraway and remote JAO (cf. Kochan and Abraham 1983:439), which certainly did not have the best resource base or most preferable climate and geographical location in the country.

The city of *Perm* is situated immediately to the west of the Ural mountains. It is a city of old traditions, and received its city rights in 1781. Between the years 1940 and 1957, it too had to change its name, and so Molotov was the denomination it had to carry during this period. Today, the city has a good 1.1 million inhabitants and ranks tenth in population size among the krai and oblast centres of the Russian Federation. In 1993, there were 3.1 million inhabitants in the Oblast altogether (Pechenegina 1996:51).

There used to be a high concentration of defence complex enterprises in Perm. 9 principal enterprises, based in the military-industrial complex, accounted for almost 50 per cent of the industrial-manufacturing personnel, 36 per cent of the commodity output, and 37 per cent of the value of the productive fixed capital of the city (Pechenegina 1996:51). For example, Perm used to be one of the most important centres of the conventional arms industry of the Soviet Union, and until 1987, the city was closed to foreigners. A contributing factor to this practice was also that the Perm area was home to several prisons and labour camps in the Soviet period, forming part of the ill-reputed Gulag archipelago.

The conversion projects undertaken within the military-industrial sphere have thus affected Perm to a substantial degree, bringing about forced restructuring of the regional industrial base and some degree of underemployment and unemployment. There are, however, deposits of crude oil, coal and diamonds in the area, the exploitation of which has helped to cushion the social unrest that might otherwise have followed. Also, the region has managed to maintain the production levels within its traditional industry sectors fairly well, including steel, chemicals, and lumber processing. At least for the casual visitor, the regional centre itself seems to enjoy a relative affluence, and politically, the region has gained a reputation for stability and tranquillity. It is a net contributor – *donor* – to the federal budget.

St. Petersburg, which regained its old name in 1991 after the Soviet-time Leningrad interlude (and after having borne the name of Petrograd between 1914 and 1928), is the second city of the Federation. From 1712 it was the capital of Russia, but this period ended in 1918, as Moscow was restored as a capital after the revolution. St. Petersburg counts its origins from 1703, when construction works started on the Peter Paul fortress in the remote marshlands of the Neva river delta, off the Gulf of Finland. At this time, the area was strategically important in the ongoing war effort against the major regional adversary of the day, Sweden. The capricious decision to erect the city there and then was made by Tsar Peter I, also commemorated as Peter the Great. The city was built at an incredible pace during the following years, largely through forced labour and at a cost of immense human suffering. According to today's estimations, hundreds of thousands of lives were lost in the process (Hedenskog 1999:80). Thus, from the very outset, there came to be a sombre streak to the history of the city.

Peter's wish to transfer the capital to St. Petersburg was not only due to strategic reasons. It was also part and parcel of his forceful campaign to modernise and indeed westernise Russia. 'Moscow and St. Petersburg came to stand as symbols for two different Russias, before and after Peter', argues Hellberg Hirn (1998:41). The competition between the two capitals has been a continuous trait, defining much of their existence over the centuries. The decision in 1918, by the Bolsheviks, to relocate the capital to Moscow at the expense of St. Petersburg had tremendous symbolical significance. In the words of Pipes (1997:206), it was comparable to a scenario where a British prime minister would decide to move out of Downing Street and relocate his living quarters, as well as his office, to the Tower of London, from which he would rule together with his ministers, under the protection of Sikh guards.

St. Petersburg's most important trump card in its competition with Moscow has perhaps been that it has traditionally been considered the home of the Russian intelligents and the mainstay of Russian culture and education. Indicatively, it still retains the epithet Russia's cultural capital. However, light and darkness have been thoroughly intertwined in the history of St. Petersburg, and the lugubrious side to this past has persisted over the centuries. The 20th century bore this out with exceptional clarity, with the city seeing some of the most violent purges during the Stalin terror. The worst disaster of all befell the then city of Leningrad during World War II, when it was subjected to the famous 900-day siege by the Nazi army. As a result of this ordeal, somewhere between 1 and 2 million people lost their lives. The siege is very much present in the political history of the city, and programmes for catering to the needs of the *blokadniki*, the veterans of the siege, are still a key issue on the municipal political agenda.

The city today has about 5 million inhabitants. The strategic location of the city had clear implications during the Soviet period, and the military-industrial complex gained a pivotal position in the local economy during those years. By the end of the 1980s, 24 out of the 30 largest industries in the city belonged to the defence sector. Therefore, here as in Perm, the city authorities had to devote considerable time and energy to the problems of conversion after the dissolution of the Soviet Union. It is estimated that industrial output in St. Petersburg was reduced by 60% in the period between 1991 and 1995 (Hedenskog 1999:53).

Today, the situation has brightened. Shipping, the electronics sector and chemical industries provide, together with the banking sector, the backbone of the economy of the city. Like Perm, it is a net donor to the federal budget. Tsar Peter founded the city as a proverbial window on the west, and so it has remained. This not only concerns its geographical location. Even though some Soviet-style phenomena still remain, the city is clearly oriented towards promoting business and tourism. Taking a stroll in downtown St. Petersburg is an experience not very different from taking a stroll in Central European metropoles such as Vienna, Prague, or Budapest, but it is worlds apart from the impressions gained from walking through the city centres of Russian regional hubs, like Volgograd or Khabarovsk. In the political realm it is still considered to be one of the most liberally inclined regions of the Russian Federation (cf. Sikevich 1996:68). As indicated above, this is also the rationale behind its inclusion in this study.

Volgograd is the city that, in this study, has been chosen to epitomise the Red Belt. According to the 1989 census, which unfortunately is still the last official census to have been conducted in the area, there were 999 000 inhabitants in the city itself and 2.6 million residents in the Oblast. The city was, no doubt, more widely known under its former name Stalingrad,[3] which is forever associated with the gruesome battle of 1942-43, marking a watershed event of World War II. As a result of the battle, the winds of fortune changed abruptly, so as to forebode the beginning of the end for the, up to then, seemingly invincible Nazi German war machine. The name of the city was changed to Volgograd in 1961, during the period of Khrushchev's second wave of destalinisation. It had borne the name of Stalingrad since 1925 when the former denomination, Tsaritsyn, was abandoned. The city was founded already in 1589, but since it was totally devastated during World War II, it had to be built anew in the post-war reconstruction period. This makes today's Volgograd, by all appearances, a thoroughly Soviet city.

The city is situated in a traditionally grain-producing area, but developed during the Brezhnev period into a centre for heavy industry and energy production. There is some oil and gas production in the region, as well as refinery capacity and a dynamic petrochemical branch of industry (Moses 1994:99). The industrial development has had definite drawbacks, though, since the southern Volga region, and with it the Volgograd Oblast, counts among the most heavily polluted areas in Russia.[4] During the post-Soviet period, the Oblast has also been beset by problems of industrial conversion, since it, too, used to be a key area for the military-industrial complex. The gargantuan Tractor plant, which according to Moses (1994:98) was 'the prototype of the behemoth Stalinist industrial enterprises', was partly tied to military production. Consequently, it was affected by large-scale dismantling of state orders to the former military-industrial complex. By the mid-1990s, there was resulting unemployment and wage arrears, which served as a breeding ground for social discontent.

Still, even though the city and the oblast of Volgograd has been chosen to represent the Red Belt in this study, it deserves to be underlined that this has not always been an apt categorisation. In January 1990, the old communist nomenklatura was swept away by a strong wave of popular discontent, paving the way for democratically inclined or independent political activists. As a matter of fact, during the period 1990-92, the city of Volgograd earned a reputation as 'one of the most liberal and antiestablishment locales in Russia' (Moses 1994:119). For a couple of years thereafter, it was counted, along with St. Petersburg and Nizhnii Novgorod, as a front runner of 'economically liberal and politically democratic' local reform (Moses 1994:96). One should not, therefore, draw the conclusion that the Red Belt is part of a political landscape that has been on the map for many consecutive years. Rather, it evolved after the State Duma elections of 1995, which proved a major success for the Communist Party of the Russian Federation, the KPRF. The Red Belt marked the beginning of a looming North-South divide in Russian politics, with a major dividing line running along the 55th latitude. This boundary threatened to separate the highly urbanised and relatively well-off regions in the North from the poorer rural areas in the South, where malcontented voters tended to cast their ballots in favour of the then principal opposition, the KPRF. By this time, the Red Belt had come to contain 'the most ardent and consistent foes' of the Yeltsin administration's economic and political agenda (Shlapentokh *et al* 1997:191). These tendencies were reinforced after the presidential elections of 1996 (Hedenskog 1999:28). However, the setting again shifted somewhat after the Duma elections in December 1999 and the presidential elections in March 2000. Vladimir Putin, and the election bloc Unity/The Bear loyal to him, managed to do highly successful forays into former KPRF territory, thereby partly dyeing the colour of the Belt.

The Respondents

Out of my 110 respondents, the geographical subdivisions were the following: there were 21 respondents from Volgograd, 20 respondents from St. Petersburg and Perm, respectively, 16 respondents from Khabarovsk Krai, of whom 13 were residents of Khabarovsk, and 3 residents of the Jewish Autonomous Oblast in the city of Birobidzhan. 33 of the respondents were representatives of the State Duma, and of these 11 were residents of Moscow proper.

As far as political affiliations were concerned, 35 respondents were representatives of communist parties, either the main Communist Party of the Russian Federation (KPRF; 33 representatives) or the relatively minor and more radical Russian Communist Workers' Party (RKPR; 2 representatives). 36 came from other political parties (Yabloko; Democratic Choice of Russia, DVR; Our Home is Russia, NDR; the Liberal Democratic Party, LDPR; Russian Regions; the Social Democratic Party; and Honour and Motherland). This group of parties might seem to represent rather strange bedfellows, ranging from a number of recognised liberal and centrist parties like Yabloko, NDR, and DVR to the grossly illiberal and ultra-right wing LDPR. However, for several reasons, I found it most adequate to let the communist parties form a category of their own, since they comprise the most homogeneous party grouping. Also, they might be expected to be especially prone to harbour some more or less entrenched Soviet-time nostalgia, which should be relevant to take into account when discussing national self-images in the contemporary Russian Federation. Of the non-communist parties, most representatives came from the centrist NDR (13) and the liberal Yabloko (9). LDPR supplied an unduly small part of the interviewees; all in all, there were 4 representatives of this party. The main reason for this disproportionately low number was that they were not represented in the regional assemblies that I studied. Finally, 39 of my respondents claimed to be independents, meaning that they were not formally affiliated with any political party or bloc. These all represented the regional assemblies, where they often constituted a considerable part of the total number of deputies. In St. Petersburg, for example, 20 out of 50 were registered as independents at the time of my interviews. In Volgograd, well over half of the 47 deputies stated to be independent, even though several of them clearly sympathised with the KPRF.

To be quite honest, 'political parties' certainly constitutes too pretentious a name to be applied across the board in Russian political life. At the time of the interviews, only three of the political groupings referred to above could rightfully be labelled parties, namely the KPRF, Yabloko, and the LDPR. The other groupings were decidedly more loosely constructed, some of them carrying the traits of election-bloc alliances, others displaying a conspicuous lack of party programmes and federation-wide organisational structure, not to speak of any stable core electorate. As for political blocs and alliances, the Russian political space is fluid indeed, and in all Duma elections of the 1990s, regardless of whether they took place in 1993, -95 or -99, new party blocs and alliances were established almost on the eve of election day. More often than not, they were founded to provide launching pads for the careers of individual political leaders, and were centred almost solely around one, two, or three such prominent persons (cf. Shevtsova 1999:93). This seldom helped to bring any clarity concerning what these alliances stood for, and what constituted their political agendas. As was mentioned in the introduction, at the time of the elections of December 1999, electoral success was virtually stunning for one such election bloc. The alliance Unity/The Bear arose out of nowhere to the position of the second largest political grouping in the State Duma, next to the KPRF. This is a vivid illustration of how amorphous the Russian political landscape continues to be after almost a whole decade of post-Soviet existence.

KPRF is still the largest and best organised political force in the Russian Federation. Due to the fact that it could, to a large extent, draw upon the organisational resources of its predecessor, the Communist Party of the Soviet Union, it got a head start as compared to other collective political contestants. Under its leader, Gennadii Ziuganov, it has since the elections in 1995 been the largest party grouping in the State Duma, as well as the biggest oppositional party. It can pride itself on having the most loyal electorate but, on the other hand, it tends to be weakly represented among the younger age cohorts. Notwithstanding the circumstance that some Soviet-time nostalgia remains among the party ranks, the KPRF has basically established itself as a loyal opposition to the governments of the 1990s (cf. Sakwa 1996:40, Shevtsova 1999:226). *Yabloko*, for its part, is the only truly federation-wide liberal party of Russia, even though it is still rather weakly represented in the countryside. The party is widely conceived of as being the preferred choice of urban intellectuals. It has participated in all elections to the State Duma since 1993, and has under its leader Grigorii Yavlinskii managed, on all these occasions, to pass the 5-per cent threshold required for representation based on party ballot in the State Duma. *LDPR* won, under its flamboyant leader, Vladimir Zhirinovskii, a resounding surprise victory, with almost 25 per cent of the party ballot vote, at the Duma elections of 1993. The political establishment suffered a virtual shell-shock as a result, and the effects were readily noticeable in Russian political life. Most political leaders and established parties now saw fit to sound a more nationalistic note, so as to forestall any further gains by the LDPR, and to win some grounds for themselves. During the course of the 1990s, however, the political star of the three-time presidential candidate, Zhirinovskii, has been waning and before the State Duma elections in December 1999, the LDPR was symbolically denied legal registration.[5]

When it was founded before the elections in 1993, *DVR*[6] was devised as a 'party of power', and was thought to be able to achieve considerable success in the polls. Due to the fact that it came to be associated with the widely unpopular economic policies of the reformist cabinet under Yegor Gaidar, this success was not forthcoming, and instead the LDPR carried the day. *NDR*, which at the time was headed by the then Prime Minister, Viktor Chernomyrdin, repeated at the Duma elections in 1995 the performance of DVR two years earlier. Despite massive back-up by the incumbent presidential administration, electoral success was limited and instead, the KPRF emerged victorious. *Russian Regions* represents, perhaps, the first more ambitious attempt to circumvent and counterbalance Moscow and, on that foundation, join together the regions in an organised, federation-wide political force. The RR emerged as a parliamentary faction in 1995, but never established itself as a solid political party. The other political groupings mentioned above, namely the Social Democrats, the RKPR, and the 'Honour and Motherland', headed at the time by Alexander Lebed, were all of marginal significance and tellingly reflect the fragmented and rudimentary nature of the party structure in the days of Boris Yeltsin's second presidential tenure.

Apart from regional belonging and political affiliation, the impact of belonging to different age cohorts has also been tentatively gauged in this study. Out of my 110 respondents, 13 were born in the 1920s (2) or -30s (11). 41 were born in the 1940s and 36 in the 1950s, whereas 20 were born in the 1960s (18) or -70s (2). A mere 15 of my interviewees were women. This was no premeditated choice of mine, and the low percentage of women among my interviewees was due to structural circumstances. For instance, in the City Duma of St. Petersburg, which has thus been deemed to be some kind of liberal stronghold in Russia, there was only one woman among the altogether 50 deputies. Finally, out of the 110 respondents, there were 16 who had an ethnic belonging other than Russian (*russkii*). Of these, 5 were Ukrainians, 3 were Tatars, and 2 were Jews. Having made all these rather arid observations, I will now turn to the empirical findings of my study. I hope that my readers will find them as interesting as I did.

Notes

1. There is still no fully adequate English equivalent of the Russian term *sub'ekt*. Even though the term 'subject' is increasingly found in English texts on Russian politics, I would maintain that this word still does not quite correspond to established uses of English. and that it may give rise to misunderstandings. Hence, I have decided to keep the references to 'region' throughout, even though the connotations are somewhat broader than would have been desirable.
2. This is apparently a sensitive issue. In Khabarovsk, as well as in Volgograd, my respondents claimed that their regions were net donors to the federal budget. the federal statistics. however, tell another story (Hedenskog 1999:31). It seems as though regional parliamentarians are reluctant to concede that their regions of residence do not belong to the high-status stratum of regions that are independent of the centre for their sustenance.
3. Hence the suggestions that the city's name be changed back to Stalingrad. In the words of one non-communist deputy of the Oblast Duma, 'No-one is familiar with Volgograd, but everyone knows of Stalingrad' (V 11)
4. Residents of Hotel Intourist in Volgograd are given two complimentary bottles of mineral water a day, as the tap water is not only unfit for consumption, but even downright hazardous to drink.
5. After some legal wrangling, the so-called Zhirinovskii Bloc was, however, allowed to run in its stead. whereby it managed to squeeze past the 5-per cent post.
6. The party was originally founded under the name Russia's Choice, abbreviated VR.

3 The Past Dimension

Elements of Pride

It is now time to turn to the past dimension and the response patterns emanating from my interviews. Given the fact that the past is so tremendously important for the make-up of national identities and national self-images alike, and departing from the view that the construction and maintenance of a viable civic national identity in Russia would be desirable, it must be said that the analysis of this dimension will reveal both reassuring and deeply worrisome features. There is no doubt that the past dimension holds aspects that seem to serve as unifying bonds across the different spectra of my investigation. At the same time, however, there are other traits in relation to the near past where different political camps appear to be miles apart. It will probably not come as a surprise to learn that this concerns the evaluation of the Soviet period in Russian history.

In order to provide a basic point of reference, I will initiate the discussion by presenting the most frequent kinds of responses among the interviewees. The total sample of my interviews may not say that much, since they can hardly be judged to be representative for sentiments among Russian political elites at large. Even so, there is some value attached to the discussion of overall response patterns, since it gives us an additional basis for detecting what seems to stand out regarding regional and other patterns that were encountered. Thus, concerning the past periods or events giving rise to particular sentiments of pride, the most popular period in the Russian past turned out to be World War II, or in Russian parlance, the Great Patriotic War,[1] as it was mentioned by 33 respondents. Next came references to the reign of Tsar Peter the Great (22), the Soviet period as such (14), the conquest of space (13), and the reform period of Peter Stolypin and others of the early 20th century (11). Incidentally, this was the very ranking order given by the deputies of the State Duma who, ergo, seemed to reflect what might be called a national average of my study.

Indeed, my results would seem to indicate that the Great Patriotic War continues to exert the function of a national mobiliser well into the first post-Soviet decade of Russian political developments. In her fine book about the cult of World War II in Soviet Russia, Tumarkin (1994) argues that the war's mobilising clout was lost towards the close of the Soviet period, and indicates that it did not regain its strength under the first years of Yeltsin's presidency. On the basis of my findings pertaining to a stratum of regional political elites, one might, however, hypothesise that whether by default or through the lack of contending candidates[2] or, indeed, for whatever reason, the Great Patriotic War still comprises a greater part of the affective glue that helps to keep the bundle of national identifications together.[3] The sentiments of personal pride regarding the War seem to constitute the most potent unifying trait of the past dimension of my respondents' national self-images. As we shall see, this observation is valid for almost all of the subgroups[4] represented in my study.

Regarding the Soviet period, Tumarkin (1994:133) argues that 'the idealized war experience was a reservoir of national suffering to be tapped and tapped again to mobilize loyalty, maintain order, and achieve a semblance of energy to counter the growing nationwide apathy and loss of popular resilience of spirit'. My own findings would indicate that, even though there are no longer any major campaigns orchestrated from above, recollections of the War at least among regional political elites appear to have continued to instil feelings of commonality, even towards the end of the first post-Soviet decade. This being so, what is it about these remembrances that so seemed to move my respondents? First and foremost, one should underline the fact that the magnitude of the victory itself was a lingering subject of pride. It was, in the words of one of my respondents, 'a victory beyond time and space' (V 4+5).

In developing this theme, several interviewees came close to the old Soviet-time version that Hitlerite fascism was defeated thanks only to the Soviet Union, and that, as a result, the world has an enormous debt to pay the Russian people. These sentiments were typified in the words of two deputies of the Khabarovsk Krai Duma:

> I would posit that Russia, first the Russian Empire, and then the Soviet Union, played a great role in the world, not least for the development of world civilisation. We won the Second World War. We did not allow fascism to spread further in Europe or to consolidate in Asia.
>
> (Kh 9)

> The Great Patriotic War was undoubtedly of such a magnitude that it shook the whole world. It was above all thanks to the Soviet Union that fascism was vanquished.
>
> (Kh 14)

Moreover, the Victory seemed to be a domain where respondents were still sure of what representatives of other countries thought. This stands out in apparent contrast to several other areas where Russia's past greatness has waned considerably. Russia's glory as the perceived chief victor of the war has lasted, and this might contribute to the continued appeal of recollections of the War. 'I never met anybody, anywhere in the world, who was not aware of the contribution made by the Soviet Union' (SD 33), remarked one State Duma deputy, while one of my respondents in Volgograd expressed his assessment with great confidence: 'I believe that you and I evaluate Russia's role in the Great Patriotic War in a similar manner' (V 16). To his mind, there was no need to further elaborate on the subject. Apparently, he took it for granted that I, too, shared his assessment of the Soviet war effort as an awe-inspiring and glorious feat, indeed as a victory beyond time and space.

Regional and Other Variations

Regionally, there were some differences to be noted. The interviews in Perm did not include all of the questions asked of later respondents, since, as has already been mentioned, these earlier interviews were conducted in connection with a pilot study. Therefore, there are only results from the three other regions on the question related to pride of the national past. These results show that Volgograd displays a distinctly Soviet-flavoured appreciation of history, whereas the respondents of St. Petersburg and Khabarovsk seemed more sympathetic to Russian non-Soviet history. It deserves to be noted that, in this sense, the Volgograd respondents seemed to be more communist than the representatives of the subgroup comprising the KPRF itself. Volgograd was at the time situated in the very centre of the Red Belt, and so, although the results may not be all that surprising per se, the contrast with the KPRF stands to be noted. The geographical overall distribution of views, and their respective ranking, is indicated in the table below, with the relevant number of respondents expressing the most popular views given in brackets.[5] The response pattern encountered in the State Duma is also shown in order to provide a point of reference:

Table 3.1 Pride of the national past by region

State Duma	St. Petersburg	Volgograd	Khabarovsk
1. The Great Patriotic War (19) 2. Peter the Great (9) 3. The Soviet period in general (6); The conquest of space (6) 4. Russian culture and science (5); The reform period of Stolypin and others	1. Russian history in general (4) 2. The Russian people (3) 3. Peter the Great (2); Alexander II (2); The Great Patriotic War (2); The conquest of space (2)	1. Peter the Great (5); The Great Patriotic War (5) 2. The October revolution (4); The Soviet period (4) 3. Catherine II (3); The Soviet super-power status (3)	1. The Great Patriotic War (7) 2. Russian history in general (4) 3. The Russian people (3); Russian and Soviet inter-ethnic stability (3); Peter the Great (3); The Napoleonic Wars (3); Russian culture and science (3)

Indeed, Volgograd stood out starkly. Here, 31 out of 54 statements concerned the Soviet period. The Soviet-time aspects that seemed to evoke sentiments of pride showed a certain amount of variation, but most frequent were references to the Great Patriotic War, the October Revolution, and the military might and status of the Soviet Union. There was a general lingering enthusiasm, geared more than anything towards the period as such:

> During the Soviet period everybody had the chance to develop. How many useful and good things were made during the Soviet period! What construction sites! What progress! Factories were built in no-time. There was an enthusiasm to be proud of.
>
> (V 8)

Thus, life during the Soviet period was idealised and depicted in a favourable light (V 7). As a contrast, the great reformers of the late 19th century and early 20th centuries were conspicuously absent from the list. In fact, none of the respondents in Volgograd mentioned the names of Peter Stolypin or Sergei Witte as objects of pride. Generally, references made to the Russian imperial past concerned times of expansionist gain, times of successful defence against aggression, or other examples of Russian greatness, for instance in the cultural field. Peter the Great turned out to be quite popular, and along with the Great Patriotic War, his constituted one of the time periods most frequently referred to.

The responses in Volgograd constitute a striking contrast to the pattern of responses encountered in St. Petersburg, where a mere 2 out of 23 references indicated the Soviet period as an era holding elements of which to be proud. Here, the single, most frequent answer was not to point towards any period in particular. If respondents did profess themselves to being proud of their history, this was often over its entirety, without singling out any specific periods or aspects:

> I am a citizen of this country and I am proud of all periods, regardless of in which colours people try to paint them today. Of late there has unfortunately been a tendency to seek the negative sides, but I believe that one, for every period, should try to find the positive ones.
>
> (Spb 11)

Khabarovsk found itself in a position somewhere in between. There, 15 out of 51 references concerned the Soviet period, and among these, the most frequently encountered regarded the Great Patriotic War, where, according to one respondent 'the people acted as an organic whole and safeguarded its interests, while not forgetting international interests' (Kh 16). Other common reference points concerned Soviet-time achievements in the fields of science, culture and social life. The following quote is quite similar in tone and spirit to the one from Volgograd:

> Above all, I would like to stress the achievements made during the Soviet period, in the fields of science, economy, medicine, education, and so on. In these fields, unusually high levels were attained during a very brief period of time. This one should, on the whole, be proud of. And still we were at war during the same time. People lived well. What sanatoriums there were, what leisure areas! All working people could go for a holiday, they could go visiting their friends or relatives. Russia has never ever experienced such a boost during such a brief period of time.
>
> (Kh 2)

Furthermore, as in St. Petersburg, several respondents in Khabarovsk asserted that Russian history in its entirety was an object worthy of pride.

This theme was, in a somewhat circular manner, elaborated on by one interviewee:

> I believe that we, in principle, can be proud of our past, albeit with some minor exceptions. We have a difficult and burdensome past, but it is our past and we can be proud of it, on the whole we can be proud of our forebears. There may have been some negative moments, but there have been mistakes made in every nation's history. On the whole, our forebears gave us a great and powerful state, they did all they could, and we can be proud of our past.
>
> (Kh 11)

Other respondents in Khabarovsk provided fine illustrations of the deeply problematical relationship between what they seemingly thought to be the centrally stipulated attitude towards the Soviet period (at least as postulated by the federal government and the predominant agenda-setters of the intellectual and media-driven debate), and the attitudes they themselves sensed that they held. One deputy, an independent devoid of any party label, expressed herself in the following manner, reflecting a reluctance to indulge in condemnations of the past:

> Even if many do so today, I do not feel ashamed of 1917. One can apply different labels, but all that was done, among other things, during this very year, was done out of sincere convictions, good ideas, endeavours and objectives. Therefore, why should one feel ashamed of 1917? This is my past, this is the past of my state, the past of my family.
>
> (Kh 12)

Thus, even though sentiments did not match those encountered in Volgograd, several respondents in the Khabarovsk Krai Duma fondly recalled aspects relating to the Soviet past. There were different rationales pointed out to me, and far from all of them related to ideological factors. Rather, what often seemed to matter was that Russia had been great, or at least perceived as great, during that period, which made for a marked contrast when compared to the contemporary situation. For example, one deputy explained why, according to him, it was quite possible, and indeed natural, to at the same time hold both the periods of Peter and the Soviet Union in high esteem:

> I am appealed by the politics of Peter I. He acted dynamically even though he had difficulties in meeting certain objectives. I also relate closely to the Soviet

period. Even though there were difficulties, people were aware of ideas that they had in common, and therefore they could achieve great things in spite of everything. Today there is a re-evaluation of the values of the time, but one must not cross them out. If one looks at the statistics, Russia has never developed as dynamically as it did during the times of Peter and the Soviet period. At this point in time there is a certain downturn, but I believe that, when people pause to think, they will find that these were the most dynamic periods of our history.

(Kh 1)

As has been pointed out above, the rankings among the State Duma deputies corresponded to the overall pattern emanating from my study. This ranking was somewhat different from that of the subgroup consisting of members of the KPRF. The notable difference in the KPRF case was that the Stolypin reform period was not included among the top five. Instead, the October revolution of 1917 was listed among the five most popular alternatives. Certainly, the omission of the Stolypin reforms was not extraordinary, since they symbolise for many the endeavours in the early 20th century to entrench small-scale capitalism in the Russian economy. The agrarian reforms, which perhaps constitute the most widely known component of the Stolypin reform package, were geared at breaking up the village communes, encouraging individual landownership and raising productivity in the rural areas. According to rather frequently encountered interpretations within as well as outside Russia, they were permeated by the reformers' desire, inspired by the tenets of Social Darwinism, to 'wager on the strong and sober'. While the accuracy of the latter assessment has been somewhat contested (Macey 1987), it is quite clear why, in the light of the viability of these beliefs, the Stolypin reforms do not seem to be very popular among the adherents of the Communist party.

Turning to the representatives of other, non-communist political parties, such as the centrist NDR, the ultra-nationalist LDPR, the liberal *Yabloko*, and a number of smaller, primarily liberal parties not represented on the State Duma's party ballot list, the Great Patriotic War was again most popular, followed by Peter the Great, the reform periods of Stolypin and others, the reign of Alexander II, and, notably, the conquest of space. That references to the Soviet period in its entirety were absent from the list should come as no surprise, given the political affiliations of the bulk of the respondents in this subgroup. However, it should be noted that the space programme, itself a prominent symbol of Soviet power, was esteemed so highly. Most significantly, it is evident that the inspirational clout of the Great Patriotic War did not seem to be restricted to the adherents of communist ideology. Rather, it appeared to be a national mobiliser across the whole spectrum of respondents (cf. Karlsson 1999).

In this subgroup of adherents to non-communist political parties there is, if anywhere, a glaring absence on the list of most popular moments in history. There were only very scattered references to the *perestroika* period (1 respondent), the defeat of the attempted coup in 1991 (2) or the dismantling of Soviet rule and concomitant democratisation around the years 1990-91 (2). If one recalls the great political enthusiasm and active engagement among liberals and democrats of those years, it is indeed noteworthy with what fatigued indifference these events seem to be reviewed today. Notably, the Khrushchev period gathered more references in this category (3). There are many interesting aspects that have come to the surface in my respondents' response patterns, but this issue of relative absence is certainly one of the most intriguing facets. The dog did not bark, and that is significant. In sum, the basic response pattern among the politically defined groupings can be presented as follows:

Table 3.2 Pride of the national past by political affiliation

KPRF	Other parties	Independents
1. The Great Patriotic War (13)	1. The Great Patriotic War (14)	1. Russian history in general (7)
2. Peter the Great (11); The Soviet period in general (11)	2. Peter the Great (7)	2. The Great Patriotic War (6)
3. The October revolution 1917 (8)	3. The reform period of Stolypin and others (5)	3. Peter the Great (4); The Russian people (4); Russian culture and science (4)
4. The conquest of space (7)	4. Alexander II (4); The conquest of space (4)	

The dimension in which the otherwise, perchance, most interesting differences could be discerned on this score was that concerning differences among the age groups, which allowed for the formulation of some interesting hypotheses. Bearing in mind the results presented above, the generational rankings consisted of the following. Again, only the most frequently mentioned aspects will be displayed:

Table 3.3 Pride of the national past by age group

1920s/1930s	1940s	1950s	1960s/1970s
1. The Soviet period (5)	1. Peter the Great (12)	1. The Great Patriotic War (16)	1. The Great Patriotic War (6)
2. Peter the Great (4)	2. The Great Patriotic War (9)	2. The conquest of space (6)	2. Russian history in general (4)
3. Catherine II (3)	3. Stolypin and others (7)	3. Culture, science (5); Alexander II (5)	3. Peter the Great (2); Catherine II (2); The Reconstruction after the Great Patriotic War (2)
4. Novgorod (2), Alexander II (2); The conquest of space (2)	4. The October revolution (5)	4. Peter the Great (4); The Reconstruction after the Great Patriotic War (4)	
	5. Alexander II (4); The Soviet period (4)		

Most striking in this context is, perhaps, the absence of the Great Patriotic War in the top five among the representatives of the oldest generation. Its mustering strength also seems to be less intense among the respondents born in the 1940s, where the reign of Peter the Great appears to be the period instilling most pride. When reviewing this pattern, one might be led to the hypothesis that the Great Patriotic War is the most compelling symbol among those that did not have to experience it or suffer its most immediate aftermath. Since the number of interviewees is scant, I will not draw any further conclusions. Let it also be noted, however, that the youngest generation is the only age-group to put references to the entire Russian history among the top five.

There was also an interesting ranking among the female respondents. This was, along with those born in the 1920s or 1930s, the only category where the Soviet period in general was referred to most frequently as a period instilling pride. Some women representatives indicated that their positive feelings towards the Soviet Union were due to the concurrent socio-economic safety net, where the availability of child care and nursery homes was a foregone conclusion, rents were low and unemployment was dwarfed in comparison with today's levels (SD 6, SD 33, V 4+5). Similarly, other women indicated that they deeply deplored the dissolution of the Soviet Union, particularly so, perhaps, since the post-Soviet state borders had separated friends, relatives and acquaintances from each other and inhibited their chances of meeting in a normal and desired manner (V

4+5, V 7, V 10, V 19, P 4). 'People long and hope for a reunion, so that we can live peacefully and the border can become what it used to be', one woman deputy of Volgograd argued (V 10). The ensuing response pattern among the women was consistent with the men's, however, since references to Peter the Great came in second position, followed by the Great Patriotic War.

Finally, among the non-Russian (i.e. not *russkie*) respondents, there was a ranking according to which Peter the Great was most popular, followed by Catherine II, the Soviet period in general, and the Great Patriotic War. It may be that this order is not very surprising, since Peter the Great was known in his day to promote the career of individuals on the basis of professional merit and personal qualifications rather than on the grounds of ethnic belonging. Catherine, of course, was herself of non-Russian origin – she was German. And the Soviet period, at least on the surface, was characterised by a downplaying of the ethnic factor.

Models from the Past?

As has been discussed above, the national past is not only a repository of recollections and myths from which to draw strength and identify elements of pride. The past may also indicate paths and lines of action to be chosen in the present and for the future. Scholars within the tradition of cognitive theory have amply demonstrated the tendency of individuals to apply successful lessons from their personal history to current circumstances (Vertzberger 1990). In a similar manner, theorists preoccupied with the diffusion of ideas have indicated lessons from the national past, along with lesson-drawing from abroad, as the major source of inspiration for leaders trying to chart a new political and/or economic course for their country (Bermeo 1992). Thus, it is natural to consider this factor in this study also, by reviewing to what extent the respondents regard models from the past to be applicable to the contemporary context. When this particular question was put, the interviewees were given the choice to indicate whether they held such lessons to be applicable partly or in full. All in all, out of the 106 references given in the five cities, 10 respondents rejected outright the idea that past models could be of any use in bringing Russia out of its present crisis. Among the remaining references, certain suggested models were quite clearly more popular than others. Consequently, 19 concerned the period of the great reformers of the early 20th century, 15 suggested learning from Peter the Great, and 26 referred to various aspects regarding the Soviet period.

The refutation of the applicability of past experiences to the solving of contemporary problems was thus not altogether uncommon among my interviewees. The general argument was elaborated on by one of the deputies of the St. Petersburg Duma:

> Unfortunately there are no such models today. It is impossible. With all due respect to our forebears, this one cannot do. It is the same thing as with children who cannot keep on emulating their parents, no matter how respected and wise these parents are. History has to develop in a spiral leading upwards, albeit downwards at times, but then upwards again. There are certain similarities, but they are in a spiral mode and cannot be repeated. One cannot look back at Russian history, one has to look around and upwards. It is no use reinventing the wheel, we do not have to start from scratch, we only have to select wisely, look through our Russian prism, reassess, and implement.
>
> (Spb 16)

In other words, this particular deputy was rather willing to keep an open mind to foreign experiences. This is what he meant when talking about there being no need for reinventing the wheel, and we shall return to that subject below. As moderate as his argument might seem to be, it was, however, gainsaid by the bulk of the respondents, who seemed more in favour of turning to the national past for inspiration on how to deal with the somewhat gloomy present.

As was mentioned above, among those who believed in learning from history, considerable attention was given to the great economic reformers of the early 20th century, above all Peter Stolypin. This was exemplified by one deputy of the St. Petersburg Duma:

> I am very much attracted by the Stolypin reforms. Had the First World War not erupted, and had Stolypin been allowed to continue his reforms, our country would have met with quite another fate. If one could correct the past today, I would absolutely have given this man more time to rule.
>
> (Spb 11)

Similarly, another deputy from St. Petersburg argued that he experienced personal pride when looking back at the days of the great reformers:

There were great politicians and economists who, from the early 20th century, carried out reforms which were conducive to the rapid development of Russia. This was especially true for the period 1907-14, when Russia's growth rate was the highest in the world, thanks to the personal initiatives of Witte, Stolypin, and Alexander II (...) They were great men, and they showed that Russia has always had a potential for normal economic reform. They should be a source of inspiration, even for the young generation of today.

(Spb 5)

No great variations on this subject could be discerned between the different subgroups, but it deserves to be pointed out that the preference ordering of the KPRF respondents turned out to be somewhat unexpected. They actually chose to rank the reign of Peter the Great to be the historical period most worthy of emulation, whereas the national unity during the Great Patriotic War came second, and the Soviet period and the reconstruction efforts after the War were mentioned only in third position. Thus, the ordering was not quite as Soviet-inspired as one might have expected. The same thing could actually be said about the preferences of the Volgograd respondents. For although the greatest number of deputies there asserted that no historical models were applicable in the first place, only 10 out of the 20 references that were given concerned Soviet times, whereas the reforms of Stolypin and others constituted the most frequently mentioned model. In Perm, St. Petersburg and Khabarovsk, the times of Peter the Great were again most frequently singled out, followed by references to the great reformers.

What Accounts for Popularity?

While recognising that the Great Patriotic War was fought and won under the leadership of Stalin, one should acknowledge two things when discussing what might account for the tendency to continue to hail and cherish its memory. First and foremost, making a wholesale renunciation of one's country's past is not an easy thing to do. Given the pivotal role of the past dimension in the construction of national self-images, it is most reasonable to expect there to be an emotional need to experience a positive, or at least not altogether negative, pride/shame balance (Scheff 1996). This does not only relate to the meso/macro level. Considering the fact that the parental generation, or at least the great-parental generation, of today's active age groups fought, bled and died in the defence of Russia, there is a more tangible need, even at the level of the family, to recognise that these near and dear people did not die completely in vain (Kh 13). It would not be an easy thing, for instance, to accept that the main effect of the war effort was, in the longer run, to prop up and legitimise an authoritarian regime at home, and to subject the peoples of Central Eastern Europe to almost 50 years of political oppression. Rather, as was discussed above, some emotional well-being can be derived from an otherwise dire situation when at least some positive and even glorious moments can be extracted from one's national past. This might make it somewhat easier to cope with a troublesome situation here and now, at least for some occasional, brief moments (cf. Tumarkin 1994:201). Also, as was indicated above, it was often pointed out by the interviewees that the internal cohesion achieved during the time of the Great Patriotic War, although at great cost, was something which showed the ability of the Russian people to close ranks in times of trouble, and thus to withstand aggression and threatening havoc. And, it was argued, this is an experience from which some inspiration could still be drawn today.

On a more general level, Hedetoft (1995) has found that, as a rule, war experiences have a most compelling force in national imaginings. War heroes, war achievements, sacrifice and the martyrdom of war are, according to him, pivotal when it comes to fostering national cohesion and strengthening the affective glue. This goes for all nations, but especially multi-national, multi-cultural states that do not benefit from the sense of belonging that may be brought by relative homogeneity. These states are, in Hedetoft's words, 'heavily reliant on state-oriented vertical symbolism, condensing sentiments of pride around myths of crises and war' (1995:133, cf. 177-178). This military dimension, he goes on to argue, is 'invested with a magical agglutination value, providing a unitary identity with symbolic fodder often strong enough to ward off the diversifying effects of different cultural-ethnic components' (Hedetoft 1995:177). So, while some aspects of Hedetoft's case might be slightly overstated here, the Russian predilection for taking pride in the wartime experience of the Great Patriotic War seems explicable, not only for idiosyncratic reasons, but also because of more general factors, pointed out within the social sciences at large. Where state-centred identity seems to be comparatively weak in general terms, it is still possible to invoke it in times of war and crises of a comparable magnitude (Hedetoft 1995:162). It is, therefore, quite natural that those great moments of coming together and fighting side by side for common goals and objectives be remembered and cherished for long periods afterwards (cf. Scholte 1996:42). And indeed, such aspects are crucial building blocks in the construction of both ethnic and civic national identities.

To my mind, there is yet another aspect accounting for the centrality of the Great Patriotic War which should be noted in this context. It pertains to the immediate post-war years, and the reconstruction efforts during that period, which were quite often referred to by my respondents as a Soviet-time model from which inspiration could also be drawn in the contemporary period of political, social, and economic disarray. According to several respondents, some of the optimism, unselfishness and sense of common purpose that characterised the immediate post-war period, would have been highly desirable in the present context. As one of my interviewees put it, 'there was ... a real enthusiasm which we are lacking today' (Kh 7). The reconstruction work of those days had quite simply displayed 'everyday heroism among the people' (Kh 12), and evidently this continued to instil pride:

When the Great Patriotic War was over, the whole energy of the people was, through the government, geared at reconstructing the economy and agriculture (...) I was only a child back then, but I saw how rapidly everything was reconstructed. People rejoiced every day, they believed in the future, they lived in the future.

(V 10)

I recall how the people rose to its feet after the war, how it stood up again in the course of a mere decade. I used to live in Dnepropetrovsk in Ukraine back then, and there as in all other cities, there was a tremendous activity of building and reconstruction... Among our people there was this desire to have the country resurrected.

(Kh 2)

Apparently, it was a widespread feeling that, even though the economy was in a shambles and people were destitute during the first post-war years, they were, in some respects, better off than the present generation. This was not only argued to be the case in view of the present day's lack of enthusiasm and optimism, but also concerned other matters. 'We have experienced a downfall in economy that we did not even experience after the Great Patriotic War', argued one communist representative of the St.

Petersburg City Duma (Spb 4, cf. Kh 2). This type of comparison, between the contemporary period and the strenuous post-war reconstruction efforts, was obviously another way of voicing criticism towards the current policies of the presidential administration. 'People were paid their salaries [back then]' (Kh 2), one Khabarovsk respondent observed dryly and, indeed, in late 1998, when this particular interview was conducted, the issue of country-wide wage arrears loomed high on the political agenda.

Contrary to my findings in this study, that the youngest respondents held the Great Patriotic War to be the finest moment in Russian history, the young generations of Russia have, at least at the public level, seemed to take a sceptical or rather disillusioned view of both the present and the past (cf. Tumarkin 1994). Post-Soviet political realities have provided rich indications that the younger generations, at least those born during the 1970s and 1980s, have lost most illusions pertaining to politics. At any rate, they might not be prepared to make a blanket acceptance of the political values cherished by their parents and grandparents. One of the respondents from Volgograd, born in the late 1940s, lamented this fact, and found it hard to accept that today's youngsters did not hold the memory of the Great Patriotic War in as high esteem as did her own generation:

> The victory in the [Great Patriotic] War [was something to be proud of], it was before we were born, but it was a victory outside of time and space. From time to time, young hooligans say that 'if you had not fought so well during the war, we would have lived better today'. This is an absurdity; people will never be able to accept that. We did as much as we could to make life easier in the occupied countries and give them a chance to resurrect themselves...
>
> (V 4+5)

Intuitively, the popularity of Peter the Great seems harder to grasp for the outsider than is the high ranking of the Great Patriotic War. The fact is that the legendary Tsar has remained a controversial figure throughout national history, and his name was brought to the forefront of the perennial struggles between Slavophiles and Westernisers, above all during the 19th century (Riasanovsky 1985). He has clearly achieved the status of being a symbol of one of the major poles of that great debate (Hellberg Hirn 1998:198), and in the contemporary period, when the question arose as to whether Russia should orient itself primarily westwards, eastwards, or inwards, following the tenets of Eurasianism (Shlapentokh 1997), he is still very much a person at the forefront of topical debates. Tsar Peter was undoubtedly a great innovator, and his at times almost frantic reforming activities, aimed at modernising Russia, certainly left their lasting imprint on the country's development. And today, as during previous centuries, politicians inclined to further reform Russia and integrate it more with the western countries hold this to be a good and praiseworthy thing:

> [Tsar Peter's reign] is a period to be impressed by. The 20-year transformation period under Peter not only opened a window on the west, but also provided a real push to Russia's development in the following epoch in history.
> (P 13)

However, even those, who maintain that there are certain lessons to be drawn from the time of the great Tsar, see a need in adding some caveats before endorsing the developments of his time. In the words of one St. Petersburg Duma member:

> What takes place today reminds us to a significant extent of what occurred in the time of Peter the Great, when Peter, in the patriarchal Russia of the Boyars, tried to inculcate new modes of governance and new attitudes to traditional values by drawing Russia closer to the West, through Western technologies and models. At times this was done too harshly, and not all things were done altogether wisely. But still today, the main direction of Peter's reforms manifests itself, and what takes place today is thus very similar. And, therefore, I would say that maybe we should not direct our attention to the successes of Peter's reforms, but rather to the problems that his reforms brought to Russia. The attempts to copy the experiences of the Western countries were harmful to Russia (...) Therefore the time of Peter the Great is not a source of inspiration as much as it is a case and a time from which to draw lessons.
> (Spb 14)

Likewise, another member of the St. Petersburg Duma told me that, while he felt proud of the historical character, the persona of Peter, he believed that several of the policies introduced by him had been detrimental to Russia (Spb 7).

When discussing the lingering attention to and prevailing popularity of Tsar Peter, one should point out that, while he certainly used authoritarian methods to modernise and rehash the country – something which may, of course, appeal to some of my respondents longing for that reputed strong hand at the helm of Russian government – he did manage to assert Russia's status as a great power in world politics, thereby putting an end to prolonged periods of internal strife and weakness, which had previously subjected Russia to imminent threats from assertive neighbours in the surrounding world. He is regarded by his admirers as the ruler who 'led the country out of the morass of breakdown and up to the level of international civilisation' (Kh 3). He led Russia from the days of the humiliating defeat by the hands of the Swedes, at Narva in 1700, to the resounding and decisive victory over Sweden at Poltava in 1709. In other words, within the course of a very few years, he made Russia an international actor to be reckoned with (Greenfeld 1992:224-226). And this very phrase, that Russia should be a state to be reckoned with, was repeated almost like a mantra, over and over again, by a great number of my respondents. To many Russians, the reign of Peter the Great might, therefore, be said to signify and symbolise a period when Russia was grand, great and on the rise, and thus, their image of his time might correspond very well with the hopes and dreams they have for the near future of Russia.

The respondents' preferred choices of historical models to be emulated seem to testify rather clearly to the kind of predicament in which Russia currently finds itself. I am, as a rule, rather inclined not to subscribe to theories of path dependence. On the whole, I am deeply sceptical of paradigms that depart from a deterministic vantage point. However, it is unmistakably the case that reformers and political practitioners, set not only on democratising Russia but also on consolidating the achievements of democracy, have a much more arduous and formidable task before them than their counterparts, those of the former socialist states of Central Eastern Europe. For undoubtedly, the latter have been able to draw some strength and inspiration from lessons learnt in their countries' relatively recent pasts. In the Russian case, however, there is quite simply nothing to draw upon. The period extending from the Soviet *perestroika*, the subsequent dissolution and onwards is, save perhaps some brief months after the revolution of February 1917, the only time in history when there has been an attempt to make democratic practices take root in the Russian political system, at least as far as the central level is concerned.

Certainly, national history might hold some lessons of relevance as regards economic reform, hence the references to Peter Stolypin and the other great reformers of the late 19th and early 20th century. Concerning political reform, however, Russian history has certainly not been satiated with experiences to inspire today's political reformers and democratisers. Here the reforms of the early 20th century has nothing to offer, since

Stolypin himself was clearly an advocate of a rather authoritarian political framework (Sakwa 1996:47). Whenever they wish to draw on experiences from the Russian past, would-be democratisers have to look further back in time. Several interviewees referred back to the *zemstvo* reforms begun in the 1860s, in the days of Tsar Alexander II (cf. Shlapentokh *et al* 1997:120-121). These were geared at establishing local structures of governance, endowed with a greater say in matters such as the upkeep of roads, prisons, and hospitals, as well as the encouragement of industry, agriculture, education, poverty relief and public health. The members of the *zemstva* were elected on a county and provincial basis, but had no executive power and had to share considerable parts of the revenue with the central government (Porter 1991).

The repeated references to the *zemstvo* system among the respondents had probably less to do with its limited formal powers than with the fact that these structures subsequently evolved into a dynamic and liberal force, often challenging the central bureaucracy (Kochan & Abraham 1983:189). Moreover, according to its proponents, it gave a boost to the emergence of a fledgling civil society in Russia and served as a bastion for the defence of human rights in the country (Porter 1991; Shlapentokh *et al* 1997:155). In the words of one adherent of the basic tenets of the *zemstvo* experiment, there might be some insight into democratic reform offered by this period:

> Regarding today's construction of local self-government, there are aspects which have already been dealt with in the Russian past, with the single exception that they were labelled differently (...) *Zemstvo* is the same thing as local self-government, that which we are trying to introduce in Russia today. If we talk about to what extent it has been implemented, we can say that we are still only at the beginning of our path. We have but taken a first step, we have established the elected bodies for local self-government and given them a certain legal foundation. One must develop this, and the *zemstva* hold many very positive aspects. We can learn from this good experience in history.
>
> (Kh 12)

Likewise, according to one deputy of the St. Petersburg Duma, 'the *zemstvo* system and the rights under it might be a pattern to follow. Unfortunately, it has not penetrated the local self-government of today' (Spb 8). And in the Volgograd Oblast Duma, where the bulk of the deputies otherwise seemed to be pretty adverse to the idea of pushing democratic reform, one deputy expressed pride of the *zemstvo* period, arguing that 'it could also be something for the contemporary period, although of course with due adaptation to current conditions' (V 1). In the days of the *zemstvo* reform, she argued, 'Russia proved herself to be capable and not worse off than the developed countries, with regards to the ability of evolving and accepting innovations. One can even say that she was capable of democracy at that time' (V 1). So, in the *zemstvo* reform attempts, there lies at least some basic experience of developing democratic procedures and practices at a local level.

However, and this is the very point I wish to make in this connection, there are no corresponding examples concerning the make-up of democracy on the more overarching state level of governance. Quite on the contrary, the numerous references to the reign of Tsar Peter I and the early 18th century have a slightly ominous ring to them, at least if taking the political perspective of democracy-bent reformers. Admittedly, Tsar Peter opened the much talked about window on the west and modernised Russia, through, among other things, introducing administrative reforms as inspired by the system of the then arch enemy Sweden. However, his authoritarian rule, symbolised by his inclination to use his famous cudgel to get things done, in a literal as well as a figurative sense, carry more than a tinge of the qualities that seem to be sought for in the calls for a strong hand in contemporary Russian politics. These peaked in the late 1980s and early 1990s in the Russian political discourse (Vainshtein 1994, Sautman 1995), and in early 2000 they seemed to account for the tremendously high ratings of President-to-be Vladimir Putin in public opinion polls, as he had displayed the qualities of just such a strong hand in connection with the renewed war effort in Chechnya (cf. Kovalev 2000).

In all, it is indeed a meagre guidance that the examples set by Peter the Great, Alexander II, or even the reformers Stolypin and Witte can give to today's much-needed political reforms. In fact, to the political scientist taking the outsider's view, it is non-existent, as is Russia's previous experience of democracy and democratic methods of rule. To be sure, given the recency of the Soviet period, any suggestions that aspects of this experience be brought back to today's political life seem somewhat less far-fetched and anachronistic, even if they surely do not denote a longing for a thorough consolidation of democratic achievements in Russia. As time goes by, and if the economic and political crisis persists, such sentiments might tend to become more conspicuous, above all when recollections of the downsides of the old system become more faint and recede into oblivion. And, in certain cases, one might of course assume that once a believer, always a believer, even if these believers are primarily to be found among the elder strata of the population. As if to illustrate my point, one of my respondents, a deputy of the State Duma representing the KPRF, concluded: 'I believe that the governing system we used to have during the Soviet period was something unique which corresponded to the interests of the people' (SD 6). There are some steadfast believers who tend to be unruffled even by turbulent times.

Even though the loyal electorate of the KPRF grows increasingly older, this might be counteracted by tendencies to casting votes in protest, provided that other, stronger contenders for attracting such voters are absent. As always, recipes for quick fixes carry populist appeal. This is certainly not to argue that the return of the Soviet system or the re-establishment of the Soviet Union are likely scenarios. They are not. However, one could well envisage that, in the case of persisting economic weakness, political calls for the strengthening of state ownership and regulations in the economic structure might increase, partly drawing upon experiences from the Soviet period. Because, as has been argued above, in the repository of models from the past, the shelves are otherwise empty.

A most vivid illustration of the turmoil of the Russian political scene during the last years of Yeltsin's presidency is that several of my respondents, in answering the question of fitting models from the past to be emulated in today's political practice, chose to invoke the ending of the *smuta*, i.e. the Time of Troubles of the early 17th century (cf. Shlapentokh *et al*, 1997:36, Sakwa 1996:45). During this cataclysmic period, Russia was effectively without rulers, while Swedes and Poles competed for taking maximum control over the inchoate Russian political space, and a series of false pretenders (the false Dmitriis) presented themselves to the throne. Two of these later attempts were crowned, literally, with short-lived success. In a watershed event, the commoner and popular hero, Kuzma Minin of Nizhnii Novgorod, raised an army that under the command of Prince Dmitrii Pozharskii eventually defeated and expelled the Polish forces, occupying Moscow at the time. Finally, the Time of Troubles ended with the establishment of a new royal dynasty, the Romanovs, which was later to count Peter the Great among its descendants. In the words of a number of my respondents, there are several parallels to be drawn to the current situation:

After the reign of Ivan IV, the Terrible, the period of the Time of Troubles commenced. During this period the situation in Russia was characterised by a disorganisation of state structures. It went on for quite some time, and to a certain extent that period can be compared with the one of the present day. Whereas, at that time, different Tsars by the name of Dmitrii appeared, there is today a struggle for the presidency which is little different from the practices of that time.

(Kh 6)

Then the situation was quite similar to the one of today. It took a popular movement to bring the country out of the crisis. This characterises the Troubles of today as well. We will doubtless find a way out of it and proceed from there.

(Kh 8)

By arguing that there is an analogy between what was going on in Russia during the Yeltsin presidency, and what took place in pre-Romanov Russia, my interviewees seemed to illustrate a number of points. First of all, they underlined that Russia was, to their minds, unduly influenced by foreign actors, and that Russia should muster its forces to get out of this predicament. Secondly, they appeared to hold that Russia was profuse with the existence of a series of politicians that, in actual fact, were incompetent and false pretenders to the levers of political power. And finally, some of them might also have wished to argue that it was time for that strong hand to exert control over Russia, in order to end its current stage of weakness and to deliver it safely out of the political and economic morass. Or, at any rate, that there be some kind of popular uprising against the prevailing incompetence.

Shameful Aspects of the Past

Concerning the less appealing traits of Russian history, I have already discussed the need to find a usable past to serve as a groundwork for national identity. There is a parallel in this sense to the German post-war experience, even though the Soviet Union imploded and was not defeated in a war by an external adversary. The relevance of the German reconstruction of national identity and the soul-searching that this may involve was pointed out by one of my respondents, a centrist deputy of the State Duma:

> The process of repentance is still not concluded among the population. There is an analogy here to the processes that took place among the German population. The first attempts were made during the 1980s, when the KPSS published certain documents bearing evidence of how millions of people suffered and were killed. This was, of course, a sad side of our past. However, one cannot change the past. I myself lived in this past, and I cannot dissociate myself from my own life. In Russia, there is a tendency to withdraw from history. People may even forget about it. The best thing would be to do as the Germans did. They internalised the tragedy brought about by German fascism. They do not want the past to return. But in Russia there is even a leftist opposition which actively strives towards the past.
>
> (SD 29)

Evidently, what is and is not considered shameful might vary among the respondents, depending on factors such as ideology. In this particular case, the centrist, non-communist political affiliation of my interviewee was discernible from his way of phrasing his answers. Even so, for all respondents, the pride/shame-balance is vital for the make-up of national self-images, and it is now time to turn to the responses encountered with regard to the negative aspects of the Russian past. While being fully in conformity with the approaches taken by Russian colleagues in the field of social sciences (Sikevich 1996), it was quite clear that this particular question roused the emotions of several respondents. It also, obviously, touched the very foundations of the affective elements of their national self-images. While one respondent found it rather 'unpleasant' that foreign scholars should come to Russia and put questions to Russian political practitioners about national shame in the first place (P 15), another interviewee took to reacting in a rather emotional manner, thereby pointing out that he found the phrasing of the question 'unscholarly'. It was also quite apparent that a long academic career, interwoven with a career within the Soviet Communist party, had served to cement his beliefs that 'objective' yardsticks could and should be applied for the assessment of what took place in the past:

> I am not in favour of introducing evaluations like shame or no shame into politology. Every phenomenon should be evaluated according to its own standards. One should seek to establish its causes, its positive and negative aspects. To be sure, there have been periods in the history of Russia and the Soviet Union that one would hope will never be repeated again. But to talk about what I am ashamed of, that is, pardon me, an unscholarly term. (V 16)

Still, I chose to retain these questions. It seemed to me that the intensity of such responses indicated that, if I wished to approach the affective strands of Russian national self-images, I was proceeding along the right path. And, indeed, my respondent's negative reaction to the question on shame amounted to a total mirror image of his previous response to my corresponding question on pride:

> Thank you, this is a most serious question. If an individual does not feel proud of his nation's past, then this is a person who is a stranger to his land. Then he is not interested in his nation's past, but rather in something else. I would hold that there is a multitude of events and processes in the Russian past which one has every reason to be proud of.
>
> (V 16)

As can be seen from these responses, national self-images and national identity are not matters to be taken lightly, and given their affective components, they are not matters to be talked leisurely or indifferently about. Discussing one's conception of the nation one is part of, regardless of whether it is defined within ethnic or civic parameters, is not like talking about the weather, and above all it would be emotionally trying to elaborate on the theme in cases of a negative pride/shame-balance. Individuals can surely regard themselves as sincere patriots and still experience very little to be proud of in the near past or in the contemporary situation (cf. Robertson 1998). Given this, it is easy to imagine that questions such as mine can trigger rather pointed responses. Another side of this is that respondents are not wont to speak at length about aspects they are ashamed of. Often, references to shameful events in the national past were given in a rather perfunctory manner, which is also reflected in the text below. There was quite simply not the same wealth of illuminating statements to draw upon as was the case with the moments of glory. Hence the relative sparsity of quotes encountered on the following pages.

The question on sentiments of shame towards the Russian past was put to 95 respondents. Of these, the most frequently mentioned period or aspect by far was the Stalin era and the Stalin terror, which was specifically referred to by 29 respondents. The second most frequent response was to state that there were no periods whatsoever in the Russian past that the respondent was ashamed of. This was the response of 19 of the interviewees. In third position came references to the recent past, namely to the war in Chechnya 1994-96 (14). This item was followed by

82 *National Self-Images and Regional Identities in Russia*

references to the Soviet period in its entirety, and to the war in Afghanistan from 1979 on. These two items were both singled out by 11 respondents.

The Regional Picture

Once again, the response pattern of the State Duma representatives displayed an almost perfect match with the national average of my study. In order to see deviations from this norm, we need once again to move on to the regions. There, one could find some noteworthy aspects which merit further discussion:

Table 3.4 Shameful aspects of the national past by region

State Duma	Perm	St. Petersburg	Volgograd	Khabarovsk
1. The Stalin period (10)	1. The Stalin period (4)	1. The Stalin period (5); The Soviet period in general (5)	1. The dissolution of the Soviet Union (6)	1. The Stalin period (6)
2. There are no such periods (6).	2. The Soviet period in general (3)	2. There are no such periods (3); Afghanistan (3); Chechnya 1994-96 (3)	2. There are no such periods (5).	2. There are no such periods (4).
3. Chechnya 1994-96 (5).	3. Collectivisation (2)		3. The Stalin period (4)	3. Afghanistan (3); Chechnya 1994-96 (3); The current situation / Yeltsin (3)
4. The Soviet period in general (3)			4. The current situation / Yeltsin (3)	

Thus, the large majority of respondents referred to at least some aspects of the Soviet period as shameful. When asked about the most bitter lessons of the Russian past, one Perm respondent mentioned the Bolshevik coup of October 1917 and its aftermath up to 1991 as the greatest tragedy of all. In elaborating his argument, he did not mince his words on the matter:

> It is quite clear to me that Russia is a country cursed by God. I do not know why. Russia has had to go through more terror and nightmares than any other country of the civilised world. We had the revolution, and as a result millions of people annihilated each other. We had the collectivisation and the Stalin regime. Again millions of Russians annihilated each other. Russia perennially

annihilates itself, devours itself. As a rule, it is the best part of the population that is destroyed, the wise, the talented. As a result, the genetic pool is harmed.

(P18)

As could be expected, among the respondents of St. Petersburg, the Stalin terror was the item most often indicated as a source of personal shame:

The 1930s and the Stalin repression [is a shameful period]. The 1930s, the 1940s and the early 1950s. The trampling of every living thought, the brute annihilation of millions of people that were guilty of nothing. I am not only ashamed of this period, it hurts me deeply to think about it.

(Spb 10)

Yet, there was one nuance which set the respondents in that city aside from the bulk of my other interviewees. Alongside the indications that the Stalin period was the one that prompted them to feel a sense of personal shame, the most frequently given response was to mention the Soviet period in its entirety. In this sense, the St. Petersburg Duma members seemed to live up to the liberal reputation of their city.

Interestingly, several of the Volgograd deputies also mentioned aspects of the Soviet past, even though the great majority of them referred to isolated events, such as the invasions of Czechoslovakia in 1968 and Afghanistan in 1979 (although these are not indicated in the table showing most frequent responses). They certainly did not engage in the kind of blanket condemnation given in St. Petersburg. All in all, 11 out of 29 statements in Volgograd concerned the Soviet period, but not all of them unreservedly so. While one respondent was cautious to point out that Russian history had always been manipulated, so who could actually trust the way it was presented now (V 11), another deputy of the regional assembly expressed doubt as to whether the reported atrocities of the Stalin years had actually taken place:

Of course I am ashamed of the repression, or rather, maybe I am ashamed of it. I cannot fully believe in it. When one encounters people who experienced the repression and have been rehabilitated today, they present it in a fashion that is different from what is written in today's history books. And I sincerely doubt what is written there. Yes, I am ashamed, if it really is the case that millions of people were destroyed, but I cannot say this objectively. Also, the conditions were special then, and if other conditions had prevailed, things would have been different... We do not know how this period will be described 50 years from now, by our children.

(V 19)

In my series of interviews this is the clearest case of a budding history revisionism, a cousin of sorts to the scary phenomenon of denying that there ever was a Holocaust. Aside from this attempt to deny the atrocities of the Stalin era, there was also one representative of the Khabarovsk Krai Duma who, despite maintaining that the Stalin terror was a shameful episode in Russian history, personally harboured some doubts whether it was actually carried out in the scale implied by media reports of today (Kh 10).

When it came to the evaluation of shameful events in Russian history, the Volgograd representatives once again stood out quite conspicuously in my sample. Among the single items eliciting a sense of shame, the dissolution of the Soviet Union was the one most frequently mentioned by the deputies of the Oblast Duma. Often, the responses along these lines related to the Russian loss of status and prestige in the international arena. Or, in the words of one of the most vocal interviewees:

Everybody wants to be strong, independent, but nowadays we are quite simply a humiliated country, and we feel ourselves to be humiliated. And we also feel that we are being taken for idiots. We feel that we are being led like sheep (...) We have by our own hands, through our own government, destroyed our own state. It is quite hard to find any parallels to this in history. So the greatest shame of them all is related to our own government, our own leaders, our own traitors.

(V 3)

In other words, one could again see that the respondents of the Volgograd Duma were deeply opposition-prone, and that a firmly entrenched Soviet nostalgia was holding its sway in the region. One should also make note of their enumeration of the contemporary situation and the Yeltsin rule to be among the most shameful periods of all time in Russian history. This is well in conformity with the vehement criticism towards the centre that, on so many occasions, was articulated by the political elite of the Volgograd Oblast. In many respects, the respondents of Khabarovsk echoed, albeit somewhat faintly, sentiments that were expressed in Volgograd. They, too, made rather frequent references to the Yeltsin period and the then current situation as being one of the most shameful aspects of Russian history.

Even though the Stalin period and its excesses were among the aspects most frequently cited as shameful by the Volgograd representatives, this was the only item pertaining to the Soviet period to be named by them in this context. In this, the Volgograd respondents fashioned a composition of the list that was similar to the KPRF subgroup's. As shown below, however, the Stalin period was actually one of the two items most frequently encountered on the KPRF's bottom-five list. Thus, it seems as if the Red Belt label is certainly more than apt to apply to Volgograd at the time of study. This was again demonstrated when considering what broad aspects were singled out as shameful by the Volgograd deputies, in other words whether they chose to mention pre-Soviet, Soviet, or post-Soviet ones. In Volgograd, a mere 3/21 respondents chose to mention exclusively Soviet aspects of history, and only 9/21 included any reference at all to the Soviet past. The corresponding numbers for Perm were 7/9 and 8/9, and for St. Petersburg 11/19 and 15/19. In Khabarovsk, sentiments were on many occasions quite sympathetic towards Soviet times, as indicated by the figures 4/16 and 10/16. For the KPRF representatives, the corresponding figures were 4/30 and 14/30. As expected, the ratios were higher among other party representatives (14/31, 25/31) and the independents (16/34, 24/34).

Other Variations

Some words should be said about the other categories also. Comprising a rather small physical number of respondents, the female interviewees only came up with two aspects that were mentioned by a significant number, namely the Stalin era and/or the Stalin terror (8) and the Chechnya war 1994-96 (4). Albeit the physical number of respondents was even less for the non-Russian politicians, it is still interesting to note that the two periods most frequently rated as shameful were the same as the women's and were given in the same order.

Coming then to the possible impact of political affiliations, the following pattern of responses was encountered:

Table 3.5 Shameful aspects of the national past by political affiliation

KPRF	Other parties	Independents
1. The Stalin period (6); There are no such periods (6)	1. The Stalin period (12)	1. The Stalin period (9)
2. The dissolution of the Soviet Union (5); Chechnya 1994-96 (5); the current situation/Yeltsin (5)	2. Chechnya 1994-96 (6)	2. There are no such periods (8)
	3. Afghanistan (5); The Soviet period in general (5); There are no such periods (5)	3. The Soviet period in general (6)
		4. Afghanistan (4)
		5. The October revolution (3); Chechnya 1994-96 (3)

Thus, the Stalin period and the Stalin repression was the period or aspect which was singled out as shameful by the single largest number of KPRF representatives, albeit along with the denial of the existence of any shameful periods in the Russian past. In other words, there seemed to be no wholesale embracing of the Soviet past among these respondents. Rather, a certain amount of critical reflection appears to have taken place. However, there were, of course, two items on the KPRF list not featured among the bottom-five list of the total population of respondents, namely the dissolution of the Soviet Union and the current situation/the rule of President Yeltsin. We recognise these items from the response pattern encountered in Volgograd.

It is a trite conclusion to underline that there is an ideological dimension at work here, for this is surely where the oppositional clout of the Communist party is displayed. Where the ideological and geographical factors reinforce each other, as in the case of Volgograd, the results turn out to be a rather flammable mixture, characterised by a substantial amount of enmity towards the Moscow centre and the current administration. The sentiments were formulated quite clearly in the statement of the communist deputy of the Volgograd Duma, who not only labelled the Yeltsin administration as 'anti-popular', in accordance with a rather widespread linguistic practice among the communist opposition at the time (cf. Shlapentokh *et al* 1997:103), but went even further and branded it 'a regime of traitors' (V 3).

In other words, there seems to be a salient cleavage concerning the assessment of the near past, which has somehow to be dealt with in the construction of an all-Russian civic national identity (cf. Berglund, Hellén, Aarebrot 1998). Obviously, this concerns the evaluation of the Soviet period, an era which considerable segments still take pride in, and an opposing and equally large faction views as shameful. It is hardly conducive to harmonious political developments if broad segments of the political elite consider a particular period to be something from which to draw strength and inspiration, whereas other sizeable segments of the political spectrum posit that those very aspects of the national past denote shameful events in history. When considering the ultimate significance of the past dimension for the make-up of the national self-image, the bridging of this cleavage should be regarded as a task to be prioritised. How to go about it is quite a different matter. There are no ready-made recipes and no quick fixes to the predicament. Probably, only time will heal. However, if it turns out that the tendencies displayed in my small sample of KPRF representatives is corroborated among a larger population, and that the condemnation of the Stalin years is widespread throughout the party ranks, this would be a promising vantage point. Parts of this cleavage might then at least be in the process of being overcome.

It is an open question whether personal and physical Others are at all times needed to construct viable collective identities. One would of course wish this not to be the case, that immaterial factors could instead be made the basis for united efforts in a manner that would not be harmful to physical out-groups. On a purely theoretical basis, at least, one might hope that a streak of shame concerning the murky Stalin period might function as some kind of immaterial, non-physical Other that could unite Russian national self-images across the board, and thus serve to cement and encourage joint efforts. Concerted attempts to do away with and overcome dark memories might, in the best of all possible worlds, be a stepping stone towards the construction of a vital civic national identity that would not be altogether marred by ideological cleavages. Sadly, however, we do not live in the best of all possible worlds.

Indeed, there are other factors which can be said to complicate the picture even further, making it a rather appropriate point to turn to generation-related factors. If one looks at the response pattern encountered across the age groups, the ranking listed below presents itself. Once again, it would seem as if the youngest generation is the least predictable:

Table 3.6 Shameful aspects of the national past by age group

1920s/1930s	1940s	1950s	1960s/1970s
1. The Stalin period (5)	1. The Stalin period (9)	1. The Stalin period (11)	1. There are no such periods (9).
2. Chechnya 1994-96 (4)	2. The Soviet period (7)	2. Chechnya 1994-96 (7)	2. The Stalin period (5)
3. The Finnish Winter War 1939-40 (2); Afghanistan (2)	3. Afghanistan (5); The dissolution of the Soviet Union (5); the current situation/Yeltsin (5)	3. There are no such periods (6). 4. The Soviet period (4); Czechoslovakia 1968 (4); Afghanistan (4)	

Thus, the youngest generation of politicians seemed least inclined to keep brooding over the misdeeds of the past. As could be seen from the question related to pride, those born in the 1960s and -70s were rather apt to mention that they felt proud of all periods of the Russian past. This case matches that result. The most frequently mentioned response in this age cohort was not to feel ashamed of any period of the Russian past whatsoever. This, then, would seem to correspond to what in the introduction was referred to as a positive self-image. It could, I believe, be taken as a promising sign if it is the case that the next generation of politicians has now mustered enough strength to get out of the self-image related quagmire, and is instead ready to develop a more positive all-Russian identity, permitting it to proceed with necessary business. One should not, however, blind oneself to the fact that the opposite might also turn out to be true, namely that this tendency could indicate that the younger generation of politicians has shunned its part of the necessary *Vergangenheitsbewältigung*, making it thus susceptible to repeat some of the mistakes committed by its elders.

Common Traits, Divisive Issues and Shame Avoidance

To sum up, the interviews have shown there to be at least some unifying traits as far as the past dimension is concerned. This is especially revealing when one looks at the sympathy generally expressed to certain aspects of the Russian past, above all concerning the experiences of the Great Patriotic War, which seems to maintain its position as some kind of unifying national icon. This also goes for the time of upsurge, reconstruction and expansion associated with the reign of Tsar Peter the Great. Furthermore, the interviews have demonstrated the prevalence of a major cleavage regarding the respondents' varying assessments of the past dimension on the subject of how to deal with the country's past Soviet-time experience. Even though comparatively few claim to take pride in the Stalin era itself,[6] the Soviet period as a whole is named as one instilling pride by a substantial number of communist-inclined respondents, whereas it is primarily non-communist party representatives who condemn the Soviet past as a shameful aspect of Russian national history. The contrast between the two opposing perspectives was colourfully illustrated by the words of one deputy of the St. Petersburg Duma:

> Russian history is speckled: sometimes light, sometimes black, sometimes light, sometimes black. Practically every process can be looked upon from two angles. Many, myself included, view 1917 as a plus, others view it as utterly negative. Some see it as a *coup d'état*, I see it as the Great Socialist October revolution.
>
> (Spb 4)

For obvious reasons, the tension created by this near dichotomy of national self-images complicates the construction of a viable civic national identity. Unquestionably, united efforts that are geared at the attainment of common goals are made considerably more difficult under the presence of deeply differing assessments concerning points of departure.

Naturally, one practicable and rather rational way for the individual to cope with the problem of assessing the Stalin period is to avoid taking sides altogether, and state that one should really not judge the actions of one's forefathers, because they certainly did what they thought to be best in a complex and unwieldy situation. This view was expressed to me on several occasions, throughout my series of interviews, and was the underlying rationale of the Volgograd respondents who appealed to me to look for objective causes rather than subjective factors, such as sentiments of shame. In all likelihood, this kind of reasoning is a highly contributive factor to the frequently expressed assertions that there are no periods in Russian history of which to be ashamed. Its appearance is understandable enough. As pointed out by Greenfeld (1992:230), given how 'singularly unpleasant' the feeling of shame is, it is difficult to sustain it over a lengthy period of time. It is decidedly more comfortable to allow oneself to slide into non-use of history.

Accordingly, in the words of one deputy of the St. Petersburg Duma, there were two sides to every phenomenon, and therefore it was not possible to categorise them according to simple dichotomies:

> I was brought up to think in a dialectic manner. Every process has got its positive as well as negative aspects, there is not only black or white. I still cling to that position. All aspects and events in history have got positive as well as negative sides. If we look to the last century of our past, at the surface we will detect violations of human rights, but at the same time, one cannot assess this or that event in a definite manner. That is the way the world is.
>
> (Spb 19)

This is, doubtless, one way of reducing the emotional stress involved in condemning postulates and practices that one formerly may have held in high esteem. The majority of respondents chose to take sides, however, and the fact remains that the cleavage regarding the assessment of the near past seemed clear and conspicuous.

Still, as was indicated above, there were additional, contentious issues, addressed in the assessment of the even nearer past. References to the Chechen war in 1994-96 were, as mentioned, in third position of the list of all-time shameful aspects in Russian history. Moreover, they were relatively evenly distributed across the different subgroups, leaving no discernible pattern, even if there certainly was often an anti-governmental tinge to the references. Interestingly, the frequent allusions to the first Chechen war hardly concerned the fact that the centre had disgracefully lost the war to the rebels. Rather, they centred on the point that the civil war had unfolded in the first place. Among the most vehement critics were two deputies of the Volgograd Duma, who were visibly angered by the fact that the short-time Prime-Minister-to-be, Sergei Stepashin, had been allowed to retain his cabinet portfolio, in spite of the fact that he had been heavily incriminated by his involvement in the Chechen war campaign. The two deputies did not mince their words:

> [Deputy 1:] In this context, I have to say how shameful an experience the war in Chechnya was for the Russian [*russkii*] people. It is beyond description. And those who were behind it, whether we talk about [the then Minister of Defence Pavel] Grachev, or whether we talk about Stepashin, those who were behind the

start of this war (...) how can they ever look people in the eye? So many human lives were lost, so many were killed...
[Deputy 2:] Yes, Stepashin has even become Minister of Justice,[7] he has returned to his portfolio. And he has given himself such a stain that it cannot be washed off for the rest of his life. And yet he has the stomach to rule again!
[Deputy 1:] Yes, these people should have been made to face a popular court to answer for their deeds.
[Deputy 2:] A Nuremberg process is what would have been needed. This is genocide, no-one is afraid of using that word any more, everybody is talking about it already.

(V 4+5)

While the bulk of comments made on the first Chechen war were not as drastic as those of the two deputies, criticism towards the actions of the centre was scathing whenever the subject was broached. Stupidity, short-sightedness, ineptitude and misunderstanding were traits often attributed to the Russian leadership on this subject (P 3, P 12, P 17, Kh 2, Kh 15, Spb 2, V 6, V 8, V 12, V 16). 'Incomprehensible' is another word often used by my respondents, and one Khabarovsk deputy pointed out why he had some difficulty in understanding what had actually occurred in the first place:

In spite of the propaganda, the majority of the people was shocked. We, as Russia, as a unitary state, declared war and made war in a part of our state towards a people that is part of our state. This does not make sense.

(Kh 6)

Indeed, the thorny issue of Chechnya pertains to most aspects of national self-images in contemporary Russia. The war between 1994-96 took place in near history and it is therefore natural to deal with it within the temporal dimension. However, it also goes to the very root of the problem of what the true extension of Russia is and should be, and what internal and external dangers the country is facing. Therefore, it lies squarely in the spatial dimension as well. We shall have ample reason to revert to the complexities of the Chechnya issue below. It is now time, however, to address in general the spatial dimension of the national self-images encountered among my respondents. Accordingly, the question is whether this other main dimension holds cleavages and common grounds of a similar magnitude as the temporal one.

Notes

1. This encompasses, strictly speaking, the period from the German attack on Russia in June 1941 up to the end of the war in May 1945.
2. Incidentally, in spite of Tumarkin's conclusion that myth-making around the Great Patriotic War has little relevance today, one of her Russian respondents, interviewed in the early 1990s, exclaims that 'Victory Day is the only holiday we have left. No one is going to take it away from us' (Tumarkin 1994:201). This, I believe, really symbolises centrality by default.
3. The lofty words used by President Putin on the 55th anniversary of the 1945 Victory in May 2000 seemed to be a case in point. A disillusioned war veteran complained that '...remembrance of that victory long ago is the sole element that binds the nation together as one family' (*RFE/RL Newsline* vol. 4, No. 90, Part I, 10 May 2000). Kathleen Smith of the US Hamilton College has in her research noted a renewed official tendency to hail the memory of the War (Abrams 1999).
4. Henceforth, when I use the term 'subgroup', I will be referring to the various geographical, party political and generational categories as laid out in the previous chapter. Occasionally, the women and non-Russian (not *russkie*) respondents will also be referred to as subgroups.
5. This presentational strategy will be used throughout in connection with the tables.
6. Still, there are those who do. Witness, for instance, the words of one of my respondents in Perm, a representative of the KPRF: 'Lenin was wise and Stalin harsh, but all in all they were giants who preserved the country' (P 3). SD 20 and V 13 provided other examples.
7. In fact, at the time of the interview (May 1998), Stepashin was Minister of the Interior.

4 The External Dimension

Threats to Security from Without

As was touched upon in the introductory chapters, our notions of Ourselves are to a significant extent constructed on the basis of opposition to Them, to the out-group. By establishing what They are, and what We condemn and distance Ourselves from in Their way of being, We also establish what We are not and what We do not ever want to become. As has also been clarified, enemy images are not the sole feasible variant of depicting these Others who comprise the necessary antipode to our images of Ourselves. However, since the study of enemy images constitutes a traditional concern among image theorists, it might be a natural starting point in this chapter. If it becomes clear that an external power is perceived by a great number of respondents as being a chief adversary, an actor responsible for many of the ills that have befallen Russia in recent years, then this would seem to be an important part of the national self-images adhered to by those interviewed.

It lies in the very nature of perceived threats to a country that they be not viewed as only coming from abroad. They might equally well be depicted as coming from within. In other words, the issue of threats to national security is related to both the external and the internal dimension of the national self-image, as well as the interface between the two. From the perspective of desired societal cohesion and state stability, the situation where enemies are primarily identified within the state polity itself is certainly the gravest one, even if negative consequences can, of course, accrue from either one of the varieties.

Turning to the response pattern encountered in the course of the study, it seems as though quite a substantial percentage of my respondents harboured the notion that Russian national security, or plainly put, Russia, was subject to some kind of threat from without. Out of a total of 108 respondents, 44% (47) believed in the presence of one or several external threats, whereas 10% (11) thought that, although they presumed there to be such threats, they were not of a military nature. Another 15% (16) held there instead to be potential future threats towards Russia's national security. 31% of the respondents (34) argued against the existence of any external threats whatsoever. One may well think that the tendency to harbour notions of threats being posed to Russia from abroad seems alarmingly high, and that little seems to have changed since the days of the Cold War. Before going into detail on this account, however, it is justified to point out that the clarity of this tendency dwindles when compared to the respondents' views regarding whether or not there were any threats to Russian security lurking from within. The prevalence of internal enemy images seemed to be constantly high over time, as well as across the geographical cases. I shall, however, leave the detailed analysis of internal threats to Chapter 6. For the time being, suffice it to underline that the preponderance of perceived domestic threats is a clear and indisputable finding which has emerged from my study. It is, perhaps, the clearest of them all and, as will later be borne out, it is related to concrete target groups, as well as to political and societal phenomena and the federal centre itself. The contrasts between the gravity of assessments related to external and internal threats, respectively, is illustrated by the following tables:

Table 4.1 Overall assessments of the prevalence of external threats

Are there any external threats to Russia's national security?	Number of responses (N=110)
Yes.	47
Yes, but no military ones.	13
No, not today but maybe in the future.	15
No.	33
Declines to answer/No answer.	2

This is to be compared with the following table:

Table 4.2 Overall assessments of the prevalence of internal threats

Are there any internal threats to Russian national security?	Number of responses (N=110)
Yes.	98
No, not today, but maybe in the future.	5
No.	6
Declines to answer/No answer	1

Thus, it is abundantly clear that the paramount threats to security are deemed to come from within. In other words, the menacing Other is predominantly to be found inside Russia itself. There are some regional differences to be discerned here. In Perm and St. Petersburg, the contrast between the responses regarding external and internal threats was most marked, whereas the tendency to discern external enemies was somewhat greater in Volgograd and Khabarovsk. However, the patterns are not altogether comparable, since the Khabarovsk and Volgograd interviews were carried out at a time which, for reasons to be elaborated on shortly, was marked by a more tense international situation. As a matter of fact, in these two cities, well over half of the respondents believed there to be some kind of external threat.

One central finding of this study is that the traditional external threats from the days of the Cold War still seemed to hold sway among my respondents. Discerned threats from the United States (23 references) and Nato (18) topped the league. Thereafter followed references to somewhat less traditional threats, namely China (17) and Islam and/or one or several Islamic states (17). The individual Islamic states most frequently encountered in this regard were Pakistan (6), Afghanistan (6) and Iran (3). Other commonly mentioned threats were geographically diffuse ones, concerning various economic aspects, such as dependence on imports of strategic goods, stiff economic competition and the flooding by imported goods (12), and the general presence of advanced weaponry, including nuclear weapons (8). Next followed yet another reference to a concrete country, namely Japan (6).

Returning to the regions, the Perm respondents were the least worried about external threats. Among those who did believe in the existence of some kind of present or potential threat, however, the Islamic factor was most frequently referred to (5 references). In St. Petersburg, China seemed to be the most worrisome factor (5), followed by Islam (4) and the United States (4). Nato, however, was only mentioned by one respondent. Somewhat surprisingly, the Volgograd respondents most frequently singled out Islam as the most acute external threat towards Russian national security (5), even though Nato (4), the United States (3), and China (3) were also referred to.

In the case of Volgograd, there is of course a geographical proximity to Islamic countries which might account for the pattern. Khabarovsk corresponded rather closely to the general picture, even though Islam seemed to be a rather distant concern. Again, geographical factors might account for this tendency. As was argued by one deputy of Khabarovsk: 'We live in a corner of the world where these questions are not that relevant. There is no discussion about them here' (Kh 14).

Among the non-geographical subgroups, KPRF members, State Duma deputies, and the oldest group of respondents, the 1920s/1930s cohort, seemed to be the most alarmist. 9 out of 13 members of the oldest cohort professed to see clear threats against Russia's national security. About two thirds of the KPRF members responded accordingly, as well as some three fifths of the Duma respondents. Thus, a Duma member representing KPRF and being born in the 1920s or 1930s would, in my study, seem quite likely to argue that Russia was subject to threats from without. Again, the time factor should certainly be kept in mind, since most of the State Duma deputies were interviewed late in the series. On the opposite side of the spectrum, the politicians in Perm seemed, as mentioned, least worried about external threats; indeed well over half of the respondents denied their existence. Similarly, just below half of the independents did not discern there to be any existing threats. Neither did a relatively large fraction of the women (7/13), nor the non-Russians (7/16), but, as it has already been noted, here the physical numbers are preciously low. A large degree of the 1940s cohort (18/40) also felt accordingly.

Not very surprisingly, perhaps, the KPRF members were most prone by far to view the United States and Nato as threats. In other words, my study does indeed seem to indicate an ideological factor at work here also. References to these two sources of threat predominated vastly, illustrated by the fact that they gathered 14 references each, whereas those placed thereafter on the list (China, Islam, Japan, and economic threats, respectively), all collected a mere 4 references each. By way of contrast, representatives of the other political parties displayed something almost amounting to a mirror image. There, Islam (9 references) was feared the most, followed by China (6), the general existence of nuclear weapons (5), different kinds of economic threats (5), and, conspicuously low on the list, the United States (4).[1] Finally, the independents displayed a slightly different pattern from those encountered among the other two political subgroups. China was the most frequently mentioned concern (7), followed by the United States (5) and Islam (5), the existence of nuclear weapons (4) and economic factors (3).

All in all, it would seem as though political affiliation, regional belonging and time (which will be dealt with shortly), impinged most on the distribution of views on the existence of external threats. Generational factors did not seem to matter that much, although the 1960s/1970s age cohort was the one most prone to mention geographically diffuse threats, such as the general existence of nuclear weapons and economic factors. Yet, here too, the United States was the single threat most frequently indicated. In the other age cohorts there was an unabated tendency to attribute the prevalence of threats to, above all, nation state actors or conglomerations of these.

Rationale for Most Prevalent Threats

It should be kept in mind that the interviews were all conducted between September 1997 and April 1999, with the bulk being undertaken during 1998. For obvious reasons, the time dimension cannot be frozen, and this has to be taken into account when interpreting the results. This period saw, above all, a growth in US and Nato activity, or even assertiveness, in different parts of the world. During this period there were repeated crises over Iraq as well as the Balkans, especially Kosovo. In this later case, the climax was reached in connection with the Nato bombing campaign against Serbia, between the end of March and mid May 1999.

As is well known, this action, taken against Russia's traditional ally - Serbia - substantially reinforced tensions between Russia and the Nato bloc in general, and notably the United States. The bombardment of Yugoslavia in particular visibly affected the respondents' evaluations of external threats to Russia. This was borne out in words by a deputy of the State Duma:

> Today it is Yugoslavia, tomorrow it might well be Russia, and the day after tomorrow it might even be England's turn, that country also has its national problems, and yes, after that it might be Sweden's turn.
>
> (SD 22)

Similarly, one of his party colleagues, a fellow communist of the State Duma, supplied the following analysis:

There is not a single self-respecting people that would accept someone dictating how it should live, according to what laws, according to what social mores, and so forth... The last example – Nato's actions in Yugoslavia, surely constitutes an aggression, an aggression which has turned the significance of the United Nations into nothing.

(SD 27)

'It is the only power which tries to dominate the whole world and it designs its foreign policy accordingly', one Volgograd representative said of the United States (V 3). And, with a greater degree of colourful detail, yet another communist representative of the State Duma, in a manner markedly reminiscent of subscription to conspiracy theories, argued:

Not so long ago, at a closed session with the Joint Chiefs of Staff in Washington, [President] Clinton named three fundamental tasks regarding relations with Russia. The first of them was to carve up Russia into pieces, as soon as possible, and into as small pieces as possible. And then, they were to install governments in these fragments who would never ever orient themselves towards the centre and try to re-establish a unitary state. And the third task was, of course, to subvert the military might of Russia at large, and subsequently the military might of these small republics. These three tasks he presented to the Chiefs of Staff, and he has started to put them into effect.

(SD 25)

In short, what seemed to be a genuine fear and frustration was expressed by a great many respondents, above all in the State Duma. In their expression of these sentiments, there appeared to be a mixture between concern about what they perceived as a notable course of events, and remorse regarding what Russia used to have but now seemed to have lost. This blend could be summed up in the succinct formulation by one deputy of the State Duma: 'In the bipolar world there was a balance. Today the United States is trying to impose its dictatorship over the whole world' (SD 27). Clearly, quite a number of interviewees expressed some yearning back to the relatively stable world of Cold-war bipolarity, where the two superpowers at least seemed to keep each other in check. What they above all longed for was, doubtless, Russia's lost superpower status.

There was thus a noticeable tendency towards a greater proneness to discern external threats at the end of the period than was the case at the beginning of this study. Whereas a mere quarter of the respondents perceived such a threat during the later part of 1997, about half did so during 1998 and during the first half of 1999, at the height of Nato's Kosovo campaign, two thirds stated the existence of external threats. While about half of the respondents completely denied the existence of any kind of external threat at the beginning of the period, the fraction to do so dwindled abruptly to around a quarter during 1998 and 1999. What is interesting in this regard is that the increased tendency to sense enemies from without did not only relate to the United States and Nato, even if those two sources of threat certainly predominated during the said period. As a matter of fact, the tendency to identify tangible threats from without seemed to increase across the board, regardless of their possible origin.

Before embarking on this study, one of my hypotheses was that concern about a suspected Islamic threat would have surfaced to a rather notable extent among Russian political elites, perhaps even taking front position as the most prominent external threat of all. The reason for such a supposition was that, in the first part of the 1990s, the two major conflicts in which Russia had involved itself, namely Tajikistan and Chechnya, had at least had some degree of Islamic dimension to them. In statements devoted to the overall political and strategic situation in Central Asia, Russian leaders had, in fact, quite frequently expressed concern that Islamic fundamentalism might wax in influence, and ultimately spread to the Russian mainland itself (cf. Halbach 1996). Such sentiments were also expressed from time to time among my interviewees:

> Everywhere where there is unrest in the world, the Islamic dimension is being articulated (...) There is a wave of militant Islamism rolling over the world, and Russia is exposed through her southern regions and her Central Asian neighbours.
>
> (P 12)

In general terms, however, the original hypothesis was only partially verified by my respondents. In comparison with the esteemed threat from the traditional enemy, the United States, fears about an imminent threat from the Islamic world were not widespread. For although it was doubtless enumerated as one of the most prominent threats, it was certainly not universally elevated to the position of *the* threat to Russian national security.

The basic rationale behind the assessment of there being a threat from Islam was spelled out to me by one deputy of the St. Petersburg City

Duma. His analysis testified to the artificiality of the inside-outside divide in the analysis of several aspects of Russian politics and Russian affairs:

> In Russia there are, as you know, people attached to Islam. If matters concerned external affairs only, things would be easier. But the added internal dimension makes the political picture much more complex. It is very hard not to heed the internal dimension... We constitute a borderline country, a zone of diffusion, a mixed zone if you will. It is difficult for us to be harsh in our relations with Islam.
>
> (Spb 12)

As another deputy put it, 'the Islamic world is situated within Russia itself' (V 17). According to one centrist deputy of the State Duma, the fear of certain ideas related to Islamic fundamentalism diffusing inside the state proper should prompt certain actions in the foreign-policy arena:

> Fundamentalist regimes, established on the foundation of Islam, cannot be a priority of our foreign policy. But we must of course maintain normal, humane and respectful relations with them. We must cooperate with them in order not to allow any expansion of fundamentalism into our own country.
>
> (SD 32)

But again, far from all discerned Islam to be a threat. Indeed, countervailing tendencies were also noticeable. One representative of the St. Petersburg Duma criticised the way Islam had had to fill the function of being the world's scarecrow, thereby mentioning Samuel Huntington's *Clash of Civilizations* (1996) as a point in fact (Spb 2). Being a scholar of solid repute, the respondent approached the theoretical domains of my study, and argued that negative consequences might accrue from the elevation of the Islamic world into a position of being the enemy institutionalised:

> I believe this to be a constructed conflict line, and a representation of the search for an enemy (...) If one seeks an enemy for the sake of seeking an enemy, one commits a serious mistake.
>
> (Spb 2)

Others chose to turn the tables completely, and argued instead that an alliance with the Islamic countries was indeed essential in order to keep the United States at bay (P 4). As an added contrast, a St. Petersburg deputy offered a somewhat unusual analysis of the situation. In his rather original reflection, he made the recommendation that Russia should team up with the Islamic world. The reason was not, however, that Russia and the remaining world needed to shield themselves from the United States. Rather, he believed himself to have located the most formidable adversary elsewhere on the globe:

> One third of the world's population are Chinese, one third are Muslims, and the remaining third constitutes the rest, among them Christians. Christians and Muslims have to cooperate, otherwise the Chinese will gain the upper hand. Otherwise we will all become Chinese and Indians. Then there will be no way back.
>
> (Spb 7)

Interestingly enough, this deputy's ideas may not have been altogether as wild as they might seem at a first glance. As was shown on several occasions, the reasons stated for the expressed fears of China were precisely the sheer multitude of people and the population growth at large. The fact that China has a population comprising way above one billion people was stated in and of itself as a legitimate cause for concern (P 18). The continued increase was also underlined as a problem to be taken into account:

> There is a threat against the whole world. There is a number of countries with a population growth that is beyond control. It is India, China, these Asian countries, and Africa (...) Today, Russia is weak from an economic and military point of view. I believe that. China is the foremost potential ... not adversary, but a state that might throw glances toward Russia's territory, the more so since we are weakened and have natural resources... But this is a problem for all mankind, and if we do not find ways to regulate the population growth in these states, then it can become a severe headache for all developed states, America and Europe included.
>
> (Kh 9)

This statement had a clearly racist undertone, and it should be stressed that it turned out to be rather exceptional in that regard. Still, a somewhat denigrating tone could often be detected in the statements about China, and, as will be discussed below, assessments to the effect that Russia should prioritise relations with China were made referring to bare necessities rather than to desires or senses of commonality. (There seemed, however, to be a sincere admiration of the Chinese model of development, but this is another and separate matter, which will be dealt with shortly.) China, as a neighbouring country, was deemed powerful and on the rise, and Russia, therefore, had to adjust its external relations accordingly, but this orientation was seldom due to brotherly love. The most frequently stated reasons for China being regarded as a threat to Russian security did not include perceived deliberate political designs but again referred to the sheer number of people. One deputy of the Volgograd Duma put it succinctly:

> I believe China to be the potentially largest threat, not due to aggressive pretence but due to sheer physical magnitude. If there is unrest, it will spread to Siberia. If there is some kind of breakdown, the popular masses will have to find new territory, and ours is next door.
>
> (V 2)

In the Russian Far East, the perceived problems took on more concrete traits. Naturally enough, the politicians of Khabarovsk had more reason to ponder over the opportunities and risks involved in cooperation with China on a daily basis than, say, the deputies of the St. Petersburg Duma. This stands to reason. Khabarovsk is situated very close to the Chinese border, and city officials and politicians routinely have to tackle issues ranging from the activities of Chinese migrant traders to joint programmes for environmental and wildlife protection. However, as for the main threat associated with China, there was no principal difference between Khabarovsk and the other regions. Among the politicians interviewed in the Far East, prevailing threat perceptions again mostly concerned the migration movements that, according to the expressed concerns, might arise on a more or less spontaneous basis:

> China is large and powerful, today one billion four hundred million people, and along the border to Russia alone, seventy million people live in the border area represented by the distance between Blagovezhensk and Semipalatinsk. They are starving, and they are lagging far behind the centre as of today.
>
> (Kh 15)

In other words, the inhabitants of the Chinese border region allegedly might feel tempted to move across the Russian border where, to aggravate the problem, population is sparse (cf. Sakwa 1996:296, Shlapentokh *et al*

1997:217-218). This was believed to be a quite feasible scenario since 'human nature is impatient' (Spb 1). The same train of thought was adhered to by another Khabarovsk deputy:

> China is a giant neighbour of ours, it starts 40 kilometres away from here. (...) I certainly feel a certain caution, a certain concern when I think of its future development... The country has an annual economic growth rate of 8 per cent, and maybe issues might arise here pertaining to natural resources. Or territory. We must take this into consideration. Here in the Far East the population is decreasing.
>
> (Kh 11)

Similar deliberations were expressed elsewhere. For instance, one respondent in St. Petersburg echoed the words of his Khabarovsk colleagues, arguing that the fact that there are 'large sparsely populated territories, richly endowed with natural resources' on the Russian side of the border, might prompt large-scale migratory movements from the Chinese side. This, he argued, would be especially likely in situations of internal Chinese tension and unrest, and he concluded that 'during the next century, China will cross this border, one way or another'. There was nothing that Russia could do to stop this by force, he went on. Therefore, the central government in Moscow had to devise as co-operative a policy as possible vis-à-vis the Chinese (Spb 1).

Friends in the Surrounding World

Luckily, from an individual as well as a collective perspective, the world seldom consists of sources of threat alone. Even though national self-images are constructed in contrast to Others, all Others need not, as noted above, be enemies. There is a Swedish saying along the lines: 'Tell me who you socialise with, and I shall tell you who you are'. And, as is so often the case, popular wisdom is indeed – wise. National self-images are also, to a significant extent, constructed in relation to friendly Others (Herrmann & Fischerkeller 1995) and, furthermore, some of them may even be important as role models. It is, of course, feasible that the inhabitants of a state polity be totally without friends in the surrounding world, even though it may not be very probable.[2] In such a hypothetical country, at least where the leadership enjoys some kind of legitimacy among its people (Holmes 1997), internal cohesion would most likely be high, since togetherness and intra-state loyalty would be built on the premise that there is a need to stick together in the face of a hostile world. Even so, as was testified by Stalin's Soviet Union, if internal stability is attained through the means of coercion and oppression, there might still be intense internal manhunts for potential collaborators and traitors on the inside.

Yeltsin's Russia clearly did not fit the description of such a hypothetical country. In the previous pages, I have demonstrated that the respondents of my study were rather prone to detect external threats. However, in their attempts to figure out the nature of Russia, the world, and Russia's place in it, they also had definite views of which states constituted Russia's most desired international partners. Even at a collective level, identity is defined by reference to, among other things, networks of intermingling. Therefore, it is now pertinent to address the sunny side of Russia's international contacts. Who, then, according to my interlocutors, were Russia's most desired partners in the outside world?

When summarising the response pattern established through the interviews *in toto*, the ten-most-wanted list indicated below emerged. It should be pointed out that respondents were allowed to mention as many states and constellations of states as they wished. Given the previous section concerning the most prevalent sources of threats, the list may hold a few surprises:

Table 4.3 Overall assessments of most desired international partners

1. China (58)	6. France (29)
2. Germany (51)	7. Sweden (23)
3. Japan (40)	8. Finland (22)
4. United States (39)	9. India (21)
5. Europe/Western Europe/EU (34)	10. Former Soviet Union/CIS (15)

To this should be added that Scandinavia, as a whole, was also quite a popular choice. All in all, it was given 10 references, separate from those concerning the individual Scandinavian countries. If this figure were to be taken into account, Sweden would be placed well ahead of France. On the other hand, it is almost certain that an accentuated interviewer effect was at work here. The interviewer being Swedish may have caused some respondents to think it polite and proper to mention Sweden.

Once again, the most interesting results emerge when the different response patterns are related to different subgroups, but prior to this, one thing should be stated clearly. When it comes to future possibilities of cooperation, the lure of the former Soviet republics seems very limited. Indeed, they were ranked conspicuously low on the list, despite the political priorities of the first part of the 1990s (Webber 1996). This finding is rather surprising, but could be explained by the fact that some deputies seemed to take cooperation with the former Soviet republics for granted, and may thus have thought that it did not warrant any specific mention. One deputy even viewed developments in former Soviet republics as security matters still internal to the Russian state (V 10).

In any case, using a similar presentational strategy to the one used regarding the past dimension, the following picture emerged:

Table 4.4 Most desired international partners by region

State Duma	Perm	St. Petersburg	Volgograd	Khabarovsk
1. China (23)	1. United States (13)	1. Germany (10)	1. Germany (8)	1. China (13) Japan (13)
2. Germany (17)	2. China (10) Germany (10)	2. Finland (8)	2. China (7)	2. United States (8)
3. India (13)	3. Europe/ Western Europe/EU (7)	3. Europe/ Western Europe/EU (7); Sweden (7)	3. Sweden (6)	3. France (6); Germany (6); South Korea (6)
4. Japan (12)	4. Japan (6)	4. Japan (6)	4. Europe/ Western Europe/EU (5); France (5)	4. Europe/ Western Europe/EU (4); Finland (4)
5. Europe/ Western Europe/EU (11)				

There are several points to be noted here. First of all, Germany was evidently a popular choice in all regions, and was even the most preferred partner in St. Petersburg and Volgograd. Both these cases are indeed interesting, since they denote that on this score, the past dimension is in fact overshadowed by pragmatic deliberations in the present tense. Given the traumatic war-time experiences in 20th century history, and the pain and suffering inflicted on the two cities by Nazi Germany, one might otherwise have expected a different turnout. As a rule, the inclusion of Germany at the top of the list of desired international partners was often stated matter-of-factly, without major elaborations. Responses left, however, little doubt about the prime reason for the wish to develop and consolidate relations with Germany, namely the big investments made by German capital and the economic might of German business interests (Spb 4, P 11, P 12, P 15). Occasionally, there was also the supplying belief that a Russian political alliance with Germany (and France) might serve to counterbalance the influence of the United States in Europe (V 14).

Secondly, the idea of having India as a partner seemed to primarily attract the State Duma representatives. Also, most Duma interviews were undertaken during the spring of 1999, when references to a multi-polar world made for popular catchwords in Russian foreign policy statements. About half of the Duma interviews were undertaken at the height of the crisis over Kosovo and the Nato bombings of Serbia, and since Nato's intervention was resented by most Russian political strands, the popularity of the aforementioned phrase is rather easily explained. To be sure, most references to a multi-polar world implied, on the one hand, criticism towards the United States and its alleged hegemonic aspirations, while on the other, they demonstrated a desire to carry on cooperation with, above all, China and India. Doubtless, the very absence of the United States from the Duma list of most preferred choices may also partly be explained by the events in the Balkans. By a similar logic, the prominent placement of the United States on the Perm list might be due to the fact that tensions between the United States and Russia were rather low at the time, viz. during the autumn of 1997.

The perspectives taken in St. Petersburg and Khabarovsk were certainly affected by their respective geographical locations. Still, the strong insistence of the St. Petersburg deputies of a need to keep up viable cooperation with the Nordic countries might seem surprising to some. Regarding Khabarovsk, the United States is a neighbouring country, and this should certainly be taken into account. By way of contrast, however, the popularity of faraway Finland in Khabarovsk should also be noted. This could hardly be explained away as an accentuated interviewer effect, and I am actually at a loss to find a plausible explanation in this case.[3] Such an effect might well, however, be relevant to the prominent listing of Sweden by the respondents of the Volgograd Duma.

Foreign Role Models

In a situation where crisis persists in the political and economic fields, and no immediate ways of solving the problems present themselves, it would seem to be tempting for political elites to begin to search for more or less ready-made recipes. As we have seen above, the Russian past offers scant guidance. Some inspiration could be drawn from the Stolypin reforms of the early 20th century as regards economic reforms, but as far as the political arena and democratising practices are concerned, no candidates from the 20th century present themselves. It is quite telling that, apart from those remarks indicating that inspiration should above all be drawn from the Soviet period, the most recent examples that are offered pertaining to the political arena date back to the 1860s and the *zemstvo* reform of local self-government. Even more revealing is the multitude of references regarding the reign of Tsar Peter I. This would only seem feasible in a state where a large number of people feel confused about where to go and why.

If this is the case, one might imagine foreign role models to be the proverbial catchers in the rye. If the well of domestic inspiration has run dry, one might try to tap foreign sources.[4] The issue of foreign models is closely attached to the more general one regarding friends and foes, in other words the categorisation of Others in the outside world. It is quite a common phenomenon that the search for foreign role models occurs in inchoate states, during stages of political and economic development (Dijkink 1996:12, cf. Neumann 1999:178-179). Thus, the question on foreign models was quite a natural one to ask the respondents. In this respect, the study also provided a sequel of sorts to other interview-based studies centred on Russian political elites. Lane (1996) asked a similar question to members of the Gorbachev-time political elite. The results engendered by my own research turned out to be quite interesting and conformed partly to the pattern earlier identified by Lane.

Out of 62 respondents, 23 denied the validity of foreign models, whereas 12 were unreservedly in favour and 26 thought that they might be partly applicable (1 respondent was undecided). Interestingly, the willingness to accept foreign models as sources of inspiration seemed to be greater among my respondents than among interviewees subject to previous, related research, Lane's study included (Lane 1996:177, Avraamova 1998:57). In those studies, the largest category of elite respondents by far denied any applicability of such models to the Russian case. Still, a substantial number in my study also held Russia to be so unique that no external models could be used. Russia had to define its own path. This was said to be due to historical traits, among others the long dominance of the Communist party, and above all, perhaps, to the fact that Russia is a vast country that straddles two continents. In the words of one vocal respondent, every attempt to force a model upon Russia was likely to backfire:

> I am opposed to all models. They have a mechanical trait which, from the very outset, will disturb the functioning of the body to which they are applied. I am convinced that every attempt to force a model upon us, regardless of whether it is Western, Eastern, or American, will prove unworkable. There are plenty of examples in the past (...) Every time, even with the best intentions, it ended up the usual way. We have got the expression *poltora*.[5] It is neither one, nor two. It is *poltora*.... In the testing of a theory, a negative result is also a result, but in real life it is only a waste of time.
>
> (V 15)

And, along similar lines, one deputy of the State Duma lashed out against the notion of applying foreign models to try to steer away from Russia's current political and economic predicaments. While doing so, she very neatly summed up the traditional arguments as to why Russia should be considered a case apart:

> I believe that Russia is unique, and to scout another country to try to find a model for our political system ... would be sheer stupidity. We have seen that on those occasions when Russia has tried to look westwards or eastwards it has ended in tragedy for us. Russia has a unique culture and her position in between east and west is one aspect of her uniqueness. Russia should be its own model.
>
> (SD 6)

'A person who blindly tries to emulate the behaviour of other people whom he admires will inevitably become a laughing stock', another respondent argued (SD 27). Indeed, the point about Russia's perceived uniqueness was raised by several other respondents. Among other things, it was pointed out that nowhere else in the world did there exist such a vast country where day-time temperatures could vary between +40 and -40°C (SD 19). The particular respondent who pointed this out had an otherwise open mind towards adopting some elements of foreign models. He warned, however, against trying to apply those aspects universally and uniformly across the vast space of the Federation. After all, he argued laconically, water melons could not be grown in Siberia, whereas they usually brought a wonderful harvest in Krasnodar (SD 19). And, along almost identical lines, other deputies underlined that, in Russia, no single universal model of development could be applied across the board, for one had to take into consideration the fact that conditions differed vastly between, say, Sakhalin and the republics of the Northern Caucasus (SD 27). One should not, for example, venture to apply identical measures in Chechnya as one did in Murmansk or in the Komi-Permyak Autonomous Okrug (Spb 2).

Be that as it may, most respondents were thus quite sympathetic to the notion of being at least partially guided by foreign models. Regarding the follow-up question on which foreign models, if any, might be relevant, it turned out that two models were by far the most popular, namely the Chinese and the Swedish ones[6] (19 and 15 adherents, respectively). The Swedish model was the most popular in St. Petersburg, closely followed by the Chinese one, whereas the order was reversed in Volgograd and Khabarovsk.

In the words of a Russian social scientist, the characteristic traits of the Chinese model include a 'gradual transition to market economy with the active participation of the state in upholding economic ties' (Avraamova 1998:57). One might be tempted to add that the Chinese model would also seem to connote not only a rather visible hand of the state in economic affairs, but also the maintenance of less than democratic, even authoritarian, political structures. The popularity of the Chinese model among my respondents was above all due to the common ideological heritage, and the stunning success of the Chinese economy. The country's political stability was also taken into account:

> China is convincingly on her way towards a leading position in the world. In practice she is edging towards the position that was previously occupied by the Soviet Union. There, the economy is developing in a stable manner, the social problems are solved, but here they are getting ever deeper. This is the model that we should orient ourselves towards, that could be used as a pattern for bringing Russia out of its crisis.
>
> (V 3)

The Chinese reforms, it was claimed, had been implemented 'without the overthrow of the political system and without ensuing social hardships' (SD 4). Not surprisingly, most supporters of the Chinese model turned out to be representatives of the KPRF, and indeed the Chinese model was by far the most preferred option within this subgroup. However, the Chinese model did not seem to hold very large appeal among the State Duma members of my study. Here, it was superseded not only by references to the Swedish model but also to the German one.

The Swedish model, for its part, did not attract those that were primarily longing for an economic boom. The model's main characteristics could be said to be that the state should 'regulate certain sectors of the economy and take care of the most needy segments among the population' (cf. Avraamova 1998:63). Even if some respondents expressed their liking of such aspects as Swedish parliamentary practice (SD 3), it seemed as if Swedish achievements within the sector of social security held most appeal:

> In our country, many people refer to Swedish socialism. In your society, you have freedom of the individual, which we appreciate, and you also have democratic traditions and a highly developed culture. At the same time, social security is given priority. A person living in your country can feel at ease, he can think about the future. I am sure that you have shortcomings, too, there is no such thing as an ideal society... Nevertheless, I believe that if we are talking about emulation, it is the Swedish example we should turn to.
>
> (Kh 1)

Several interviewees also pointed out, however, that the Swedish model seemed in recent years to have lost much of its popularity in the Russian media. And, it was argued, where the Swedish model had lost some ground, the Chinese model had instead gained (V 9).

Finally, the German model, spelling out market economy with a considerable amount of social responsibility displayed by the state, as well as representing a federal model with both a strong centre and strong autonomous *Länder* (cf. Shlapentokh *et al* 1997:156), ended up in third position, even if it was listed far behind the two aforementioned alternatives. Here, it turned out that references to the German model constituted the most frequent response among the representatives of the non-communist political parties, and, as previously mentioned, in second place among the State Duma members. However, its high ranking among the adherents of the non-communist parties is quite interesting, since it seems to indicate that, even here, the US model has lost a great amount of clout as an inspirational force. Indeed, it was seemingly superseded even by the Swedish model in this category.

Similar scepticism towards the US systemic model has been borne out by other investigations among political elites and the public alike (Lane 1996:177, Avraamova 1998:54-64). Avraamova (1998) gauged the popularity among the public of three alternative models of socio-economic development, which she labelled the liberal model, the social-democratic model, and the paternalistic model, respectively, and here, the likeness to the US, Swedish, and Chinese models is striking. Avraamova's results corroborate the findings of this study, indicating that the paternalistic model was most popular throughout the period of 1993 up to 1997, when it was favoured by between 53 and 68 per cent of the respondents. The social democratic model, which was ranked second highest, was preferred by between 26 and 40 per cent. It seemed, however, as if the popularity of the social democratic model rose somewhat during this period, whereas the paternalistic one displayed a corresponding slope downwards. In Avraamova's study, then, the reverse trend, as pointed out by some of my respondents, was not corroborated.

The liberal model (according to which the state should guarantee its citizens their individual political rights and ensure the rights of free enterprise but provide minimal social protection) was, on the other hand, kept at a level of low rankings throughout the period, gaining the adherence of at the most 8% of the respondents (Avraamova 1998). One could presume that these figures reflect the relative failure of the early years of Gaidar-led economic reform, where market economy was brought to the country at an accelerated pace through a national version of shock therapy, and where minimal consideration was given to the necessities of maintaining a social security net for the less competitive strata of the population (cf. Shevtsova 1999:4). After all, it is quite natural for the inhabitants of a country to denigrate a foreign model when it has already been tested without apparent success. In such a case, there is likely to be 'a reversal of attitude', since dependence on the model is taken to be evidence of 'non-identity' (Dijkink 1996:12). One might well assume that such a situation breeds not only rejections of the models in question, but also negative attitudes toward the country of origin (Dijkink 1996:12). Such boomerang effects would hardly be likely to affect Russian attitudes toward Sweden, as it is probably considered to be too small and politically insignificant to worry about, but concerning views on the United States, things might very well be different. This might, in turn, contribute to the tendency of viewing that country as a threat, as brought out above. However, there is more to the picture than simple enemy images.

China and the United States – Denigration, Fear, and Inferiority

My respondents' attitudes towards the United States are, on several occasions, deeply contradictory. For it is quite indicative that the only remaining world superpower is put at, or at least close to, the top of the list of most preferred partners, as well as that listing the most prominent threats to Russian national security. The outlook on China has the same Janus-faced characteristics. Indeed, as was pointed out above, assessments of China and Chinese policies have often had a somewhat disparaging note to them, and recommendations that the Russian federal government prioritise relations with China seem largely to have been made out of necessity: 'We have to have good relations with China, because China is the future' (P 6), and 'It is best to have them as friends' (P 20), mused politicians in Perm. Along similar lines, it was pointed out elsewhere that as China was developing so dynamically, it would soon become one of the most powerful states of the world, and hence, there was a need for partnership (Kh 10).

Of course, there was also the factor of sheer vicinity. 'One will always have neighbours and neighbours will have to be prioritised, regardless of whether they are small or large' (Kh 11), one Khabarovsk respondent pointed out. This line of argumentation was in many cases deemed valid for relations with China as well as with the United States:

> Our neighbour China and our neighbour America ... are the countries that we have to stay friends with and cooperate with, whether we like it or not (...) The foremost partners are China and America, that is where we find the greatest population, the greatest territory and the greatest potential.
>
> (Kh 14)

In my opinion, then, the formula 'whether we like it or not' neatly sums up attitudes in relation to China. To cooperate with the great neighbour is something that Russia simply has to do. Even if there were occasional statements by KPRF representatives speaking of at least previous friendship and brotherhood (V 7), the reasoning that there had to be cooperation out of necessity was the most prominent idea about how to deal with China. This pattern is also highly relevant for the understanding of the United States' favourable listing among the most preferred partners.

The fact that Russian politicians and public alike have, for a very long time, harboured mixed feelings towards the United States, is hardly a novel phenomenon. It is well known that, during the Soviet period, while Soviet politicians used to apply the United States as a yardstick regarding economic matters and military might, they at the same time condemned it and predicted its ultimate downfall and demise. A well-known case in point is Nikita Khrushchev's famous bragging exercise, when he promised that the Soviet Union would catch up with and overtake the United States within a period of 20 years. It was deemed to be a most central achievement on the part of the Soviet leadership when it, in the heyday of the Brezhnev regime of the early 1970s, reached nuclear parity with the United States and was given corresponding political recognition of this fact (Jönsson 1984). All this time, however, the United States was deplored for ideological reasons, as well as for being morally defunct and suffering from decrepit spiritual values. Thus there was, at the elite level, a curious mixture between feelings of material inferiority and moral and ideological superiority.

Judging from the responses elicited from my interviewees, this complex structure seems to have been retained to this day, at least at the regional political elite level. The adverse feelings towards American society and American values had ample representatives. It could concern, for instance, such seemingly mundane examples as American humour encountered in films: 'It is raw. It is coarse. It is empty. It is dangerous (...) I do not allow my son to watch such films' (V 8). Or a negative view could be taken regarding the values prompting Americans to undertake sacrifices for a common good, such as for example in connection with the World War II. There, the same deputy mused, Russians were motivated by their 'unity and spirituality', whereas the whole of Europe 'had surrendered', and 'the American soldiers fought for money' (V 8). As a matter of fact, it was argued, 'America has lost all cultural values' (V 13). Quite simply, according to another diagnosis, 'the States is a coarse country, it is not civilised' (V 8). And one liberal interviewee confessed that 'the influence of American culture disturbed [her] a great deal' (Spb 10). The reason for this was that 'it is a pop culture bereft of spirituality, humanity and compassion, and now it imposes itself on our country' (Spb 10). Furthermore, and according to other interlocutors, the American model of development had nothing to offer, because 'the Americans do not constitute a nation, and we do... The American model is a model of development for a rootless people' (Spb 3). The model was designed to fit 'the American national ideology', voicing an 'extreme individualism', something which did not go well with the needs of 'the Russian mentality and soul' (Kh 6).

Furthermore, it was pointed out quite spitefully that the United States does not have much to brag about by way of national history. Sweden, too, was brought into the picture in this regard, again because of my origin:

> We have deep historical roots. In Novgorod, in Pskov, in Yaroslavl, in Leningrad (sic), wherever you go, you come across granite rocks, rocks that are thousands of years old... You can sense the past, you can see our ancestors' graves; it is our past. They gave their blood for us, against the Tataro-Mongols, but maybe also before that. There is much to be proud of here. In this sense we are richer than you are, and you are richer than America.
>
> (Kh 11)

Not surprisingly, the mixed feelings also pertained to assessments of contemporary international politics, and what level of cooperation should be upheld with the United States. As was touched upon above, the United States was prominent on the list of the most dreaded external threats to Russia, as well as on the list of most preferred international partners. In a repetition of the Chinese pattern, most of my interviewees seemed to include the States on the latter list not as much out of affection as out of necessity. The political and economic preponderance of the United States could hardly be wished away, and thus, whether one liked it or not, Russia had to accept realities and cooperate with the United States, for the sake of its economic well-being. It did not mean, however, that there had to be love and devotion, or as one respondent put it:

> There is no reason for Russia to throw itself into the arms of the United States. And those arms are not held out to us anyway. The European countries are more important, they have old and solid traditions of parliamentarism, freedom and democracy which they respect and cherish. We can learn a lot from them.
>
> (P 18)

Along similar lines, one of his colleagues stated: 'We do not love them, but they are hardly a threat to us today' (P 14). Another deputy took a slightly different view, pensively probing the pros and cons in his assessment of the prospects of Russo-American partnership:

> We must cooperate with the United States, the same way as we do with other states of the world, as regards science and technology, but we are, after all, closer to the European house. The Americans cannot come to meet us in that manner, they will pursue their own advantages, and try to squeeze out their European adversaries. Maybe we can have some use of the Americans at some point, but it might be a short-lived success and we might stand to risk more.
> (Spb 20)

Yet another respondent re-emphasised the point that Russia does not really have much of a choice, for one can hardly close one's eyes, wish that the United States was not there, and then act in accordance with this wishful thinking:

> As far as relations with the United States are concerned, they will continue to develop (...) If a state has a leading position we must continue to reckon with it, whether we like it or not.
> (Kh 10)

So, here as before, the expression 'whether we like it or not' seemed to be quite an apt and convenient one. On the other hand, it was quite clear that the United States is also admired by a large number of respondents, albeit reluctantly from some quarters. This is not only because of its economic might and achievements, or its status as the sole military superpower of the post-Cold war world. One communist respondent, otherwise pretty scornful of many aspects of US society, proudly recalled that 'even the American army is equipped with helicopters that have been constructed by Russian engineers' (Kh 6). Most often, though, undiluted admiration seemed to be granted for other reasons. One of them, which has certainly come to be a conspicuous theme due to the domestic Russian debate of the 1990s, is the defence and support extended to compatriots abroad (Melvin 1995, Kolstoe 1995). In this regard, parallels were drawn to the Russian politics vis-à-vis the diaspora Russians residing, first and foremost, in Estonia and Latvia. Numerous references were made to what the corresponding US policy would have been, and this was so in all the regional centres under study.

Admittedly, some of these references seemed to be involuntary slips of the tongue, whereas others were quite clearly unreserved in their admiration of the way the United States is reputed to back up strong words with strong deeds, if needs be:

> Above all, the Russian-speaking population in the Near Abroad should know that they are representatives of a state that is so strong and powerful that it will come to their assistance, should they be humiliated. I think that the Americans constitute an excellent example in this respect. Wherever one of their citizens reside, and whoever he is, America always hurries to his defence. This is very important. And the Russian citizens should also feel such support.
>
> (Kh 10)

This recommendation was given by a representative of the Khabarovsk Krai Duma, and a colleague of his was even more articulate in his admiration of US resolve:

> In this regard I believe the American position is very good. Wherever a Russian-speaking individual resides, in whatever country it may be, the state should come to the defence of this individual. No matter how great or small he is. This is the most important thing. When this individual feels this, his patriotism will reach the same level as the American one. I believe that the Americans are the most nationalistic and patriotic people in the world. They are the ones who most obviously display these qualities.
>
> (Kh 16)

Even more colourfully, one deputy of St. Petersburg suggested that 'if an American sailor gets killed in any state of the world, the whole of America is raised to its feet' (Spb 9), and, he argued, Russian leaders would do well to consider acting equally forcefully in similar cases. In all four regions of the study, a substantial number of interviewees were very clear about this. One of my respondents, from Perm, added himself to the choir of voices invoking the aptitude of the US analogy:

> Every Russian must be defended. The new states must be made aware that they are pursuing a policy that is harming the Russians. We must defend the individual human being in the same way as the Americans do. Human rights must not be violated, regardless of whether this takes place in Chechnya, Russia, Estonia, or Kazakhstan.
>
> (P 4)

Indeed, even if there were some instances when the respondents chose to add a more cautionary note to the assessments of this particular US policy, the bottom line was a positive evaluation of US resolve:

> [The Russian policy] should be stricter toward those states where the rights of the Russian-speaking population are violated. (...) I even support an economic blockade, if the rights of the Russian-speaking population are grossly violated. (...) Other states, like America, defend every citizen, and can even use force of arms to do this. As a mother and a woman I am categorically against the use of violence, and I hold that one has to act through diplomatic means. But I do not rule out economic blockade.
>
> (V 19)

There were other aspects that were also added to positive assessments of the United States. Most of all, these dealt with the organisation of the US federal model and the relations between the federal centre and the states (Spb 18), as well as referring to the solid and venerable US constitutional groundwork. Similarly, the relative inter-ethnic harmony of recent decades in the United States was given its due by several interviewees. On balance, however, it must be said that negative references predominated, and this tendency was quite clearly reinforced over time. Without a doubt, this had to do with perceived American heavy-handedness in the international arena, above all in relation to developments in the Balkans and the Middle East. Often, when negative assessments were made of the US acting as the world policeman, remorseful remarks were made about what Russia used to be in the days of the Soviet Union and what it is today:

> In the days of the Soviet Union, we were regarded as a very great great power. Our ships were to be seen alongside the American ones in the Indian Ocean, in the Mediterranean. And they had an influence in the Persian Gulf, too... But, unfortunately, we have lost this position today.
>
> (V 14)

However, some respondents argued that Russia, still being a great power, had a special right to wield influence over certain parts of the world. And in developing this train of thought, they argued that the United States in fact had given itself such a right, making it only pertinent that Russia do the same:

In those regions that are vital for the safeguarding of our national security [Russia has a right to wield special influence]. This point of view does not differ from the one expressed in the United States. The interests of the state and its population must be prioritised. If a country, in any region, constitutes a threat to Russia, our country must respond accordingly, as would any country.

(Spb 15)

We shall have reason to return to this very issue in the next chapter. The main thing in this context is that it was once again expressed with abundant clarity that the United States constitutes the yardstick against which Russia should be measured. It stands for might, even if most of the interviewees seemed to think that it does not stand for right. Maybe, however, it is also deemed a luxury that one can do without, if needs be.

Quite separate from the issues of might and glory, there are also issues connected with day-to-day realities. And, as has been argued above, if one can take refuge in areas where greatness is still felt to be bestowed on the collective body of which one is a part, it might be easier to bear the uphill battle of the personal economic plight. However, the domestic arena has also to be confronted, and here one has the clear impression that the bulk of my interviewees could identify precious little to rejoice about. Several important issues related to the interface between the spatial sub-dimensions are equally troublesome. It is now time to turn to these subjects. Let us start with the question regarding whether or not Russia should be considered a great power, brimming as it is with implications for policies towards the outside world.

Notes

1. It deserves to be noted, however, that 4 representatives of the ultra-nationalist Liberal Democrats were included among the 'other parties' group. Of these, 3 representatives mentioned the United States, which inflated that particular figure.
2. That is tantamount to the situation of Albania after the Sino-Albanian rift under Hoxha, and possibly in Kampuchea under the Khmer Rouge regime.
3. A friend of mine jokingly suggested there to be a 'bandy effect'. Being a metropolis of this exotic game, Khabarovsk is likely to have seen visits by Finnish national teams which have probably performed rather well. I would still argue, however, that this does not account for the fact that Finland is listed ahead of Sweden, which normally performs even better at this sport!
4. Dijkink (1996:12) argues the other way around, and holds that calls for the adherence to domestic models of the past might ensue as a reaction to the unsuccessful application of

foreign models. To be sure, there will most often be an interplay in time between the application of foreign and domestic historical models.
5. The expression means 'one and a half'.
6. Some caution is called for in interpreting these results. There might be an accentuated interviewer effect at work here also. Even though several of them hastened to assure me that their mentioning of Sweden as a positive model had nothing to do with my origin, this potential impact should be kept in mind. However, in Lane's (1996) study, references to 'the Scandinavian model' were the second most frequently mentioned foreign source of inspiration, serving, perhaps, to mitigate my concern for such an effect.

5 The External/Internal Dimension

Still a Great Power

There is one argument that is referred to with the frequency of a mantra by a large number of my respondents, namely the expressed desire that Russia be a state to be reckoned with. The contrast between the Soviet period and the contemporary situation is most starkly illustrated by the controversy surrounding the diaspora Russians (*russkie*). According to a frequently cited figure, there are about 25 million of them residing in the so-called Near Abroad. This amounts to some 17 percent of the total Russian population of the former Soviet Union (Sakwa 1996:345). Whereas these Russians used to be citizens of the Soviet Union, a superpower on a par with the United States, albeit more feared than respected perhaps, they are today left in a situation where the protests of the self-proclaimed great power, the Russian Federation, are only occasionally heeded. No doubt, the fact that Russia is practically without fool-proof levers with which to influence these former Soviet republics in the desired manner, is one that may be hard to accept by those who retain sympathy or maybe even nostalgia for bygone days. Even so, the recipe to mend the situation proposed by one KPRF representative in Perm turned out to be unusually blunt:

> The Baltics and partly the Caucasus, are the main problems. A re-establishment of the Soviet Union by peaceful means would be the real solution... Everything else is only half-measures.
>
> (P 6)

A party associate of this politician invoked a popular mandate for a policy platform, prescribing a future reintegration of the former Soviet Union. This was what people really hoped for, she argued, adding:

> When I visited Transdnistriya,[1] I found not only elderly people to be nostalgic. Also, normal healthy people in their best working age told me 'Take us back to Russia!'
>
> (SD 33)

In fact, nowhere seems Russia's loss of great power status, as compared to Soviet times, to be more conspicuous than in the specific arena relating to the diaspora Russians. The aforementioned comparisons with US policies in this field are, for the most part, undertaken rather reluctantly, and a component of envy can clearly be discerned. The handling of the policy area related to the diaspora of Russian-speaking people, and their precarious situation in some of the former Soviet republics, unavoidably ushers in comparisons between what is now and what used to be. Whereas these people used to be citizens of one of the two superpowers of the world, they are now residents of independent, in many cases Western-oriented states. In some states they are barred from citizenship and corresponding rights, unless they are able to pass pretty demanding tests, documenting their knowledge of the new, non-Russian state language. According to a liberal respondent, the mild reactions of the West towards exclusionary practices directed at Russians in Latvia and Estonia indicated that 'Russia's interests are disregarded or quite simply ignored' (Spb 18). And, he went on to argue:

> It is possible that I exaggerate here, but I would say that certain legal elements [concerning legislation in Estonia and Latvia] remind me of what there used to be in South Africa not so very long ago, when society was subdivided into whites and blacks. In a similar manner there are attempts to subdivide society into Russians and Estonians, into Russians and Latvians (...) The fact that a large number of people are in practice bereaved of vital civil rights, and the fact that this does not upset Sweden or the West at large, is one example of the fact that Russia's interests are ignored.
>
> (Spb 18)

On the whole, there seemed to be wide agreement to the effect that the Russian state had an obligation to care for the well-being of its compatriots in the Near Abroad. The responsibility to protect Russians was not regarded as limited to the territorial confines of the Russian Federation. Precious few were unclear on this point. Of those respondents who expressed their views concerning in which areas the situation of the Russian was the most acute, 33 spontaneously referred to certain Baltic states, whereas the Central Asian or Caucasian states only received a few mentions.

Regarding the question of how to safeguard the interests of the diaspora Russians, non-military means were most favoured by far. Indeed, there were few respondents who did not explicitly rule out the military option. In connection with the references to the American model, however, there were several respondents (10 altogether) who suggested that Russia should use all means at its disposal to safeguard the well-being of its countrymen abroad. Most deputies had a preference for diplomatic means, while some also argued that Russia should not hesitate to use economic sanctions if necessary. A minority held that the problem should not be countered abroad, but that the best policy option would instead be to let the Russians come to Russia, and once they were there, treat them generously. In general, several respondents did not hold current governmental policies regarding these matters in high esteem, and argued that policies should definitely be made more active to redress a situation perceived as unjust.

The question of whether indeed the restrictive policies of, for instance, Latvia and Estonia are justified is not a matter to be discussed here. It is, however, evident that a situation, perceived as unjust by residents of Russia, cannot but make them ponder over just how great a power Russia really is at the present time. This leads us directly to the question of whether Russia should at all be assessed as a great power at the current point in time.

On this score, there were several aspects where the samples of my study indicated interesting results, and where there were great similarities between the four cities. First, there was the continued belief that Russia is a great power and that it still has some kind of mission in the world arena. Substantial majorities in Perm, St. Petersburg and Khabarovsk argued this to be the case. In sum, out of 102 respondents, 82 held that Russia retained or probably retained its great power status (74/8), whereas 20 held the opposite to be or most likely be true (15/5). The greatest number of those in the latter category represented the Volgograd Duma, where more than a third of the respondents found it hard to characterise contemporary Russia as a great power by any standards. Again, the disposition towards vocal opposition against all things that the Yeltsin administration stood for shone through:

> Quite frankly, I cannot characterise Russia as a great power. That is not a secret, not for us Russians, anyway. When the Soviet Union existed, I could label it a

great power. But today, our situation is far removed from what it used to be... When I meet my electorate, I urge them to unite and attain the goal of making Russia a powerful state. That is what the Russian people needs.

(V 19)

The Volgograd estimations of current Russian affairs were, in general, deeply pessimistic, and the assessment of the question of Russia's great-power status was no exception to this.

Concerning the majority of respondents, namely those residing outside the confines of the Volgograd Oblast, several reasons were expressed as to why Russia should still be labelled a great power. Even so, there was hardly any rosy red optimism. Among the reasons most frequently stated were Russia's physical immensity, its possession of nuclear arms, its rich history and cultural heritage, and the sheer numbers and talents of its population. Several respondents chose, however, to underline that Russia had lost a great deal in comparison with the Soviet Union's assets. The military potential remained, however, even if there had been a downward turn with regard to capabilities in this area as well. Furthermore, one of my respondents in Perm expressed some hesitation about the adequacy of basing the country's status in world community on military criteria:

It goes without saying that a state that possesses nuclear arms has to be perceived as a great power [...] Alongside the United States, it is Russia that masters nuclear technology. It might well be that there are minuses attached to this, and maybe this is not the kind of greatness we would like to have. But as long as that basis exists, this [state] will continue to be a great power.

(P 20)

It is a lingering impression that a great many of my respondents expressed their belief in Russia as a great power, since it was inconceivable for them to imagine anything else. A typical response was to commence with a lengthy prelude, underlining the multitude of capabilities and resources that Russia has lost in comparison to the Soviet Union. Even though the epithet 'Burkina Faso with missiles' was repeatedly flouted in the Soviet press in the days of Gorbachev and is still frequently used by Russian media today, it was apparent that this label denoted a vision of reality that the majority of my respondents chose not to be party to. It is a case in point that the largest category of those arguing in favour of a continued Russian great power status referred to non-military factors only

(39/82), while a very limited number (8/82) cited military reasons exclusively, the rest claiming there to be a combination of these factors accounting for the Russian great power position.

Quite often, after having denigrated Russia's power potential in comparison to the material base of the Soviet Union, several believers in Russia's continued position among the most prominent state actors in the global arena ended up by referring to Russia's undeniably vast geographical land mass and extensive physical resources as the prime reasons for the categorisation. One example of this kind of argumentation proceeded accordingly:

> Russia is a great power in aspects related to the military, natural resources and human resources. It will take you two or three weeks by train to travel from the western border to the eastern one. No other country is equally large. By air it will practically take you twenty-four hours.[2] We also have very many inhabitants, wise people who are well versed in state-of-the-art technologies and other things. We can compete with any country.
>
> (Spb 13)

Another variant was represented by a LDPR State Duma member, who chose to argue almost defiantly that, although Russia had lost out economically and found itself on a slippery slope concerning military capacity, immaterial factors pointed indisputably towards the uncontested classification of Russia as one of the leading powers of the world:

> Concerning intellectual and cultural potential we score higher than the West. In the West there has never been and never will be such authors as Pushkin or Dostoyevskii. We also have a richer language, and I do not know whether, anywhere in the world, there is another language as rich as Russian. It all adds up. We have got everything. We have one of the best schools. And look at the Olympics during the last thirty years. Look at physics, chemistry, biology, mathematics. There, we are always at the top. These are good indicators of our traditions. We have a good potential everywhere, our businessmen do not work worse than yours, indeed possibly better. Our own dark chocolate is finer and better-tasting than Snickers, and people have rapidly realised this. This is the way it is across the spectrum. What took you 30 or 40 years to achieve, we need only 5 years to complete.
>
> (SD 28)

While this was a rare specimen of self-congratulating complacency, the quote is still indicative of a trend that comes through in my material, namely the tendency to anchor and legitimise Russia's great power aspirations in achievements of the past tense, as exemplified by the references to Pushkin, Dostoyevskii and the Olympics. Also, this particular respondent chose to point towards the future, telling me to wait for just five years, after which we would see the results. This is in keeping with a widespread tendency protruding from my material, namely to mortgage the future in order to be able to claim that Russia is a great power. Indeed, the magic word here seems to be *potential*. 36 out of those 82 who claimed Russia to be a great power did so by referring to its great potential, as regards natural riches, military might, intellectual resources, and the like. Thus they, at least partly, contradicted themselves, for in explaining why Russia should be considered a great power today, they came up with reasons founded in estimations of the future. Witness, for instance, the statement by another of my respondents, also a deputy of the State Duma:

> Due to its scale, its nuclear arms, and its future, yes [Russia is a great power]. And concerning the third aspect, 'its future', it has always been there, it is still there, and it will remain there. Temporary violations, that were permitted to occur by those in the government of our state, who pursued American policies and American interests, have undermined our economy, but they have still not undermined Russia's greatness (...) Therefore, I say it again, particularly from the point of view of tomorrow, our Russia is still great and will remain great.
> (SD 25)

Several respondents made their desired prospects for the future part of the explanation of why Russia was to be attributed great power status today. They wanted to believe, and so they believed. Even though there seemed to be nothing on which to found this belief, but the will to believe itself, they, in a more or less unreflecting mode, regarded this as valid evidence.[3] So whether this was circular reasoning or tantamount to conjuring up a *fata morgana* in order to feel better or whether, indeed, this was their reasoned estimate, they seemed in this manner to point towards a better tomorrow.

The Right to Influence Foreign Countries

Granted then that the bulk of my respondents still regard Russia as a great power, what implications does this have for their views on Russia's international role and conduct? Quite obviously, the notion that Russia is a great power cannot but influence the view of the government's way of handling the perceived plight of the diaspora Russians. It is almost inevitable, in this context, that the aforementioned parallels to US practices come to the fore. Russia's perceived great power status has in all likelihood, however, further implications for the assessments of how the country should design its foreign policy actions. This also holds true for the issue of whether Russia has the right to influence political developments in foreign countries. Some respondents were very clear on the matter:

> We talked earlier of Russia being a great power. That means that she, in effect, has the right to influence the whole world, to influence all regions.
>
> (Spb 5)

These thoughts were articulated by one of my respondents residing in St. Petersburg. One of his colleagues was somewhat less self-assured, even though he held that Russia clearly had a right to cling to its traditional spheres of influence:

> In countries where Russia used to have an influence, she should continue to exert it. She should not give up that which has been achieved with such great effort. This may seem like chauvinism, but it is not. It is normal patriotism, just like the one of the Americans, as well as of the Swedes and Finns.
>
> (Spb 3)

Thus, this respondent held it to be normal and legitimate that Russia wield spheres of influence in today's world.[4] In this, he was joined by a large number of others. In fact, it turned out that a vast majority of the respondents adhered to a great power frame of mind in this respect. On the specific issue of whether Russia had the right to influence political developments in other countries of the world, the response pattern turned out to be the following:

Table 5.1 Overall assessments of Russia's right to influence foreign countries

Do you believe that Russia has the right to influence political developments in countries outside its own borders?	Response (N = 89)
Yes.	60
Yes, possibly.	7
No.	17
Unclear/does not know.	5

There were similar majorities across the political spectrum in this regard, and so the pattern was in no way restricted to the Communist party representatives. Indeed, it turned out that the representatives of the other political parties were equally convinced that today's Russian Federation retained a right of influence in foreign countries beyond its borders. The independents displayed a similar pattern. Neither were there any significant regional variations to be observed. Among the State Duma members, however, 24 out of 34 asserted that Russia had this right and, in such a manner, the Duma members seemed to hold a greater majority in favour of such assertiveness than did the representatives of the regional assemblies. This seems hardly surprising, since politicians active at the federal level would, as a rule, tend to be more interested in international matters than the average regional parliamentarian.

With a view to the generational cohorts of the study, there was least hesitation on this matter among the youngest politicians, i.e. those that were born in the 1960s and -70s. Out of 18 respondents, no-one answered a clear 'no' and 15 answered in the affirmative that Russia had a right to influence political developments in other countries. Although the physical numbers here are limited, one might still feel tempted to say that this coincides with the confidence usually associated with young age. And despite the same reservations about numbers, one could also note a clear majority among the non-Russian respondents in favour of Russia retaining spheres of influence (11/13). The female respondents constituted the only subgroup where there was, however scant, a majority against Russia reserving such a right for itself (6/11).

The tendencies were also clear-cut with regard to what parts of the globe should be influenced by Russia. When asked to specify which geographical areas they had in mind, the largest group (29 respondents) mentioned the partly overlapping categories consisting of the former Soviet republics, the Commonwealth of Independent States (CIS), or the Near Abroad. Most of these references were made to the group consisting of the former Soviet republics, which means that Estonia, Latvia, and Lithuania were not excluded.[5] The second largest group of references concerned all neighbouring countries (13), which evidently presupposed rather far-reaching rights for Russia. Next came allusions to 'all areas where Russia has national interests to defend' (9), which incidentally were made by State Duma members only. Several respondents also held that Russia might legitimately wield a special kind of influence in areas 'where Russians live' (7) and in the eastern part of Europe (6).

In summary, it seemed as though a considerable part of my respondents had yet to rid themselves of Soviet-time conceptions of the world. Russia was, according to this outlook, still a great power. It was a force to be reckoned with and, as such, it had to have a special say in matters concerning the former Soviet republics. The Near Abroad did still not seem to be the Real Abroad, and the national borders delimiting these newly independent states appeared to be perceived as rather soft. In this sense, at least, certain aspects of the Soviet Union continued to live on in their minds.

Reintegration – Scheme or Scam?

Did they, then, retain any hopes or desires that the Soviet Union might be re-established? For this would, undoubtedly, have been the ultimate manifestation of being unable to free oneself from a Soviet state of mind. When the CIS was established in late 1991, Soviet-time nostalgics pegged their hopes to this very institution, hoping that, some time in the future, it might function as a device for the re-establishment of the Soviet Union. Increasingly, however, the CIS came to be seen, both by Russian politicians and by political practitioners in the other CIS states, as a vehicle for the implementation of Russian great-power interests within the CIS area (Webber 1996). The most obvious example of this use being put into practice was perhaps the CIS peacekeeping operation in 1992, in Tajikistan's civil war, where token forces from Central Asian CIS states acted as a fig leaf and legitimating device for the forceful Russian intervention which turned the war's tides of fortune (Petersson 1997). As time went on, however, it became clear that the CIS had mainly become ornamental, and that it constituted little more than a forum for the exchange of views between the different national leaders of the former Soviet republics (Webber 1996). Even though some tangible progress appeared, at times, to be made in predominantly the military and economic spheres, it was a lasting impression that there was a huge gap between the lofty words on cooperation schemes, uttered at the CIS summit meetings, and the scant number of agreements that were subsequently implemented.

At the time of the presidential campaign of 1996, Boris Yeltsin got an edge on his main opponent, the communist Gennadii Ziuganov, by posing as a great champion of increased integration between former Soviet republics. However, at this time, he had largely abandoned the CIS format. He concentrated instead on the development of a free trade area and customs union together with Kazakhstan, Kyrgyzstan and Belarus, subsequently to be joined by Tajikistan, and even more so on developing a closer-knit political union on a separate basis with Belarus. This political union had also to travel down a bumpy road, however. Despite the fact that, practically each year, different and ever more expanding drafts about the union were presented and adopted, obstacles remained vast and, as in the case of the CIS, gaps between words and deeds persisted. Matters were not helped by the fact that the main champion of the Russia-Belarus union was the wilful President of Belarus, Alexander Lukashenka, who displayed deeply authoritarian traits and was distrusted and even shunned by Western countries as well as by the liberal opposition in Russia.

This, then, is the background regarding developments within the CIS. So, what did my respondents have to say on the subject? Did they still believe in the institution of the CIS, or did they have more faith in the customs union or the political union with Belarus? Alternatively, did they distrust the projects altogether? Also, did significant numbers of them still harbour hopes of the re-establishment of the Soviet Union? It is now time to proceed to the results obtained concerning these particular aspects.

Most respondents viewed the prospects of the CIS as rather dim. Even though a majority claimed to see merit in the basic idea (71/107), there was disillusion concerning the progress made so far. Furthermore, this is a case where the centre perspective, as represented by the State Duma members, seemed to differ substantially from the regional ones, as illustrated by the following table:

Table 5.2 Assessment of CIS integration projects by region

Assessment	State Duma	Perm	St. Petersburg	Volgograd	Khabarovsk
Positive.	8	9	7	12	11
Pros and cons.	10	3	6	5	-
Negative.	10	2	5	1	1
Unclear.	3	5	2	3	4

Among the State Duma representatives, there was a markedly low degree of all-out endorsements of CIS integration projects, and quite a number were downright negative about the basic CIS idea. There were illustrative statements to the effect that the CIS represented 'mere decorum' (SD 21), that it amounted to 'a dream, a myth devoid of substance' (SD 7), that it was 'still-born' (SD 1), or even more condemning, that it in essence was an 'unhealthy creation' (SD 22). The most frequent diagnosis, given to explain the lack of headway made within the CIS framework, was that the leaders of the CIS states were not seriously interested in promoting cooperation and integration. The reason for this was attributed to their fear of losing their own holds on power. Predictably, several deputies also pointed out the glaring discrepancy between words and deeds.

Thus, little love was lost on the CIS institutional structure and, instead, several of the State Duma members were inclined to argue for an integration effort that shelved political matters and focused squarely on economic ones. Somewhat erroneously, several respondents were in favour of treating the European Union as a role model in this regard. Moreover, 8 of the Duma respondents explicitly favoured the formula adhered to in the case of the Russian-Belarusian union, and thought that this might also be an appropriate recipe to follow for working with other CIS states. At the other extreme, the support of the CIS idea was overwhelming among the deputies of the Volgograd and Khabarovsk *Dumy*, and a great number asserted that they were wholly in favour of the idea. Here, as well, the Belarus formula was given wide acclaim. 6 of the deputies stated spontaneously that the Russia-Belarus union efforts were positive and that they should also be emulated in other constellations involving Russia and other former Soviet republics.

Aside from these regional differences, no greater variations could be found across the spectrum of different political affiliations with regard to assessments of CIS integration. There was, however, a slight tendency that integration efforts were considered more positive within the KPRF. The independents tended also to be predominantly in favour of CIS integration projects. All in all, the pattern could be laid out in the following manner:

Table 5.3   Assessment of CIS integration projects by political affiliation

Assessment	KPRF	Other	Independents
Positive.	19	11	17
Pros and cons.	7	12	5
Negative.	7	7	5
Unclear.	3	3	11

For a persuaded reintegrationist, or even a Soviet-time nostalgic, there were two logical ways of looking at CIS reintegration efforts. Either the CIS was still seen as some kind of starting point for launching serious reunion plans and, in that case, the outlook of this category would tend to be positive. Or, if using yardsticks to measure what had actually been achieved within the CIS frame, which is precious little by any standards, frustration would tend to reign, whereby the reaction was most likely to be negative or, at the very least, indifferent. There would seem to be a good case for arguing that there is a certain time factor involved here. The more time that passed, without any substantial breakthroughs or tangible results achieved within the CIS, the more negative people would be likely to become. In order to pursue this line of argument, I checked the response pattern against the time factor, but it did not seem to cancel out the differences seemingly caused by regional belonging or political affiliation. This tentative finding will, however, have to be corroborated by a thorough analysis with a greater material.

The reintegration issue gives rise to further questions, regarding for example the aforementioned political union between Russia and Belarus. On this particular point, there were visible differences of assessment between the subgroups of my study. Whereas opinions were wholly positive among those State Duma members and KPRF respondents who mentioned the phenomenon (9/9 and 15/15 positive, respectively), feelings were mixed among the Perm politicians (5/9 positive; 4/9 negative), the St.

Petersburg deputies (3/5 positive; 2/5 negative) and the representatives of the non-communist political parties (7/11 positive; 4/11 negative). Whereas the prevailing communist view was that the Russian-Belarusian case represented a showpiece of how reintegration efforts should be run, respondents of a more liberal bent were concerned about the course of the union's development:

> Integration is always good, but it is not always possible during the period at hand...Under which conditions it takes place is quite another matter. I would not like to integrate with Lukashenka, but I would like to integrate with Belarus.
> (Spb 10)

It is not remarkable that positive assessments of the Russian-Belarusian union dominated so clearly among the KPRF respondents. I would even dare to say that these views were partly due to wishful thinking, and that many of them would still like to see as much as possible of the old Soviet Union restored. Indeed, there were a few who were quite clear about this, and even clung to the view that this would happen, sooner or later. It was not only KPRF respondents who argued along these lines, for they were also joined by several independents:

> I believe that we are moving towards a reunion of all countries [of the former Soviet Union]. Whether we like it or not, Belorussia is already part of our set-up. It is the same thing with Ukraine: we are one country (...) Within ten or fifteen years all these countries will come together again.
> (Spb 13)

Quite clearly, then, several KPRF representatives underlined the fact that they personally favoured a re-establishment of the Soviet Union (cf. Sakwa 1996:44). Certainly, it is hard to tell what amounts to beliefs and what are merely liturgical orations about what it is possible to achieve. Even so, the statements were most definitely made:

> The Soviet Union was established through a natural process – possibly exempting northern Caucasus and the Baltic states – and its parts belong naturally together. It should be re-established. My party endeavours to re-establish the Soviet Union (...) What has fallen apart must come together again.
> (P 6)

Assessing the Former Soviet Republics

There is one more facet to be touched upon concerning the estimations of the Russian-Belarusian union. While some referred to it in positive terms, there was a traceable undertone, namely that, whilst an integration with Belarus certainly offered a decent starting point and was a thing to be desired, respondents would like even more to see an improved and closer relationship with Ukraine (cf. Sakwa 1996:192). As has been touched upon previously, Ukraine, and the capital Kiev itself, have over the years constituted centrepieces of Russian national self-images. We need only recall the proverb about Kiev being the mother of Russia, and the analogy that losing Ukraine was like having an arm chopped off. 'We belong naturally together with Ukraine and Belarus', one respondent observed (V 13). If made to choose between the two states, Ukraine seemed to be the partner of preference for a great number of the interviewees.

Partly for these reasons, intermittent intransigence displayed by the Ukrainian government, as well as its desire to steer the country closer to the West, has not been taken kindly by Russian reintegrationists. Indeed, one of my respondents in Perm explained that 'the wish of Ukraine to work together with Nato is perceived as a stab in the back' (P 17). Several respondents argued that tangible headway in promoting viable reintegration within the CIS frame would only be possible if Ukraine could be won for the cause (Kh 2, Kh 4, Spb 4, V 3, V 4+5, SD 32, P 6). That Ukrainian leaders refused to play ball was evidently the source of some frustration:

> We are simply not satisfied with the position of Ukraine, it is our humble [*skromnyi*] brother, but, nevertheless, the country does not take the standpoint we would wish it to. The model we want is the one represented by the union between Russia and Belarus.
>
> (V 3)

This statement, by a KPRF representative of Volgograd, resonates an audible echo of bygone days, complete with family metaphors. It connotes that the former union republics should know their places and the Russians, i.e. *russkie*, should still have a right to determine the fates of their little brothers.

Another tendency that has protruded from my material deserves to be underlined. It is actually a corollary of the fact that reintegration with Ukraine and Belarus tended to be appreciated the most. Notably fewer seemed to be enthusiastic about the five-member customs union, comprising Russia and Belarus, as well as Kazakhstan, Kyrgyzstan and Tajikistan. It cost too much, went one argument, and it was Russia that had to bear the brunt of the expenses (P 12). According to some respondents, this was actually in keeping with the trend of the whole Soviet period (cf. Sakwa 1996:37). At that time, Russia had constantly had to subsidise its junior partners:

> Russia belonged to those that were disfavoured during the Soviet period. Russia was drained culturally and economically throughout. When we are told today that the integration processes have such a tremendous importance for Russia, I simply do not believe in it. I believe that the creation of these [NIS] states put us in a better position.
>
> (P 20)

> Earlier, Russia used to prop everybody up [in the Soviet Union]. That went for the Central Asian states in particular. Russia helped all, built everything everywhere. But then Russia turned out to be poorest of them all.
>
> (Kh 2)

This particular statement might certainly be a matter of developing the simple overextension argument that Russia undertook too much, with too little resources to back it up. At times, however, respondents clearly expressed sentiments that went beyond this. On such occasions, it rather seemed as if the arguments bordered on sheer racism towards the former Soviet Central Asian brethren:

> Kazakhstan did not even exist as a country prior to 1917, but was established thanks to 1917. In Uzbekistan and Tajikistan, clan-based societies were still in existence. The Soviet power took the Central Asian states out of the Middle Ages.
>
> (V 13)

If expanded, the arguments that Russia was drained of its resources by the Central Asian states might serve as a handy device for accounting for not only the dissolution of the Soviet Union, but also Russia's present-day economic misery. Even though this line of reasoning has not been all that prevalent among my interviewees, it still testifies to the functions of scapegoating and out-grouping in situations of economic and social distress. These practices may reduce the agony and pain, since the blame is put on somebody else's doorstep. And quite clearly, those respondents that seemed to subscribe to such a logic of events expressed noticeable disdain for the Central Asians. The following quote is definitely a case in point:

> What did the Kazaks ever do on their own? Without the participation of the Russians? What did the Tajiks or the Uzbeks ever do? Practically nothing of importance! At the very best, Turkish workers go there and build special objects. Because nobody there builds any factories. But when the Russians came, they built, they worked, they created. They stayed on there and lived peacefully.
>
> (V 13)

This is not the first time we have come across this type of mechanism, nor is it the last. We will have ample reason to revert to the issue of Othering below. At present, suffice it to say that it recurred in this context also.

Russia's Mission

It is clear that, while we are squarely in the spatial dimension, discussing issues relating to the outreach of the Russian state, we have also touched upon the temporal sub-dimensions of the present and future tense. Above, I have noted the tendency among my respondents to mortgage the future in order to justify their classification of Russia as a great power. Before leaving the external and external/internal sub-dimensions of the national self-images, let us discuss one more aspect that itself is intertwined with the cluster of issues surrounding the question of Russia's status as a great power, namely the issue of Russia's role and mission in today's world.

I have argued elsewhere that ideas connected with the future tense are of less importance than the past sub-dimension to the national self-image and national identity at large. One cannot rule out, however, that predictions of a future where Russia is once more to be great and grand might, at some point, have considerable appeal to large segments of the population. Especially under bleak social and economic circumstances, there might be consolation to be gained from the belief that not only will things be brighter in the future, but the future will in some respects even be glorious for the Russian state polity. Thus, there were some expectations on my part that this might reveal itself to be a frequent theme.

As pointed out earlier, notions of a desired national mission normally constitute parts of national self-images. Ideas pertaining to such a mission would seem less than trite for respondents from a country characterised by a rich and eventful imperial history, as well as a near past entailing a superpower status which, in turn, contributed to the bringing down of the empire itself. If one blames foreign-policy adventures and Soviet-time military inventions in remote corners of the world for contributing to the economic plight visible from the *perestroika* period and onwards, it would seem logical to distance oneself from the view that Russia should play a global role. Similarly, the concept of an international mission is thus closely connected with the question of whether Russia is a great power or not. As we have seen, a great majority in all subgroups of my study held this to be the case. So, what did all this entail for the outlook on Russia's role in the world politics arena? As it turned out, a clear majority of interviewees in all cities argued in favour of the continued existence of a specific Russian mission in world affairs:

Table 5.4 Assessment of the existence of a specific Russian mission in world politics

Do you believe that there is a specific Russian mission to fulfil in today's world?	Number of respondents (N = 105)
Yes.	76
Yes, maybe.	5
No.	18
Unclear.	6

Thus, in spite of the general weakening of Russia's international position, a majority of the respondents still believed in the existence of a global mission for Russia. What is more, this picture was obtained in all of the four regions, as well as among my State Duma respondents, albeit with certain variations in intensity. The same holds true for the generational and party-political subgroups. Indeed, all categories seemed to subscribe to the idea that Russia still has a specific role to play. The respondents in Perm and Volgograd seemed least sure about this, but, even so, majorities were in favour in both of these regions also.

The relative consensus ends there, however. There is, in fact, a vast array of suggestions as to wherein Russia's mission lies, and these can be subdivided into three major clusters of tasks. The first one pertained to the traditional notions of Russia as a great power, the second still subscribed to these ideas, but also depicted Russia as a general do-gooder, due to its inherent traits, whereas the third variant seemed to suggest that Russia was, as it were, above day-to-day world politics and could inspire through its very existence.

The first cluster contained the most popular choices of tasks. The one, single aspect most frequently referred to was that Russia should act as a *stabiliser* in world politics and *promote international peace* (14 references). Even though this suggestion was launched in all political camps, it seemed somewhat reminiscent of the Soviet days when, according to the official rhetoric, the Soviet Union was steadfastly promoting peace and security across the globe (Thibault and Lévesque 1997). Quite clearly, this was a task with a global reach and, in this sense, the Russian great power status seemed to be perceived as rather unaffected by the twists and turns of the previous decade. To an even greater extent, the same could apply to the suggestion that Russia act as a *balancer* in world politics (8). This indicated classical geopolitics and realism in action, and it was quite obvious what, it was felt, had to be balanced to benefit the rest of the world, namely the United States. This is in conformity with the overall scepticism and, at times, animosity towards the United States, as recounted above. There was also, however, a less ambitious variant of the balancing role, namely the idea that Russia should merely balance developments in Europe (1), but the phenomenon needing a counterweight was still the same, namely the ambitions of the United States.

The second cluster was different in kind, as it was more concerned with promoting peace and understanding, through Russia's unique position in the world, between the West and East, between Europe and Asia, as well as between Christianity and Islam. This task bore different labels, but it was claimed by many that Russia was exceptionally well suited to act as an intermediary between the opposing pairs (12). This was not only because of the Russian geographical position, straddling two continents, but was also due to the fact that Russia itself constituted a multi-cultural, multi-confessional mix of peoples and was therefore in a better position than any other country to bring the two worlds closer to each other. '*Bridge*' and '*link*' were the two key metaphors most frequently used in this context (cf. Sakwa 1996:287). Occasionally, the metaphor 'buffer' was used (5), which seemed to connote that Russia, simply through its immense physical magnitude, served a peacekeeping function by keeping the West and East apart. To a certain extent, this was in keeping with the traditions of Russia's plight during the centuries of the Mongol yoke, which was often alluded to by my respondents. While stemming from similar deliberations about the conflict potential between the West and the East, there is certainly a difference in implications between the two sets of metaphors. With the 'bridge' and the 'link' there is a basic optimism that Russia could make an active difference, whereas the concept of the 'buffer' seems to implicate a decidedly murkier future.

Let us mention, finally, the third cluster of responses claiming Russia to be so unique and special as to have gained the right of serving as an *example* to the world (14). There was, according to the suggestions, a plethora of domains in which the country could perform such a role and, here, the respondents had negative as well as positive examples in mind. Positive examples included beliefs that Russia could show 'how a former socialist state could integrate into world society' or 'how vast natural resources could be put to good use in an economy'. Furthermore, Russia could 'constitute a civilisation of its own between East and West', 'show its special path of development', 'retain the serenity of its culture', and similarly, 'act as a spiritual example'. Negative examples concerned, on the other hand, aspects such as 'how a formerly imperial state could renounce its heritage'. Also, by way of negative examples, Russia could 'act as a negative pattern for the rest of the world' and 'take on experiments that save the rest of the world from undertaking them'.

In essence, there was after all also a fourth, large cluster of responses, consisting of those who argued that Russia had an international mission to fulfil, but who then failed to deliver any specification as to wherein that mission lay. To be sure, notions were quite often fuzzy as to the nature of Russia's global mission. 16 of the respondents did not manage to specify, when asked to elaborate. In addition, several quite hollow-sounding attempts were made at offering further clues, like 'influence world politics', 'be an international partner', and 'pursue its foreign policy vis-à-vis all countries'. As in the other clusters, differences between the various subgroups were slight. There were no conspicuous variations regarding the types of mission favoured by representatives of different regions or political affiliations. The only manifest dividing line was that, in general, regional politicians did not appear to have given a lot of thought as to whether Russia had an international mission to fulfil. It was here that the vagueness was most notable. Even though most of them answered almost reflexively that there was, indeed, a global role for Russia to play, they were quite often hard put to elaborate further. Concretion was greater among the State Duma members who, again, are generally somewhat closer to matters of foreign policy.

I would venture to say that the confusion, which often surrounded the issue of the mission, serves as an illustration of the quandary in which Russia has found itself during the last decade or so. It is well enough to say that Russia should play a global role, but it is apparently more difficult to specify its nature. Evidently, if there are problems in determining what the state polity as such is and should be, it is consequently rather difficult to decide on its national mission (cf. Ringmar 1996). As one of my Perm respondents put it, 'it is a large problem that there is no national idea, no national programme in today's Russia' (P 20). And, again, if the country's status as a great power is mostly due to its glorious future prospects, then the definition of its global role may well have to wait a little longer.

Notes

1. Transdnistriya is the predominantly Russian-speaking region in present-day Moldova.
2. Here, however, I find it necessary to point out that the respondent's experience in cross-country travelling seemed a little outdated. The flight from Moscow to Khabarovsk took me eight hours using the services of Aeroflot. Yet, it is not the exactitude of the statement, but rather the way of reasoning that is of interest here.
3. Along these very lines, Sakwa (1996:290) has noted a general tendency among Russian politicians of the 1990s to believe that "Russia is fated to be a Great Power", though how and why this should be the case was never adequately explained'.
4. This was also the way the question was phrased from the outset. On this particular point, however, I experienced the only case where my analytical terms did not seem to be translatable into Russian, and where I did not seem to get across to my interviewees. Quite simply, my respondents did not understand what I was after, so I had to rephrase the question.
5. Estonia, Latvia, and Lithuania are the only former Soviet republics that have consistently remained outside of the CIS. As the expression 'the Near Abroad' was hatched by Russian politicians in the early 1990s, it remained somewhat unclear whether the three states were considered to be part of this category.

6 The Internal Dimension

What Is Russia?

We have now, finally, worked our way in to the very core of the national self-images. What, then, would be the best way to begin to address issues pertaining to the internal dimension of national self-images among Russian politicians? There are several conceivable opening gambits, but for many reasons it is natural to start with the name of the state itself. As if to illustrate how blurred the distinction between inside and outside at times can be, there is a significant overlap here with the external/internal sub-dimension.

In the Russian Constitution, which came into being through an affirmative majority vote in the national referendum of December 1993, the name of the state polity is spelled out in the very first paragraph. This posits that 'the Russian Federation - Russia is a democratic federative rule-of-law state with a republican form of government'. I shall return to the subject of Russia as a democratic state below. Here, however, it is the ensuing part of the paragraph which is of more immediate interest. As if to try to foreclose disputes on this very matter, the text goes on to state that 'the names Russian Federation and Russia are of equal validity' (*Konstitutsiya Rossiiskoi Federatsii* 1996:4).[1]

At the time of the Constitution's adoption, the calls for a re-establishment of the Soviet Union were rather frequently heard, at least from the left-wing part of the Russian political spectrum, and Zhirinovskii-type boasts that Russia would soon be resurrected to its former imperial size may also have affected the formulations employed in the first paragraph. Regardless of whether national self-images primarily pertain to an ethnically based or predominantly civic nation, emotional attachments are, in all probability, mostly geared at Russia, not the Russian Federation. While Russia frequently evokes emotional reactions, attitudes towards the Russian Federation often seem to be characterised by fatigued indifference, at best. Therefore, and at any rate, there might well be a need for a constitutional clause stipulating that there is to be no difference between the concepts.

What, then, did my respondents have to say on this score? The question I wished to address was whether, in addition to the obvious difference as far as emotional content was concerned, there were also diverging views regarding the geographical extension of the two concepts. My contention is that there still appeared to be divided opinions on what the true delimitations of Russia should be. Whereas the borders of the Russian Federation presented no problem, since it is a well-defined subject of international law, confusion still seemed to reign whether 'Russia' should be interpreted as historical Russia, say in the Petrine period, or whether it should primarily be interpreted as pre-revolutionary Russia, or whether it, in actual fact, should be regarded as synonymous with what used to be the Soviet Union. If it is perceived by a significant number of the Russian political elite, as well as the populace, that Russia's geographical extent should rightfully be greater, and that injustice has been done to Russia in this regard, there might, unfortunately, be future breeding ground for politicians purveying expansionist political platforms.

It struck me at times that some of my respondents, even though few of them were schooled social scientists, managed to sum up the problematique as succinctly as I could after having devoted several years of study to these specific theoretical domains. For instance, one Duma deputy clearly recognised the manner in which the differentiation between the two concepts 'Russia' and 'the Russian Federation' is quintessential for the national self-images of Russians:

> This is certainly a question about self-identification. Russia is a kind of symbol, this word has a historical and symbolic load, and it is very ambiguous, since Russia is, first of all, the Russian Empire. Russia as Russia starts with Peter. This means that everything is associated with the concept of Russia: expansion, war, and the construction of the Empire, which went on until the mid 19th century. So it remains today. Simultaneously, this is also a state which developed energetically during different periods, and this state was during and before Soviet times quite often at the forefront. Therefore I would like to say that, even if this seems paradoxical, the Soviet Union was to a significant extent also Russia. According to many parameters, this was Russia. And what the Russian Federation is still remains to be seen.
>
> (SD 24)

Indeed, the respondents were quite divided as to whether the concepts of Russia and the Russian Federation were to be regarded as synonymous from a geographical point of view and, if not, wherein the differences lay.

Therefore, it would seem as though some of them had not actually taken the stipulations of the Russian Constitution to heart. One could definitely say that some confusion seemed to reign in the matter:

Table 6.1 Comparison between the concepts 'Russia' and 'the Russian Federation'

Are the concepts 'Russia' and 'the Russian Federation' identical or different from a geographical point of view?	Number of indications (N = 74)
Basically identical.	45
They are different.	24
Unclear.	3
Declines to answer.	2

Among the four cities, Khabarovsk stood out as the place where there seemed to be least confusion. 13 out of 16 deputies asserted that, to their minds, the concepts were basically identical. In the other regions, however, opinions were divided to a far greater extent. Many of those arguing in favour of the principal similarity between the concepts did so by referring to the constitutional clause stating that this was one and the same thing:

> I can tell you this right away: they are identical. If the question is designed to see whether I would like to widen the territorial borders, then I do not see such a need. I am a citizen who obeys his Constitution. The Constitution says that they mean the same thing. I recognise our Constitution.
>
> (Spb 5)

Moreover, normative aspects were provided as arguments for why the two concepts should be treated as synonyms:

> One must not, and I will not, recognise any difference. That would be to say that Russia is only there for the Russians, and that would be to open up for nationalism.
>
> (Spb 7)

> They should be congruent... If individual republics go for their own objectives and interests, this may again lead to disintegration and conflict.
>
> (P 19)

It is even more interesting to look at those lines of argument that held the concepts to be different. In all four cities, a large number of reasons were given as to why there was a difference. One respondent argued, for example, that it was hard to say how large Russia is, since this has varied so much through the ages (V 12). Another held that Russia has a glorious past, a glorious culture, and a population which by far outnumbers the population of the Russian Federation. Russia was, to this respondent, 'a symbol of faith for Slavs living outside the borders of Russia. It is a symbol of faith in a future reunion, this time in an economic sense' (P 11).

Likewise, others claimed that Russia was larger than the Russian Federation, like the respondents who saw Russia as being tantamount to the territory where Russians reside:

> Russia is not only what we have today, it is something larger. Russia is above all Russian people. Russia is partly that which Russia has lost, I am thinking of those territories where, for centuries, predominantly Russian-speaking people live.
>
> (V 15)

> According to my understanding, Russia is not the state of the Russians [*russkie*]. It is Great Russia, Little Russia, Belorussia, all Slavic peoples (...) Russia is where Russia is spoken, where Russian is the prevailing language.
>
> (SD 29)

In a similar, yet somewhat more restricted vein, another deputy included in Russia the territory of the Russian Federation, along with northern Kazakhstan, eastern Ukraine and Belarus (V 17). While recognising that, from the point of view of the affected neighbouring states, certain negative consequences might ensue from such a conception, one Volgograd deputy tried to justify this by referring to history:

> When we talk about the borders of the Russian [*rossiiskii*] state, we should refer to the borders delimiting the borders of the real, compact residence of the Russian-speaking population, even if this happens to be outside the parameters of the current Russian [*rossiiskii*] state. This is unambiguous. It is not a matter of expansion, it is a matter of drawing the official borders in accordance with the permanent, age-old living patterns of people.
>
> (V 15)

There was a small number of respondents who went even further in their zeal. According to one rather extreme voice that echoed the one-time words of ultra-nationalist Zhirinovskii, the Russian lands were to come together again, and this would mean that, among others, all former Soviet republics and Finland would once again become part of Russia (P 4). Also, one deputy seemed surprisingly unaware of the fact that the Baltic countries are no longer part of the Russian Federation. She labelled inter-ethnic developments in Estonia and Latvia as an internal threat to Russia's national security, and made the assessment that the Estonian and Latvian peoples residing in the Baltic countries 'comprised part of Russia too' (V 10). In this particular instance, however, I would say that this was hardly the matter of an ideological statement. Rather, it struck me as a remarkable instance of ignorance of what had actually taken place in the world since 1991.

There were also those who argued the opposite, namely that the Russian Federation was actually larger than Russia proper. One interviewee, for instance, claimed that Russia hardly amounted to more than European Russia up to the Urals, Siberia, and the Far East (Spb 8). One of his colleagues undertook to make a delimitation according not to geographical factors, but to religious ones. According to him, Russia was equal to the Russian Federation, with the sole exception of Muslim islets within the Federation (Spb 16). Another respondent found the Russian Federation to be tantamount to what existed during the time of the Soviet system, whereas Russia, according to him, stood for non-Soviet, bourgeois, capitalist power (Spb 9).

From this wide array of answers one may conclude that the confusion of what Russia is, geographically and otherwise, seemed to be substantial among some deputies. And if one encounters such a picture among a regional political elite, one may presume that the confusion will not be less among the electorate. This key aspect is of course very relevant to the questions of what the Russian self-image is, and what constitutes collective identities in today's Russia. For if one does not know what constitutes the state entity itself, it is also hard to know what to be loyal to. One respondent found an apt analogy to express the nature of this predicament:

> The national interests of Russia have not yet been defined. Those interests that used to exist in the Soviet Union are today subject to redefinition. The value systems are revised at the top as well as among the population. One cannot speak of destruction of things that are not there. There is no object around

which such great antagonisms can arise. It is like at a pottery, the clay is still formless, and any form can thus far be acceptable.

(V 15)

Moreover, as previously indicated, some interviewees held in the first place rather low opinions of the state called the Russian Federation. According to one of the St. Petersburg deputies, this very polity was nothing more than a sheer artefact, for which he really could not muster the motivation to feel any attachment:

Today we create the Russian Federation, tomorrow we will create the Russian Confederation, that is up to the politicians. But Russia has been and remains.

(Spb 13)

One deputy of the Volgograd Duma went even further. Rather than expressing his indifference to the idea of the Russian Federation, he claimed that the very denomination was so laden with negative connotations that, to him, it seemed difficult to construct a viable civic national identity around it:

[The term] is associated with a time when a number of national conflicts arose among us, when we had to live through the Chechen ordeal, when we had to experience a series of unpleasant things within foreign policy. The emergence of the Russian Federation as a state is associated with the whole complex of problems we experience today. Therefore, I cannot see anything positive with this combination of words. Rather, it is perceived as insulting.

(V 12)

These sentiments were summed up by one respondent who remarked that 'the Federation is not acceptable, neither as a state design, nor as a denomination' (V 15).

In order to return to the discussion on the can of pickles, I believe that the above findings bear out with some clarity that the extent or even the shape of the can is in no way undisputed or self-evident. Rather, to several of my respondents, it seemed to be most unclear. Perhaps the analogy made to the potter's clay was the most illustrative of them all, despite the fact that it was highly dubious who was considered to be the potter and whether, indeed, it was considered justified to picture but one potter in the workshop. However, regardless of what is being moulded here, whether it be depicted as a can or as a shapeless piece of pottery, it is now time to turn to the inside proper, to its characteristics and traits. We shall return to the issue referred to in the opening paragraph of the Russian Constitution, namely democracy. And again, we shall see that tensions prevail.

Is Russia a Democratic State?

It has already been noted on numerous occasions that the interviewees representing the regions frequently chose to express themselves in a manner that was deeply critical of the central government in Moscow. Given this state of affairs, it did not come as a great surprise to find that an overwhelming majority of respondents claimed that Russia could in no way be called a democracy at the current point in time. Moreover, there was a striking confluence of views among the deputies of St. Petersburg, Volgograd, and Khabarovsk,[2] even though Volgograd, as usual, proved to be the city were the harshest criticism was voiced. Let us, first of all, turn to the general pattern emanating from this part of the study:

Table 6.2 Assessments of democracy in Russia

Would you characterise Russia as a democratic state today?	Response (N = 89)
No.	43
No, not entirely.	32
Yes.	12
Unclear.	2

This is scathing criticism. Some respondents, notably KPRF members, even argued that there had been democracy during the Soviet period, but that things had changed for the worse:

> During the period of Soviet power we had democracy in several respects. That is a fact. If we had any problems they were solved through the party channels. Really. But today the humble individual, the citizen, is defenceless in legal and other matters.
>
> (V 13)

Another deputy argued that there had been more democracy in the years following the Stalin period than was the case today (Kh 4). Along similar lines, one State Duma member articulated a clear-cut verdict:

The Soviet power is referred to as a totalitarian regime, but it appears saintly when compared with the system we have today. I believe that the Soviet system was more democratic than the one we have today. People complain that they were not allowed to leave the country in those days, that one could not travel freely, and so on. But I do not consider freedom to be the main thing. I do not recall which political philosopher said that 'Freedom is the most important thing; freedom to work, freedom to have acceptable living conditions'. We do not have that kind of freedom [today]. Today it is hard to get a job. We used to have free education, everybody could study, people got their pensions, health care was free, but that is no longer true. To be sure, our borders are open and we have the right to travel, but how large a portion of the population can make use of that privilege? Thus, we have lost the freedom we used to have. Nowadays, we have the right to express ourselves freely, but this is more or less decorum, since the mass media distort what is being said.

(SD 6)

Even though the comparison with the Soviet period was not undertaken by all of those who saw democracy as being on the way down a slippery slope in Russia, several other interviewees argued that, somewhere in the 1990s, developments had taken a turn in the wrong direction. Thus, it was posited that there had been more democracy in the Russian state polity during the period expanding from the end of the 1980s to Yeltsin's showdown with the Congress of People's Deputies in October 1993, than was currently the case. Indeed, according to a deputy of the St. Petersburg City Duma, 'the elections that were held in late 1989 and early 1990 were the most democratic ever held in Russia' (Spb 20). In a similar fashion, others argued that things had become worse since after the aborted coup in 1991 (V 9) or since around 1995, when, according to one respondent, the attempts to democratise the Russian society were given up altogether (V 18).

Speaking of comparisons with past periods, and given the fact that much has been written about the disinterest of younger people in Russia with regard to politics, it is pertinent to turn to the question of how my generational subgroups differed on their assessments of the state of democracy. Here, it seemed as if those comparatively young people, who were already actively engaged in politics, were those who were most satisfied with the efforts to consolidate democracy in their country. On the other hand, the oldest age group, consisting of those who were born in the 1920s and 1930s, was apparently least impressed by purported democratic advances. This is interesting, as they constitute the group with the greatest potential for making comparisons with different stages of the Soviet period:

Table 6.3 Assessments of democracy in Russia by age groups

Would you characterise Russia as a democratic state today?	1920s/1930s	1940s	1950s	1960s/1970s
Yes.	-	3	3	6
No, not entirely.	1	15	12	4
No.	9	15	14	5
Unclear.	-	-	1	1

Again, this might be an interesting hypothesis to try to corroborate among a larger selection of respondents. It deserves, however, to be pointed out that the communist representatives amounted to less than half of the respondents who expressed their view on democracy in the oldest age cohort. Therefore, party affiliation did not account for the whole inclination toward pessimism in this subgroup. Yet, even though age groups, as well as regional belonging, seems to have influenced the picture to some degree, not surprisingly, political affiliation appears to be the most determining factor as to whether one wished to characterise Russia as a democratic state or not. The figures on this score are quite telling, and are worth presenting in a tabular format:

Table 6.4 Assessments of democracy in Russia by political affiliation

Would you characterise Russia as a democratic state today?	Communist parties	Other parties	Independents
Yes.	1	6	5
No, not entirely.	4	15	13
No.	24	5	14
Unclear.	1	-	1

Quite clearly, the Communist party representatives were the ones who felt most aggrieved by the prevailing situation. This would probably have to do with the fact that, in the words of one State Duma deputy, the largest political party was left outside of government structures. This, he argued, was tantamount to 'semi-democracy' at best (SD 19). Even though this particular situation shifted, during the relay of different governments between May 1998 and September 1999,[3] communist representatives were prone to feel that their political party was unduly marginalised by the executive. It is noteworthy that the only communist respondent who argued that she believed Russia could today be described as a democratic state, did so out of her conviction that democracy was a phenomenon to be resented in the first place (V 19).

In contrast with the communists, the respondents representing other political parties took a more positive view of political developments in Russia. Thus, about three fifths of the representatives of non-communist political parties deemed there to be at least partial democracy in Russia, and there were as many respondents who gave an unconditional 'no' as an unconditional 'yes' to the question of whether or not Russia could be labelled a democratic state. It should be noted that the largest individual party contingent within the category of other political parties was made up by representatives of the NDR, which, for substantial periods of time since its inception, was rather privileged by means of access to the levers of government. At the time, it was commonly referred to as 'the party of power'.[4]

The independents represent, as could be expected, a middle-of-the-road category. Here, the majority of the respondents is evenly distributed between the categories of 'no, not entirely' and an unconditional 'no'. Even though many independents, such as those in Khabarovsk, turned out to harbour considerable sympathy towards the Communist party platform, this category comprised deputies of all political shades and, therefore, the response pattern found here is quite likely to be a median expression of the one established within the communist and non-communist political camps.

Thus, my impression is that there certainly was a significant ideological factor impinging on the assessment of whether Russia should be regarded as a democracy or not. This is corroborated by the regional pattern, where the Red Belt city of Volgograd had the largest number of respondents who totally denied that Russia had any democratic traits whatsoever. St. Petersburg, on the other hand, with its relatively liberal sentiments, was the city where the degree of recognition of progress towards democracy appeared to be the largest. While being fairly critical in their assessments, the deputies of Khabarovsk found themselves somewhere in between, with a rather large amount indicating the intermediate category as their favoured choice. The predominantly negative response pattern seems to have been reinforced by regional factors, such as the feeling of undue discrimination due to party affiliation experienced in Volgograd, or the sense among the dwellers of the Russian Far East of being victims of central neglect. While the question was never put to the respondents in Perm, the following pattern emerged concerning the other cities:

Table 6.5 Assessments of democracy in Russia by region

Would you characterise Russia as a democratic state today?	State Duma	St. Petersburg	Volgograd	Khabarovsk
Yes.	6	3	2	1
No, not entirely.	13	9	4	6
No.	14	7	13	9
Unclear.	-	1	1	-

Most of those who argued that Russia had taken several steps towards democracy held that these had, above all, concerned free and regular elections, and the mass media's freedom of manoeuvre. Within these spheres, the achievements were rightfully, and almost consensually, perceived as both epochal and monumental (V 16, Kh 9). Moreover, the formal and legal framework was now in place and slowly but steadily, it was argued, the country was approaching the goal of attaining democracy as far as substance was concerned:

> Russia is, of course, no consolidated democracy. But, undoubtedly, the country has set out on a democratic path and, undoubtedly, reforms are being undertaken with the objective of turning Russia into a democracy, and this has produced some results. There can be no doubt about that.
> (SD 30)

According to the more sympathetic commentators, therefore, Russia was on the right track, even if there was still quite some distance to be covered:

> One cannot say that it is a fully-fledged democracy. We will be able to say that we have democracy the day our economy makes people more equal. Therefore, we have come further towards democracy within the political sphere than within the economic one. But we already have democracy if we compare it to what we used to have. We are less democratic than you are, but more democratic than China.
>
> (SD 13)

> Under great torment, Russia is heading towards a democratic state. It is very difficult to say how long it will take to perfect the journey, since Russia is an unpredictable country. But still she is trudging on.
>
> (Spb 20)

One cannot help noticing that path metaphors are frequently employed as regards Russia's democratic project. In this sense, there is a continuation of a linguistic practice widely used in the Soviet era, where positive phenomena were frequently alluded to through the use of path metaphors, expressing the notion of approaching some distant but desired goal. As I have shown elsewhere, there was one chief contending root metaphor in those days, namely the one holding phenomena that looked appealing at first glance to be mere camouflage and smoke screening (Petersson 1990). Incidentally, this kind of linguistic practice is still widely adhered to by critical commentators of the status of Russia's democratic strivings. As will be elaborated on shortly, democratic features are branded, by some quarters, as actually hiding phenomena that comprise antitheses of democracy.

What, then, were the obstacles encountered on the path towards democracy, and what kinds of malpractice did the newly acquired labelling purportedly hide from plain view? Granted that the picture was in general considered fairly bleak, there were some grievances that were reported more often than others. First of all, there were very frequent references to the situation of the mass media, where the presidential camp had a notable dominance. 'Democracy... is used as a cover for the struggle with the opposition', one interviewee held (SD 25, cf. Kh 14). Special consideration was given to the situation within national television and to the electronic media (Kh 3). 'If the opposition is given the opportunity to appear on television once a week, the government circles appear once an hour', one deputy lamented (Kh 8). Likewise, one Volgograd respondent argued:

> It is not because I am a communist, but if we want democracy, then let everybody have access to the free word, to television, and the electronic media. Then the people will realise who is right and who is not.
>
> (V 21)

Several others mentioned the immense concentration of resources in the hands of so-called media barons (Spb 9), such as Boris Berezovskii and Vladimir Gusinskii:

> And today, when Berezovskii and Gusinskii dispose of their TV channels at will and pursue their own policies, what kind of democracy can we talk about? What kind of freedom of speech can we talk about?
>
> (Kh 2)[5]

A related viewpoint was that rights associated with electronic mass media were exercised in conformity with the wishes of those who supplied the money, and this was obviously considered less than ideal (Kh 3, Kh 8). Might made right, and the opposition had no chance of making itself heard. One interviewee, an independent of the Far East, went quite far in his criticism:

> Today's regime, today's situation, is such that there cannot be said to be democracy in any sense of the word. We have a form of dictatorship, not the dictatorship of the proletariat as in 1917, but a dictatorship exerted by a certain group of people who dispose of a certain material and economic potential. One cannot talk of democracy of any kind, since this is a group which dictates the rules of the game.
>
> (Kh 16)

In this context, the situation during the election campaign leading up to the presidential elections in June and July 1996 was frequently alluded to:[6]

> The presidential elections of –96 showed clearly what our democracy is worth. One single candidate could use all financial and power-related levers, and so on, whereas the other candidate could not enjoy anything of the kind.
>
> (Kh 1)

Ziuganov lost at these elections, and we have to respect the elections. However, while people were deceived and told that the President was well, there was no equal access to the media, there were not equal financial opportunities regarding contributions from the budget, regarding foreign advisors. It must not be like that in a democratic country.

(SD 33)

Another frequently raised point concerned the vast constitutional powers of the president. This correlation of forces was unsatisfactory, it was claimed, and the president was far too powerful in relation to the parliament. It was even sustained that the executive had usurped some of the powers that should have been the due of the legislative (Kh 6). For one of the communist respondents in the Khabarovsk Krai Duma, it was quite clear under what circumstances the current situation was brought about. The constitutional framework had been laid down following Yeltsin's dictate, and as a consequence, the incumbent president was furnished with greater powers than any ruler in Russia's past, Stalin and Ivan the Terrible included:

The Constitution was adopted under the influence of the shots at the White House [in October 1993]. The powers of the President surpasses that of any previous general secretary of the Central Committee [of the Communist Party of the Soviet Union]. Not one of them had such power. Nor did any tsar, prince or other ruler of this country. Nowhere did they have such personal power.

(Kh 8)

In a similar vein, one of the Volgograd respondents asserted:

Boris Nikolaevich [Yeltsin] is tsar, god, and hero. With all respect for his age and for him as a Russian, I wish to say that he has, by far, too many prerogatives. This is not democratic.

(V 19)

Thus, the President was purportedly in a position to disregard the views of the legislative altogether. According to the critics, all this made him more of 'a monarch than a president' (SD 12) or 'an autocrat' (SD 1). Several respondents argued that this was no democratic state, it was a 'presidential republic' (SD 12, Kh 6, Spb 3, Spb 4). To the minds of many adherents to this view, therefore, the tilt towards the executive had to be rectified, in order to make it possible to talk about democracy in the first place (Kh 5, Kh 6). Apart from making a mockery out of the notion of separation of powers, the president's boundless power allegedly brought about bribery and corruption in the executive, and a chronic distrust and lack of legitimacy among the populace (Kh 5).

Many respondents asserted that there was democracy as far as the formal framework was concerned, but that the real substance was lacking. It was frequently pointed out that there could not be democracy as long as there was such inequality and poverty among the least fortunate segments of society.[7] 'People are deprived and deceived', one respondent from Khabarovsk claimed (Kh 3). Similarly, two interviewees, who were otherwise rather positive in their assessments, stated:

> We are on the road towards democracy, but we are walking with uneven strides (...) You cannot say that Russia is a democratic state, as long as such vast numbers of people are destitute.
>
> (Spb 10)

> The situation is bad as regards economic democracy, since there are still large monopolies, such as Gazprom and others. There is a lack of small enterprises, and there are huge gaps between the rich and the poor. So, one cannot say that there is a fully-fledged democracy.
>
> (SD 13)

The incessant problem of arrears, as far as wages and pensions were concerned, was repeatedly mentioned in this regard (V 10, V 12), since it was rightfully held to aggravate the differences between the prosperous and the destitute:

> Is it really a democratic country where more budgetary means are spent on the organisation of elections than on wages, pensions and education? There are some territories where people have not been paid their wages for two years.
>
> (SD 33)

Indeed, the widespread arrears constituted breaches of basic human rights, some critics held (V 10, V 12). In a colourful manner, one deputy of the St. Petersburg Duma depicted the plight of youngsters growing up in the Russian countryside:

> Some distant regions in Russia have been rendered totally penniless. In certain regions there are children who have never seen money in their lives. They laugh at their parents and do not believe them when they try to explain that money is

small pieces of paper which you hand over in the shop in order to get a bicycle instead. This is the result of the totally irresponsible policies of the centre.
(Spb 1)

The worst thing of all, according to one critic of this very centre, was that it was aware of the problems but just did not care:

They do not pay any attention to the protests that are being voiced. We can see this. People already lie down on the railroad tracks, and this does not upset them at all. Since this is the way it is, this is not democracy.
(Kh 16)

Furthermore, several respondents expressed concern over the legal sphere, and quite clearly there were those who regarded the judiciary as the weakest link in the desired chain of Russian democratisation:

Democracy is still weak. Telephone law[8] still prevails. The right of the strongest boss still prevails. There is an insufficient number of judges who are able to settle disputes of different kinds. The judges are still not satisfactorily qualified, they cannot work without relying on Soviet methods. They are used to working by decree. I believe that it will take another 20-30 years, 1 ½ - 2 generations before Russia can start to call itself a democratic state.
(Spb 3, cf. Spb 8, Kh 5)

Another perceived shortcoming was that an extensive body of legal acts, not least on human rights, had yet to be adopted by the legislative (Spb 8, Kh 5). It was furthermore pointed out that civil society and the political parties were poorly developed (V 1). Democracy may have taken root in the Russian capital and the large cities, but in the countryside, one respondent said, authoritarian modes of rule were still the practice (Spb 5). It was also held that local self-government had to be further developed (V 1). On the whole, the perceived symptoms were many, but the basic diagnosis was the same. There was something fundamentally wrong with this patient, the state of democracy in the Russian Federation.

Democracy as a Smoke Screen

As can readily be seen from the analysis and the quotes above, all kinds of views were subsumed under the general heading of criticism towards the implementation of democracy. Deficient democracy has, in actual fact, become a handy container for all strands of criticism, major and minor, towards negative phenomena in contemporary Russia. Indeed, there is even a tendency to put less blame on the unsuccessful practitioners of democracy than on the concept per se. It seems as if democracy, to the minds of many critics, is the common denominator of the political, economic and social misfortunes that have befallen Russia during the last decade. There is, of course, a deeply disturbing side to this, since the lofty word of democracy risks being corrupted and tainted in the public mind, rather associated with its opposites than anything else (cf. Sakwa 1996:371).

Therefore, it is important to note that, low as it was, the number of respondents who argued that Russia is a democratic country was still somewhat inflated. The reason for this is that the terms democracy and democrats denoted negative concepts for one category of respondents, implying opportunists and turncoats (cf. Lebed' 1995:414, P 3). This is where the employment of the root metaphor of the camouflage again becomes relevant. According to vocal critics, democracy had come to be interpreted as something connoting insincerity and deceit (SD 5, SD 31, Spb 20). This had to do, no doubt, with the tendency among a large part of Soviet time apparatchiks and bureaucrats, to switch from being communists to being democrats literally overnight (Shlapentokh et al 1997:144).[9] This did not do much to cement the general trust in democratic politicians:

> It is highly unfortunate that those who talk the loudest about their participation in the construction of a democratic society, are themselves the largest opponents to democracy. I am a communist, but I consider myself a true democrat. For us, democracy has turned into a dirty word, and the reason for this lies in those who are in power and who started the transformation. Today, the worst partocrats within the KPSS have unexpectedly turned into so-called democrats and talk about this a lot.
>
> (SD 31)

> Once they have become elevated to power, they forget what the concept of democracy means. From October 1993 onwards we have seen these new democrats, who call themselves democrats without being it.
>
> (Spb 20)

Clearly, the sometimes far too speedy conversions had done nothing to boost the reputation of democracy among the political practitioners. 'We are negative to democracy within citation marks', underlined a disillusioned KPRF member in Perm (P 3).

Even more aggravating, and as was alluded to above, there was a faction of respondents who, on the one hand, argued that Russia was a democratic state but, on the other hand, held that democracy, at least in its Russian version, was negative per se. For instance, one non-communist member of the State Duma argued that there was actually too much democracy in Russia, indeed more than anywhere else in Europe. This was, however, to Russia's detriment:

> Today the newspapers publish anything they want to. There are no ethical norms stopping them. It is the same thing with politics: politicians do as they please. There is total arbitrariness. We have a democracy without limitations. You can criticise Russia on account of there being too much democracy, not for the absence of democracy.
>
> (SD 29)

Along similar lines, one deputy of the Volgograd Oblast Duma lamented the situation of his parents-in-law:

> People have become used to the practice of those days when the television was state-run, and the newspapers were state-run, that once they wrote something, it was true. That was the only way it could be (...) My parents-in-law are 80 years of age, and in one newspaper they read that something is white, and in the other newspaper they read that the same thing is black. They do not understand. But if someone would put it the way it is, that it is black, white, red, then it would be OK (...). This affects the psyche of the elderly people, they have been used to believing. They continue to believe that this is the way it is.
>
> (V 21)

In this particular case, however, it seemed to be open to question who actually had the greatest difficulties to adapt, whether it was the respondent himself or his elderly parents-in-law. He seemed generally to have substantial problems in coping with the situation himself.

Another strand of criticism that was levelled at the very concept of democracy was given by a Volgograd deputy of the Communist party. The way she saw it, democracy led to juvenile problems, increasing prostitution and accelerating unemployment. Against this background, the undisputed, newly acquired freedom of speech was quite simply of no avail, she argued. What use was there in the media voicing any kind of criticism towards the President, when the President himself continued to disregard all reservations regarding his policies, she asked rhetorically. So far, she concluded, 'we have only seen the negative aspects of democracy' (V 19). And, reasoned another critic, the negative aspects of the democratisation process had strangled what was originally encapsulated in the concept:

> I always tend to say that this word, democracy, is a beautiful word which the Greeks have given to the world, but it has become so soiled by dirt and blood.
>
> (V 16)

To the minds of this category of interviewees, things were only prone to get worse. There was one more version of the conceptual criticism, however. Not only did democracy bring harmful phenomena with it in its wake, but it was also, following the logic of a Volgograd representative of the KPRF, inculcated in Russia as a consequence of machinations by external powers wishing to destroy first the Soviet, and then the Russian state. Thus, he hinted, it was all part of a conspiracy:

> The democracy which was dragged in here conceals negative phenomena. In 1917 communism was dragged in here, now democracy has been dragged in here. Of course democracy means freedom, but freedom for capital to penetrate our territory. This goes for all spheres of life and relations between individuals. Even people can be bought. That is why the democracy that was dragged in here was a negative phenomenon. The world community watched this; there may have been ulterior motives for its participation.
>
> (V 2)

Arguably, one specific desire hovers above this category of responses, claiming that democracy is detrimental to Russia. Some kind of alternative was apparently longed for. While complaining about all the negative phenomena and discomfort that democratisation is seen to have brought to the Russian polity and society, some respondents seemingly yearned for a change. Presumably, such a transformation could be brought about through the return to some past practices or, at any rate, through the advent of the reputed strong hand to the helm. This tradition has undeniably 'deep roots in Russian political thinking' (Sakwa 1996:47). A number of interviewees certainly seemed to indicate that a strongman would be able to put the Russian house in order. One Volgograd respondent, an independent, appeared to discern such a need when he reflected on the current disarray on the Russian political scene:

The struggle between democracy and totalitarianism has still not vanished from the arena, and at every single moment there might be a need for a strong hand, a harsh order, since we have a situation characterised by a certain anarchy, a certain disunity and disintegration.

(V 15)

'We wait for someone to think and judge for us', one of his colleagues asserted self-critically. 'We wait for someone to wield the cudgel. Such is our mentality: the Tsar is going to judge us' (V 2). Quite clearly, in the current state of political chaos or near-chaos, one prominent task for such a person would be to deal with adversaries without and within Russia. The subject concerning internal enemies has attracted great attention in the political discourse of post-Soviet Russia, and it apparently looms large in the political concerns of the public. It is maybe the single aspect with the greatest potential ramifications for the construction of civic national identities in Russia, and as such, it deserves to be dealt with at some length. It is now time to turn to this very subject.

The Internal Threat

As has been shown above, the overwhelming majority of my respondents held democracy in Russia to be less than perfect. In fact, most of them held the deficiencies to be greater than the assets. A great number of them had become aware that the relative laxity of social control, as compared to the Soviet times, could contribute to the spreading of messages and the multiplication of phenomena opposed to peace and stability within the Russian state polity. The expansion of such sentiments could, at times, threaten the very ideas of democracy itself. As was pointed out by one State Duma representative, the scary thing about democracy is that it can nurture the seeds of its own destruction (SD 29). 'Democracy is democracy with freedom and information and all that, and with pro-fascist organisations in the streets', noted another observer (V 1). The acquaintance with this classical dilemma has certainly not been a pleasant one to post-Soviet Russian politicians. When non-democratic movements use the channels of democracy, the access to free media and the freedom of expression to spread hate propaganda and xenophobic views, democracy certainly in a sense sows the seeds of its own destruction. Doubtless, phenomena like these have alerted Russian politicians to new or at least reinvigorated threats from within.

The ideas of prevalent internal threats is not a new phenomenon in Russia. Rather, it could probably be labelled an old Russian tradition to be more prone to discern and detect internal enemies than external ones. One need only remember the examples of Ivan IV and his instigation of the brutal secret police directed towards his own subjects; the perennial struggles of Tsar Peter with internal opponents by way of noblemen and traditionalists; the times of the Civil War following upon the February Revolution and Socialist October; and, ultimately, the darkest chapters of them all, the Stalin time atrocities, where total war was waged against the domestic population, against those who were labelled kulaks, wreckers, conspirators, Trotskyites or indeed whatever seemed to be the theme of the day. Also, the phenomenon of discerning internal threats was not overcome after the demise of Stalin. As pointed out by one Russian analyst, it was common practice in Soviet times to pinpoint internal enemies in order to deflect incipient social discontent (Shevtsova 1999:114). And, in the very last years of the Soviet Union, one academic study showed for example that internal threat perceptions predominated vastly over external ones among a stratum of the educated public (Melnikova and Shirkov 1990). It is true that there was certainly no shortage of perceived external enemies during any of these periods, but I am not arguing the case of total dominance here, rather the case of prevalent emphases.

Neither am I, in any way, inclined to subscribe to determinism which, as previously stated, I certainly consider to be a poor guide to knowledge and understanding of particular cases at hand. I merely wish to point out that it need not be a novel phenomenon that Russian politicians show themselves to be wary of internal enemies. Also, it need not be brought about by current economic and political crises or the advent of free expression only. Earlier periods in the Russian state polity have also proved themselves to be fertile grounds for the social construction of internal enemy images. One interviewee actually stressed the vital importance of enemy images for the construction of a viable national identity:

> In today's Russia it is a great problem that we have no national idea, no national programme. This makes it hard to look for enemies, and if it is hard to look for enemies, it is also difficult to determine who one's friends are (...) In today's Russia, friendship is understood as alliance against somebody else.[10]
>
> (P 20)

As a matter of fact, in cases where no enemy image immediately presents itself in the external realm, it appears to be distressingly easy to solve the dilemma by turning one's gaze inwards, conjuring up an enemy image from within. One perceptive respondent, a deputy of the Oblast Duma in Perm, recognised this well-known Russian tendency to identify scapegoats in difficult periods:

> Throughout the existence of Russia there has been a quest for external and internal enemies in times of trouble. Today these people try to pit people of different nationalities against each other.
>
> (P 17)

The question is then, what did my study indicate by way of the prevalence of domestic enemy images? How did my respondents treat my questions on internal threats to Russian national security? It is time now to turn to this crucial aspect, concerning the internal dimension of the national self-images.

As mentioned in Chapter 4, my respondents were clearly more prone to fear a threat from within, than from without. As will soon become apparent, the internal threats were perceived to come in many guises, including, as two of my Perm respondents chose to put it, 'our own stupidity and ineptitude' (P 17, P 18). In any case, several interviewees made it patently clear that the most frightful threats towards Russian national security were those posed by domestic sources:

> The most horrible thing is not the external threat, but the internal one.
>
> (Kh 8)

> There is an old Russian proverb: 'I am afraid of my friends, my enemies I can handle'. I believe that the most prominent threats are to be found within.
>
> (Spb 4)

> I cannot see any individual state that, today, constitutes a threat towards Russia to the same extent as Russia constitutes a threat to itself.
>
> (V 9)

It deserves to be noted that, in contrast with the threat perceptions regarding the external dimension, there were no temporal variations in the proclivity of the interviewees to perceive domestic threats. Indeed, the pattern was remarkably stable over time. Out of 108 interviewees, 92%

argued that there was a domestic threat in the current situation, and another 3% argued that, although there was no conspicuous threat for the time being, one might potentially arise from certain quarters. A mere 5% completely denied the existence of domestic threats. Moreover, there were three named sources that were by far seen as the most troublesome and worrying, with other sources trailing. The list of the most frequently expressed concerns had the following configuration:

Table 6.6 Overall assessments of most prevalent domestic threats

1.	Separatism and/or nationalism in general	(31)
2.	The socio-economic crisis and its consequences	(27)
3.	Chechnya and/or the Northern Caucasus	(24)
4.	Islamic fundamentalism in general	(13)
5.	Corruption/organised crime	(12)
6.	The politics of the incumbent president/government	(11)
7.	Fascism	(5)

The tendency to single out internal enemies is likely to have significant reverberations on the make-up of national self-images which, in turn, may affect internal cohesion in a number of ways. When united against an enemy, external or internal, it might be easier for the majority to strive together for the achievement of common objectives, but there is also, undoubtedly, an ugly and dark side to it all. Out-groups are targeted within and repression might follow. In the words of one respondent, it would have been preferable if an external adversary had existed to facilitate intra-group loyalty and unity. This, however, was hardly the case and, indeed, my interviewee contended, this boded ill for cohesion within Russia:

> We have lived through the War, and then we saw the enemy before us, he united us, we came to each other's rescue, and we received each other because we had common concerns. Now there is no self-evident enemy, but an internal enemy image is forming instead of an external one.
>
> (V 4+5)

There was a striking consensus between the regions regarding the prevalence of the three threats that were deemed to be most salient. There were, however, slight variations between the different categories of respondents as to the relevance of the other perceived hazards. First of all, it seemed to be quite contested whether or not Islamic fundamentalism should be appraised as a threat. The State Duma respondents made very few references to the phenomenon, as did the deputies of the Volgograd Duma and the representatives of the KPRF. The oldest and youngest age cohorts, the women and the non-Russians (perhaps not surprisingly, as they were in several instances Muslims) seemed not to worry about the presence of fundamentalist Islam. It was, in fact, the St. Petersburg deputies who were most alarmist in this regard, putting the Islamic threat at the very top. Numerous references to corruption and organised crime were made by all subgroups, save the KPRF representatives, the Volgograd respondents, and the members of the oldest age cohort, who all seemed to be rather unruffled by this phenomenon. Finally, only the independents and the women claimed the non-existence of domestic threats often enough to make it appear among the five most frequently made responses within their respective subgroup.

The Nationalist Card

The dangers of nationalism and separatism to the future of the Russian Federation were pointed out by all categories, making it the single, most frequently alluded to source of threat. One metaphor used by several respondents concerned 'the nationalist card' which, allegedly, was wilfully played by certain actors in current Russian politics. Those who used the expression evidently held that the consequences of using such a card could be dangerous for Russia:

> Of course the nationalist card can be played. There might be a threat here, it is the classical path along which the Union disintegrated (...) And today this card is used in Northern Caucasus, again we have the nationalist issue and also the Muslim card. There is a certain threat here. Also in Tatarstan one can envisage it being played. And in Yakutia...
>
> (Kh 11)

The general tendencies of separatism within the Federation were thus frequently alluded to, as was the interrelated risk of ethnic strife. Pursuing this line further, I put the question directly to the respondents whether they perceived a risk for the future disintegration of the Russian Federation:

Table 6.7 Assessment of the risks of disintegration of Russia

Do you see any risk of the future disintegration of Russia?	Number of responses (N = 90)
Yes.	61
No.	29

When viewed as groups, the Volgograd respondents and State Duma deputies were the most pessimistic by far. They seemed much more convinced of the imminence of a future disintegration than did their colleagues in St. Petersburg and Khabarovsk.[11] In St. Petersburg, the most frequent stance was not to believe in any future dismemberment of the Russian state. It was often stressed by the deputies of St. Petersburg, and to a lesser extent by those of Khabarovsk, that the risk of disintegration had been considerably higher some two or three years ago. They also argued that the spectre of secession was often raised by local elites who, in truth, were not intent on breaking away, but rather used such threats as a bargaining chip or as a means of political blackmail against the centre.

Some of the respondents attributed the risk of future disintegration to discrepancies regarding legal rights and obligations between the regions of the Federation. It was argued that the fact that the republics were, above all, given greater leeway in the retention of taxes, and had managed to acquire the rights of having their own attributes of statehood, such as flags and passports, might further whet their appetite (V 15). Clearly, this line of reasoning contained a strand of criticism towards the federal centre, which had permitted this development to occur in the first place (cf. Shlapentokh et al 1997:143). Several deputies also criticised the practice in some republics to call their elected head of administration 'president'. This only served to unduly elevate the status of the regional leaders, and could enhance the prospect of their attracting wide popular support for separatist platforms (V 18). The concept of 'independent fiefdoms' was often aired by those who discerned a risk of future disintegration (V 4+5, Kh 2). This scenario, which had apparently been discussed frequently among the active political practitioners, as well as in the domestic political debate (cf. Shlapentokh et al 1997:104), was not deemed to pertain to the national republics alone. However, they provided, as it were, the first link in the causal chain.

Of the interviewees who chose to specify in what geographic regions the risk of dissociation from the centre was the highest, the greatest number mentioned the Caucasus, and more specifically, in what at the time amounted to a *post factum* manner, Chechnya. All in all, 13 respondents spontaneously referred to the Caucasus in general, and 12 referred to Chechnya in particular. The only other region mentioned by a significant number of respondents was the national republic of Tatarstan (8 references), probably not as much due to prevailing secessionist tendencies, as to the far-reaching power-sharing treaty that the Tatarstani team had managed to negotiate with Russia back in 1994. Also, one can safely assume that there were recollections of the Tatarstani referendum of 1992. A consequence of this was, it will be recalled, that a constitutional clause was inserted into the Basic Law of Tatarstan, stating that the republic be regarded as an independent subject according to international law, albeit with a special relationship with the Russian Federation. One evident conclusion that can be drawn from these results is that the absolute bulk of references to regions, that might disintegrate from Russia, concerned areas chiefly populated by Muslims.

As was mentioned earlier, the Caucasus factor was the internal threat mentioned third on the overall list. Evidently, one main rationale was the perceived risk that the region might be a hotbed of Islamism and centrifugal forces that could spread to the Russian mainland itself. One deputy suspected that foreign hands had been pulling strings to bring about these developments:

> I think the whole of the Caucasus might explode. I think it is a policy that is well thought through. If they did not succeed in defeating Russia from without, then let it explode from within.
>
> (V 19)

In this sense, he suggested that the internal enemy was actually inspired and supported from without (cf. Shlapentokh *et al* 1997:103). This line of reasoning, however, was not very frequent. Even if the Caucasus thus seemed to be regarded as a perennial hot spot and breeding ground for domestic threats to the Russian state, the thought of the region seceding from Russia gave rise to some emotional responses:

> Why should Russia lose the Caucasus? I cannot envisage the Caucasus without Russia, nor can I envisage Russia without the Caucasus. These are our lands.
>
> (V 19)

There were, however, also opposing views. As has been pointed out, the St. Petersburg deputies were the most sanguine about the risks of secession and disintegration. In fact, individual respondents from this city argued that, even if Chechnya was given full independence, it would eventually return to the Russian fold. It would do this, they argued, since harsh economic realities would force it to do so. Thereby, the example of Chechnya could actually serve as an example, the effects of which, on the whole, would prove positive for the Russian Federation:

> We should recognise Chechnya *de jure*. They should be given the possibility to live on their own. The prognosis is that this will not be successful. The euphoria over independence would probably not last more than ten or fifteen years... Even if they were helped by Turkey [sic] or other Islamic states, it would soon be obvious what economic difficulties the new republic would face, and this would function as a cold shower for the other republics.
>
> (Spb 14)

However, as indicated earlier, several respondents predicted that the buck would not stop at the national republics. They argued that the Russian regions, the oblasts and krais, might be next in line (Kh 1, Kh 3). And, if such a scenario were to materialise, one deputy argued, 'Russia would exit from the political arena and cease to exist' (Kh 2). The situation was deemed to be worrisome and, like other colleagues (Kh 8), she traced much of the origin of the situation to Yeltsin's exhortation to the republics in 1992, where he urged them to grab as much sovereignty as they could swallow. This she considered 'sheer stupidity' (Kh 2). Her prediction, however, was that common sense and rationality would in the end prevail and that the scenario of independent fiefdoms could be avoided:

> I believe that today and within the nearest century, as during the Soviet period, there will be enough wisdom among our peoples to retain their original traits as well as their sovereignty, and still maintain the unity of peoples in the great Russia. Pray to God that there will be no parade of declarations to the effect that 'I am Tatarstan!', 'I am Chuvashia!' 'And we are the Far Eastern Republic!' That would be a kind of stupidity that would come to nothing, nor would there be any Russia left. And, within a century, there would be no Tatarstan, no Chuvashia (...) I believe prudence will prevail in the end.
>
> (Kh 2)

Regarding potential separatist candidates among the Russian regions proper, there were occasional references to Krasnoyarsk. This was attributed to the then newly elected governor of the area, the former general Alexander Lebed. Indeed, in Volgograd, there were remarks that verged on hatred against the controversial politician:

> [Let us take] the elections that were recently conducted in the Oblast [sic] of Krasnoyarsk, [and the victory of] General Lebed. This potentially means an enormous risk of Russia's destruction. He is a second Yeltsin. Yeltsin ruined the Soviet Union. Lebed will ruin Russia. He will give away the Kurile Islands and the Far East if only he gets elected president of Russia.
>
> (V 3)

The particular respondent who said this was on the whole highly pessimistic, alarmist even, and chose to refer to the imminent 'annihilation of Russia' (V 3).

The Straw on the Camel's Back: the Socio-Economic Crisis

The alternative that was mentioned second on the list of domestic threats to Russia's national security involved factors pertaining to the economic crisis, and the popular reaction that might ensue, perhaps even throwing the country into civil war:

> The social destitution might lead to war. It might well be like in 1917.
>
> (V 8, also V 19, SD 20)

> The discontent is so great that the authorities could be blown away in three seconds flat. That happened in 1917, it all happened during a day back then. It can be repeated again today.[12]
>
> (V 4+5)

All in all, 23 deputies claimed more or less to harbour such drastic concerns, and this factor was ranked second by deputies in all four cities. The risk was alluded to in spite of the famed patience of the Russian people. The proverbial straw might at any minute be put on the camel's back:

> Consider, for example, the case of the Oblast of Volgograd. We have got the Tractor factory, and Volgograd tractors are known all over the world. *Krasnyi Oktyabr'* is an enormous steel factory, but it does not function today. And this

concerns an enormous number of people, there are 30 000 workers at these factories. 30 000! And today these people are on the streets. This would be an internal threat to any country. Just imagine such a thing taking place in your country. What would happen then? There would be demonstrations, manifestations and other things, would there not? But today we are waiting for something, we are patient. But what could happen tomorrow is obvious enough.

(V 13)

Another Volgograd deputy was even more outspoken. In describing the economic woes of the country, he could not hide his anger while paying special attention to the then ongoing miners' blockade of the Trans-Siberian railway.[13] In their protest against unpaid wages, the Vorkuta miners blocked the traffic on the railroad, by quite simply sitting down on the tracks:

If the people continue not to receive their wages, there will of course be a threat [to national security]. The miners demonstrate this already. Earlier on, the miners were helped and supported, but today there is an anti-popular regime in charge. Today, one can already hear non-economic political slogans and demands. They demand Yeltsin's resignation. Obviously, he and the ruling regime is not to their liking. And, if they go on making empty promises, then maybe Yeltsin will have to lie down on the tracks. Or else they will make him lie down on the tracks... The people have been brought to the edge of desperation. When the Russian bear is sleeping, one should not wake him up.

(V 21)

Obviously, the references to these issues were accompanied by harsh criticism of government policies. Moreover, it deserves to be noted that this line of argument was followed not only by communist representatives, but also by several non-communist deputies. Still, in one respect, the assessments of the KPRF members is of special interest. Their listing of the most prevalent internal threats to Russian national security reads as follows, and it certainly contained some striking features. While they rated the social and economic crisis at the top, their list held another, even more interesting item:

Table 6.8 Assessments of most prevalent domestic threats (KPRF)

1. The socio-economic crisis and its consequences	(11)
2. The policies of the incumbent president/government	(9)
3. Separatism/nationalism in general	(8)
4. Chechnya and/or Northern Caucasus	(6)
5. Islamic fundamentalism in general	(2)

What I wish to point out here is the fact that the policies of the then incumbent president and government were ranked as the second most severe threat to Russian national security. In other countries the political discourse may well be rough at times but, still, one is hard put to recall other contemporary cases involving democracies, or aspiring democracies, where the popularly elected head of the executive is ranked as a serious threat to security by representatives of the most prominent party in opposition. Of course, physical numbers are slight here, and far-reaching generalisations have to be avoided. Still, I feel at liberty to make the observation that there indeed seemed to be a sea-wide cleavage between the President and his entourage, on the one hand, and the opposition led by the communists, on the other. This cleavage may well be predominantly instrumental but, even so, it would seem to stand in the way of common identifications and the kind of internal cohesion required to usher in joint action for common and much needed goals. It certainly presents Boris Yeltsin's successor, Vladimir Putin, a daunting task to deal with.

The Chechnya Factor

As a matter of fact, the republic of Chechnya and its intransigence in its relation with the federal centre conveniently encapsulates several threats in one. Not only was Chechnya itself frequently named in this context, but it also epitomised several other worries that were referred to by my respondents, such as the perceived tendencies towards nationalism and separatism ripping up the country. Other elements could also be made out. Most notably, these included the spectre of fundamentalist Islam, as well as the threat emanating from terrorism and organised crime, the latter of which, according to the official rhetoric, was a prominent theme during the first war, between 1994-96 (Petersson and Wagnsson 1998; Kh 1).

Accordingly, Chechnya would seem to be the perfect scapegoat, the perfect internal Other on which to put the blame for domestic shortcomings. Therefore, it is interesting to note that the respondents' reactions towards the first war were almost unanimously negative (cf. Petersson and Wagnsson 1998). And, as we have seen, this war came in third position as the most shameful element of the Russian past. In other words, the perception of Chechnya as a threat did not automatically make for an approval of the deployment of military force against the breakaway republic.

Quite on the contrary, several interviewees alluded to the possibility that the Yeltsin administration, and the so-called power ministries, had actually created a fundamentalist chimera, a formidable adversary, where there previously had been none:

> Some Russian politicians created [late Chechen President Dzokhar] Dudayev with their own hands... Today this is an Islamic state which wishes to extend itself not only within the region of Transcaucasus, but also to the Northern Caucasus.
>
> (V 6)

> Things used to be satisfactory in relations between the religions, but the events in Chechnya ruined a lot.
>
> (V 14)

In fact, it seemed to be the contention of quite a number of respondents that the federal government, through its actions, had set in motion a train of events which had now run out of control. There could be no turning back, but the consequences were dire and, according to some, the developments could have been avoided from the outset:

> I have been quite surprised by the pig-headedness with regard to Chechnya. If the politicians had acted more wisely, and if they had taken stock of the situation in a better way, then Dudayev would still have been alive, and Chechnya would have been a part of Russia, even if it remains so formally today too. Many human lives would have been spared, and such large damages would not have been done to the country.
>
> (P 17)

'The fact that troops were deployed to Chechnya in December 1994 cannot be undone' (V 16), another deputy remarked. This unfortunate act, he went on to argue, created cracks that multiplied and spread throughout the Federation:

> To address the problem in this manner, by creating a dead-end street of the Afghan type, was far too rash. Today's situation, with its proclaimed independence, pride, *sharia* laws and public executions is, in fact, a result of the inept Russian way of handling the matter.
>
> (P 12)

On the whole, however, no great amount of love was lost on the Chechens by the interviewed politicians. Indeed, the deputy referring to the Afghan scenario confessed to harbour some mixed feelings on the matter. Similarly, one liberal deputy of the St. Petersburg Duma remarked:

> I have never been a supporter of the Chechen side, even if there are fairly many among the intelligentsia. But it is my country, and those are my soldiers, my officers who die there, and this torments me.
>
> (Spb 5)

In fact, while the war of 1994-96 was criticised almost without exception, it was quite clear that many respondents were fairly suspicious about the Chechens' designs and intentions. There were two familiar reasons expressed for this. First, developments bore witness to the dangers of separatism inherent in the Russian Federation (P 4, P 93, P 20, Kh 1, Kh 4, V 6, V 16, V 19, SD 29, Spb 3). And secondly, this danger was associated with another allegedly appalling threat, emanating from fundamentalist Islam, which one deputy described as an entity possessing the power to 'invade and dismember the Russian state' (SD 29).

Following the argumentation of my respondents, one may well draw the conclusion that, although the Yeltsin administration had been less than subtle in its policies towards Chechnya, neither did the Chechen leadership seem to have been overly sensitive (cf. Kovalev 2000). If it had really striven to avoid distancing itself to such an extent from the tenets of Russian civic national identity, and if it had tried to refrain from so conspicuously taking the part of an internal Other, it would have desisted from certain actions that underlined the contrasts with the Russian body politic at large. Above all, the introduction of Islamic law, *sharia*, and some quite drastic applications thereof on the territory of the Chechen republic, in the years following the peace agreement in 1996, seem to have angered and even frightened several of my respondents:

> Concerning Russia in general I do not wish to make any comments [about Islam], but such a case as the public executions in *sharia laws* is a savage one. I do not know whether this springs from the roots of Islam or from individual believers of Islam. Whichever is the case, it cannot be accepted.
> (P 7)

> When heads, hands, and legs are chopped off in accordance with *sharia*, it is something which is totally incomprehensible to me.
> (P 17)

Quite clearly, there was something about the *sharia* laws, and particularly the public executions in the centre of the capital Groznyi that was fundamentally challenging to the basic ideas of civilisation, nurtured by several of my interviewees (P 5, P 12, Spb 3). And even if one respondent wryly suggested that capital punishment be administered publicly – 'the way [separatist leader Shamil] Basayev would have done it' – to those Russian politicians who permitted a further disintegration of the Russian Federation (Spb 3), it was quite clear that this did not conform with his views on civilised behaviour.

One final aspect of the comments on the Chechen war deserves to be mentioned. This war, which seemed so incomprehensible to many, was another case in point regarding the distance between the centre and the regions. While politicians (and especially the public) had difficulties in understanding why, in 1994, the war was initiated in the first place, their regions ended up having to pay with both money and human lives for its realisation. This added, naturally enough, to the sense of alienation experienced in the regions:

> We do not care whether Chechnya is a part of Russia or not. But our people die there, and our money is spent there. The economic resources that are generated around the Caspian region, that Chechnya benefits from, we never ever get to benefit from. We are upset about this. The interests of the Perm Oblast are not congruent with the interests of individual bankers, politicians, and others in Moscow.
> (P 20)

One representative of the Khabarovsk Krai Duma, situated at an even greater distance from Chechnya, remarked:

> The consequences [of the Chechen war] are still felt by us over here in the faraway Khabarovsk Krai. Even we have soldiers that have fallen, even we have children that have lost their fathers and their mothers.
>
> (Kh 12)

And yet, seldom was the feeling of powerlessness, alienation and disbelief expressed more vividly than by a woman deputy representing KPRF in the State Duma. For her story combined all of these dimensions:

> When I see what happens in Chechnya, Ossetia, Ingushetia, this is totally incomprehensible to me. It is incomprehensible to me as a politician, as a human being and as a woman. In my home town, a small town with 25 000 inhabitants, boys who had just left high school were drafted. They were not at all prepared for this. There was no voluntary element whatsoever, 12 persons were drafted. They had not even fought a single day when they were hit by friendly fire. A grenade hit the bus and all of them died.
>
> (SD 33)

There is really not much one can add. War always has an ugly face. Here, however, several of my respondents seem to have experienced this particular war as being both incomprehensible and meaningless at the same time. Even if the dangers of nationalism and separatism in general, and the developments in Chechnya and the Northern Caucasus in particular, were ranked among the most prominently perceived domestic threats against Russian national security, it is also quite clear why so many of my respondents held the Chechnya war of 1994-96 to be one of the most shameful events in Russian history. This war brought with it only death and destruction, and neither the individual nor the collective gained the slightest shred of national glory. This war did nothing to boost Russian national identity, however defined.

Before commencing with my interviews, one of my initial assumptions was that Islam, internal and external, would be perceived as one of the paramount threats by the Russian politicians I approached. As was indicated by the figures above, there was indeed such a tendency. However, in comparison with the three major sources of threat indicated by my respondents, the purely religious factor of Islam or Islamic fundamentalism was not deemed to be of any greater magnitude. In other words, the enemy image related solely to the faith of Islam did not seem to play such a pivotal role. In trying to explain why Islam should not be depicted as a threat, and why inter-religious relations were in fact quite harmonious and peaceful in today's Russia, several respondents chose to argue that this was thanks to the Soviet education system and Soviet-time upbringing at large. This was a line of argument supported primarily by representatives of KPRF, who found it natural to present these aspects in a favourable light:

> We are such a generation that we are quite simply international. We do not see them as purely Islamic, they are half Russian. Take Central Asia for instance, where there are many mixed marriages (...) Once again, I think the conflict is an artificial one. Their faith is different, there is a mosque, and there is a church, so what? Of course the Communists partly changed their world view, but we never hated the believers. And we have, for instance, the belief in the bright future. And they think that they have some kind of protector who will come to their rescue when things are rough. That might be Buddha, that might be Jesus. Every human being believes in something, religious or anti-religious, he has some kind of platform to lean on.
>
> (V 4+5)

One deputy who labelled himself independent expressed himself along similar lines:

> We were brought up during the Soviet period. We did not attribute any special meaning to whether people were Orthodox or Muslims. It was not until ten years ago that this question became important.
>
> (Kh 14)

However, when amplified through and reinforced by the geographical factor, as well as political and separatist sentiments within the Federation, another story emerged. This could be seen through the manifold references to Northern Caucasus or, more specifically, Chechnya. It has been made quite clear above that there was widespread suspicion towards the Chechens, even though few sympathised with the first war. Had this investigation been conducted during the second half of 1999, or in early 2000, distrust would certainly have been voiced by an even larger number of my respondents than was the case in the observations dwelt upon here.

This would also suggest the hypothesis that whenever, be it in Russia or elsewhere, there are different components of, per se, salient enemy images reinforcing each other, there is the risk for quite an explosive mixture. In recent years, the tendency among Russians to denigrate people originating from the Caucasus has been clear enough,[14] even though it has not been alarmingly widespread (Petersson and Wagnsson 1998). However, when this largely dormant sentiment was combined with popular alarm over the domestic bomb scare, in the wake of the mass killings in the apartment buildings in Moscow, Volgodonsk and Buinyaksk in the autumn of 1999, popular denigration of Chechens and Chechnya exploded. This provided fertile domestic ground for the subsequent harsh campaign against the Chechens. Slanted news reports helped to whip up the warmongery even further. Most probably, if similar events were to take place centring on, say Tatarstan or Bashkortostan, similar public moods could equally well be aroused.

In other words, on the basis of the response patterns emerging from my interviews, I would tend to hold that there is a certain latency about Russian enemy images vis-à-vis Islam. The picture is complex, however. On the one hand, respondents argue that Russia has to uphold good working relations with Islamic states, in order to see to it that Islamic fundamentalism does not extend its field of activity far into Russia proper (SD 32). In this sense, they underlined the artificiality of the inside/outside divide when analysing Russian politics. 'The Islamic world is inside Russia', as one of my interviewees expressed it when asked to elaborate on his views on Russian relations with neighbouring Islamic states (V 17). On the other hand, several respondents, predominantly belonging to the KPRF wing, underlined that Russia had a history of harmonious relations between the major religions. This was true to the Soviet period as well, they argued, and the religious factor continued to be of minor significance at the current point in time.

Single Examples of Anti-Semitism

As my esteemed colleague put it when advancing his argument involving the slightly salted pickle, there is a certain risk of question-begging when conducting structured or semi-structured interviews to uncover identity-related traits. In my list of questions there was no item that specifically covered the attitudes of my respondents towards the Jewry in Russia. However, it deserves to be pointed out that only two of my respondents aired anti-Semitic sentiments - one in Volgograd, and one in Khabarovsk - in connection with my question on internal threats to Russian national security. Of these two respondents, the deputy of the Volgograd Oblast Duma turned out to be most ardent. He expressed the view that the Russian government was totally in the hands of Jews, and that this was the reason for the economic and political misfortunes of recent years:

> We have a government in Russia where no-one is Russian [*russkii*]. No-one is *russkii*, no-one is even *rossiyan*.[15] How can it be that way? More than 80% of the population is Russian, but in the government there is less than one per cent. Would that be allowed in Sweden? (...) I do not say that all of them are Zionists. We used to have an artist by the name of Levitan. His nationality was Jewish, but he was Russian [*russkii*]. His mind was Russian. But today? If the government undertakes anti-popular actions, then I do not think that it is a government of the people. And then it is a non-Russian [*nerusskii, nerossiiskii*] government (...) Those who run the country should think about this. There are many Russians [*russkie*] who could run this country. The current situation cannot bring with it anything good.
>
> (V 21)

Lest misunderstandings arise, I wish to underline once more that this expression of adamant anti-Semitism was actually an exception. There were but two cases of anti-Semitism, the above and another more moderate one, that were aired openly throughout the series of interviews. Even so, they illustrate the unfortunate tendency to look for scapegoats and identify internal Others, who might conveniently account for the fact that Russia has experienced a seemingly never-ending series of political and economic crises. This is a dangerous tendency which could bring about very unfortunate results. And, apparently, when my respondents laid out their images of Russia, few of them seemed to hold that Russia was whole, united and devoid of internal threats. Thus, the notion of internal subversion seemed to be integrated into prevailing versions of national self-images. This is certainly not conducive to the successful launch of projects aimed at achieving something bearing a semblance of civic national identity. However, as shall be revealed here next, there is another variety of this phenomenon of Othering which, if not remedied, might have pronounced effects on intra-national cohesion in the Russian Federation. In a sense, the views of the anti-Semitic Volgograd respondent constituted a variant of the theme often encountered in the regions, namely the view that the problems in the social, political, and economic spheres are to be blamed on the federal centre itself.

Centre-Periphery Relations

The regional challenge to the centre's domination of the Federation is a real one. As was mentioned earlier, there was a time in the early 1990s when the then President Yeltsin courted the regions to try to garner their support in his ongoing clash with the parliamentary structure inherited from the days of the Soviet Union. During his trip to Tatarstan in 1992 he uttered, as will be recalled, the famed words that the regions should actually 'take as much sovereignty as they could swallow'. And this the regions did, above all the national republics, in the manner recounted in Chapter 2. Simultaneously, as the centre became increasingly weak, under the impact of an ailing president and an equally feeble economy, a situation occurred which by many analysts has been described through the formula 'weak centre, strong regions'. The centre really had no sanctioning power if the regions chose, for instance, to withhold their tax payments. And still, there was envy and remorse in the regions, directed perhaps more at Moscow as the capital city, than at Moscow as the federal centre. Under its crafty mayor, Yurii Luzhkov, Moscow was turned into a city with a lure for people with money to spend and invest. Certainly, this evoked some frustration among the residents of less well-off areas of the Federation.

According to several voices in the regions, the combination of a lack of interest from the centre and the general shortage of resources was a devastating one, made even worse by the fact that the capital itself managed to make the best of the situation and achieve high living standards. This main line of argumentation is well summed up by the words of a Volgograd deputy:

> It is no accident that Moscow today is flourishing, at the expense of the rest of Russia, the resources of which are being depleted. It is in Moscow that you find the great financial oligarchies, there are the main offices of the great oil companies, the energy companies. All taxes and 50 per cent of the budgetary means end up in Moscow. The Russian government pursues an impertinent policy vis-à-vis the regions. They make us handle all the problems, but they do not allocate us any means to enable us to deal with them. Decree upon decree is written that transfers more and more responsibilities to the regions, but we are given less and less means to shoulder them... Quite understandably, the incumbent government enjoys 90% support in Moscow. The living standards are pretty high there. It is possible to find jobs there, it is possible to exist in a decent way there. But all this takes place at the expense of the regions.
>
> (V 3)

In short, Moscow came to be associated with above all two things in the regions, namely an inept political centre of the Federation, symbolised by the increasingly weak President, and a money-hungry, well-funded financial capital, which seemed to attract the bulk of the country's sorely needed revenue. In other words, 'Moscow was accused by the provinces as a parasite that lived at their expense' (Shlapentokh et al 1997:132) The exuberant celebrations surrounding Moscow's 850th anniversary in 1997 was certainly a case in point (P 20). To say the least, the general situation was hardly conducive for building an atmosphere of trust and understanding between the centre and the periphery. Sharp criticism was often formulated toward Moscow, and rebukes were as numerous as they were vocal. Taken together, these tendencies clearly threatened to undermine the cohesiveness of the Russian state polity.

The negative sentiments regarding Moscow were also, in keeping with the simple logic of Othering, instrumental in laying the groundwork for viable regional identities. As argued by Shlapentokh et al (1997:152), 'people increasingly began to identify themselves as residents of their region and less as citizens of Russia'. One member of the State Duma, who was also a resident of Moscow, was perceptive enough to realise where this dynamism might lead the country:

> The thing is that the formation of political, economic and all other elites in Moscow is dissociated from the regions (...) The self-identification in the regions is exacerbated, this is the main thing. Most often, people there do not identify themselves as citizens of Russia, but as inhabitants of their region... This is a potential source of disintegration, and it is a very serious one at that, which might operate in a long-time perspective.
>
> (SD 24)

Likewise, another State Duma member, not however a Moscow resident, observed:

> If you were in Moscow, which is also a region [sub'ekt] according to the constitution, and went just 300 kilometres outside the city, you would find that Moscow there is looked upon as a state of its own.
>
> (SD 33)

So, obviously, there were political actors in Moscow that were aware of these regional sentiments. I shall now make a final excursion to the particular regions featured in this study, and in the course of this exposé, it will be borne out that the picture of regional self-identifications and regional withdrawals from Moscow seemed to be the rule, rather than the exception.

In Volgograd and St. Petersburg, there was a much more critical stance towards the policies of the Moscow centre than was the case among the Perm respondents, while Khabarovsk was somewhere in between. The century-old competition between Moscow and St. Petersburg seems to have played a significant role, as does the Red Belt location of Volgograd. Whereas a substantial number of the Perm politicians expressed an understanding of the need to strengthen the centre in relation to the regions of the Federation (Petersson 1998a, 1998b), most of the deputies of the St. Petersburg City Duma and the Volgograd Oblast Duma clearly chose to take the opposite view. According to them, the regions had to become stronger, and Moscow had to stop meddling. It was pointed out that the centre had to realise that Russia did not end at the Garden Ring (Spb 8).

The predominant mood was clearly one implying intra-state tension and frustration. This was put most vividly by an angry and disillusioned member of the Khabarovsk Krai Duma:

> The centre does not take any real interest in us, it spits at us and does not care how we live and survive here.
>
> (Kh 10)

It is quite clear that, in cases where such moods prevail, there is already an internal Other on which to build strong regional identities. However, this Other is neither a group of fiery separatists nor a band of Islamic fundamentalists, nor is it any other ethnic or religious grouping on the outskirts of the Federation. It is the very centre itself, and this can only be deemed as a rather hazardous development. If sustained and reinforced, consequences may be thorough-going.

St. Petersburg, Volgograd and Khabarovsk all seemed to have their fair share of specific problems in their dealings with the centre. They can most easily be summed up inter-city competition, Red-Belt location, and vast distance to the centre, respectively. In St. Petersburg, 9 out of the 19 respondents argued that the age-old competition between the present capital and the previous one was still a problem affecting today's politics. Aspects of this competition were said to cause problems in daily political life:

> Of course, there have always been such problems. The foundation of it all is the Moscow mentality. They do not want to accept that St. Petersburg is the cultural capital.
>
> (Spb 4)

One respondent demonstrated vividly that the competition between the two cities was still alive and kicking. He accused Moscow of deliberately trying to turn St. Petersburg into the second city of the Federation. In other words, in his view, his city still held the prime position. Several respondents claimed that St. Petersburg was unfairly treated concerning the allocation of financial means, above all when compared with the city of Moscow itself:

> Of all the financial resources of the Russian Federation, Moscow retains more than 70 per cent. We have 7 per cent, in spite of the fact that we have half the population of Moscow.
>
> (Spb 5)

> Today we cannot compete on even terms. Moscow has got 8 million inhabitants and St. Petersburg 5, but Moscow's budget is 5 times that of St. Petersburg's.
>
> (Spb 10)

The special pride in being an inhabitant of St. Petersburg was repeatedly displayed. There were various reasons for this. One view was that St. Petersburg was traditionally the city of the intelligentsia and aristocracy, whereas Moscow was the city of shopkeepers and merchants (Spb 7). Another held, for example, that St. Petersburg had proceeded much further along the route to democracy:

> [The deputies of] the Moscow City Duma seem like kids in their relations with Luzhkov, they constitute a team that is totally controlled by him. Here we have a talented, democratic opposition and, together with the executive branch, they do what the city needs.
>
> (Spb 8)

It was also argued that Moscow's envy of St. Petersburg produced a striving in the capital to, as closely as possible, control political events in the second city. Indeed, Moscow was said to have meddled in the St. Petersburg mayoral election campaign:

I believe that the present governor was elected with certain support from Moscow-based capital.

(Spb 18)

According to another voice, the Moscow Mayor still tried to exert control over his St. Petersburg colleague:

If one looks at the relations between Luzhkov and [the St. Petersburg Mayor Vladimir] Yakovlev, it is obvious that Luzhkov always tries to act the Big Brother.

(Spb 15)

The most characteristic trait among the Volgograd deputies was the widespread feeling that their region was unjustly discriminated against by the centre. Out of the 21 respondents, more than half were quite explicit on this score. Among other things, it was argued that the Oblast, of all of the 89 regions of Russia, was the one that collected least allocations from the centre when measured in relation to its budget (V 6). Others did not go quite that far, but pointed out that Volgograd was definitely discriminated against when compared to the neighbouring Oblasts of Saratov and Astrachan (cf. V 7):

The allocations to us and the allocations to the Oblast of Saratov differ about 100 times.

(V 19)

As for the reasons behind the unfairness towards Volgograd, the most favoured explanation pertained to its location within the Red Belt:

The centre regards us as a red zone, the Red Belt... The government and the President are against communists. They are against a communist being elected as head of administration in the Oblast. They use all means to continuously remind us of this, even though it is not allowed in a democratic state.

(V 19)

'Maybe they want to demonstrate that the communists have worse conditions', another deputy mused (V 18). The situation was regarded as unfortunate, not least because agriculture in Volgograd had to cope with unpredictable weather and climatic conditions. This, it was argued, should have called for some subsidies from the centre, in order to establish buffers, lest misfortune befall the farming sector, but the region had seen nothing of the kind (V 4+5, V 7).

A number of respondents claimed that the Oblast had been hard struck by the fact that the centre had reduced its orders from certain strategic industries in the area. This was the case with the huge Tractor factory, and the steel mill industry, *Krasnyi Oktyabr'* (V 13, V 10). It also applied to factories more squarely within the military field of production (V 10). The withheld orders from the centre had further sharpened the economic crisis in the Oblast, increased unemployment rates and reduced standards of living (V 10, V 11). One interviewee pointed to a specific aspect of the negative discrimination. Since there were certain deposits of crude in the Oblast, branches of Gazprom, as well as various oil companies, were quite active there. However, while depleting the resources of the region and drawing upon local manpower, the giant companies were registered in Moscow and, thus, also taxed there. Hence, Volgograd was not given its due, the old story repeated itself and the profits ended up in the capital (V 2). In all, the general sentiment was one of resentment and vexation concerning the region's position vis-à-vis Moscow.

As far as Khabarovsk was concerned, the most characteristic trait among the deputies of the Far East was that they felt their geographical location to be to their disadvantage. Khabarovsk was out of sight of Moscow, therefore it was also very much out of mind. The region was, it was felt, very far from being favoured by the centre:

> It is like in a large family, all children should be regarded as equal by their father. But unfortunately, the centre has its favourite children today, as well as those who are not as much in its favour (...) The inequality has above all financial consequences. We notice this here in the Far East, as we are situated so far away.
>
> (Kh 7)

The perceived problem was aggravated in the JAO, which was not only distant from the centre, but also, comparatively speaking, territorially insignificant. In consequence, one of its representatives lamented:

> The JAO is so small a territory with so small a population that, seen in relation to the whole width of the Federation's problems, we in principle amount to nothing more than a grain of sand.
>
> (Kh 16)

Even though a few deputies argued that there were no specific problems between Khabarovsk and the centre, bar the geographical distance, the majority of answers indicated otherwise. Several of the deputies called attention to the transportation costs (Kh 4, Kh 5, Kh 8, Kh 9, Kh 10, Kh 11), and the fact that these significantly hampered the development of industry in Khabarovsk Krai (cf. Shlapentokh *et al* 1991:181). As long as the centre was unwilling to reduce railroad tariffs, the regional economy of Khabarovsk would not be able to flourish:

> The Far East lies very far away from the central Oblasts, and therefore it is not competitive. Why not? First of all, distances are vast and thus transportation costs are prohibitive. If the state cared about these territories, it would furnish the transportation rates in such a way as to make our products competitive... A machine is produced here at, say, a price of 1000 roubles. But in order to transport it into [central] Russia you will need to add another 4000 roubles, due to the transportation rates.
>
> (Kh 8)

One deputy unhesitatingly drew his conclusion about the consequences of this situation:

> Khabarovsk Krai, like all of the Far East, has from an economic perspective been cut off from Russia.
>
> (Kh 5)

Similarly, a large number felt that the centre had to lower the energy costs levied on Khabarovsk (Kh 4, Kh 5, Kh 8, Kh 10, cf. Shlapentokh *et al* 1997:208). The Krai had been unlucky enough not to have had any power stations allocated to its territory during the Soviet period, and today, this cost it dearly:

> In those days, great hydro-electric plants were built all over the country. No doubt the thought was that a unitary tariff would be used everywhere in Russia. Today, however, individual regions like Krasnoyarsk Krai pay only a trifle, whereas we have to pay enormous amounts. This is to say that our products do not stand a chance of competing with those that are produced in Krasnoyarsk (...) We are punished because we happen to be part of a region where no hydro-electric plants were built.
>
> (Kh 5)

Energy tariffs had to be reduced, it was concluded, lest the regional economy be caught in a blind alley. This reduction was all the more desired, since the Krai needed compensation for its harsh climatic conditions.

Also, in view of the Krai's sparse population, migrants were required from other parts of the Federation but, in contrast to the Soviet period, the centre offered no inducements to promote such migration (Kh 11). This also meant that the region's rich mineral supplies could not be tapped. Furthermore, during the Soviet period the region had been home to a large military-industrial complex. As defence-related production units were now being dismantled, unemployment continued to grow and this, too, warranted compensation from the centre. So far, this had not been forthcoming. Said one disillusioned respondent about the desired programmes for improving the region's infrastructure:

> We need to make big investments, which the Khabarovsk Krai cannot make on its own. But maybe the government does not want to help, or maybe it just does not have the means.
>
> (Kh 8)

If looking only to Moscow for assistance, however, the politicians of Khabarovsk seemed destined to be stuck in a vain waiting for Godot.

Notes

1. An English translation of the Constitution is provided in Sakwa 1996, Appendix 3.
2. This particular question was not in the pilot study.
3. Yurii Primakov included a representative of the KPRF, Yurii Maslyukov, in a prominent position in his cabinet, which was formed in September 1998.
4. At the time of the Duma elections in December 1999, however, the heyday of the party was over. It did not manage to pass the 5-per cent threshold of the vote on the party list that is required for representation in the State Duma.
5. There was a distinctly anti-Jewish tinge to the statements of this respondent, whose rather anti-Semitic views have been dealt with elsewhere.
6. Incidentally, the body of international election observers, within the framework of the Organisation of Security and Cooperation in Europe (OSCE), reached the conclusion that the incumbent President Yeltsin had been unduly favoured through media coverage and media access. So these were apparently not only the complaints of dissatisfied and frustrated Russian politicians ('Election for the President of the Russian Federation', 1996).
7. This view, that economic rights should be incorporated into the general concepts of civil and human rights, could be regarded as a heritage from the Soviet period. It was a

principle that was also nurtured by the Soviet government in the international arena. Witness, for instance, the UN Declaration on Social and Economic Rights, which was adopted following an initiative originally taken by the Soviet Union. It seems as though this principle continues to be hailed by Russian politicians, although in view of the large discrepancies between the haves and have-nots in society, it would seem that it is not taken to heart by all in contemporary Russian society. (The dwellers of the newly constructed red-brick buildings, the so-called New Russians, would probably distance themselves from such a view.)

8. The term refers to the malpractice of Soviet times, where party bosses could just pick up the receiver, dial the appropriate number, and 'order' desired verdicts from the formally independent judiciary.
9. As pointed out by Shlapentokh *et al* (1997:144): '...a number of local politicians who were formerly Communists publicly changed their views, some sincerely and others not, and they joined those who praised democratic values and a market economy'. Cf. Shevtsova 1999:109.
10. Apparently, this line of reasoning on the centrality of enemy images is not the exclusive domain of political practitioners in the East. As a matter of fact, it can also be encountered among Western scholars, for example: '[R]emoving and forgiving requires knowing who the enemy is. The problem was that the enemy in the postcommunist period was not identifiable' (Cohen 1999:84). Similarly, three distinguished Russian scholars, one of whom is active in the US, refer to 'open or hidden enemies' of the Russian regime (Shlapentokh *et al* 1997:144). Thus they seem rather accustomed to viewing the world in such a manner.
11. This particular question was not put in the pilot study.
12. Indeed, this line of reasoning is in conformity with Kingston-Mann's (1999:7) observation that, ever since the reign of Catherine the Great, 'officials, scholars, and social critics [in Russia] tended to judge economic policy first according to its role in fostering stability or disruption in society...'.
13. The interview was conducted in mid-May 1998.
14. This is certainly not a new phenomenon. Relations between Russians and Caucasians, particularly Chechens, have been troubled for centuries (cf. Sakwa 1996:204-205, Lapidus 1999:49-50).
15. For reasons stated in the beginning, this sentence is not translatable into English. The translation would be that 'no-one is Russian, no-one is even Russian', which, of course, does not make sense.

7 Concluding Remarks

Now that my story has been told and the journey is almost completed, it is time to reflect upon the major patterns that have emerged. What did my respondents recount and what kinds of pickles did I produce from the metaphorical can? What did my findings indicate concerning predominant national self-images in the regions? All told, there is reason to confirm the initial assumption that the image of what Russia is and what it ought to be is not uniformly held across the four cities under scrutiny. Rather, it would actually seem as though the national self-image is most vividly held regarding the past dimension, whereas, as far as contemporary times are concerned, regional belonging has shown itself to be more important. This in itself is a rather discomforting thought. There seems to be precious little affective glue to be found in the present dimension. Instead, the apparent emotive mobilisers are to be found further back in time. As was noted above, the Great Patriotic War retains its forceful appeal across the generational, regional and political spectra. Also, the feats undertaken by Peter the Great continue to inspire widely different quarters, albeit with some added caveats. However, this raises some broad but crucial questions: Is this really enough? Are common historical myths and memories, no matter how inspiring, sufficient for welding the bonds of togetherness that, in the longer run, are necessary to keep such a vast state polity together? Will there not have to be some forceful unifying strength that identifies common tasks to be performed in the present for the sake of achieving a better tomorrow? Or is belonging to this particular state polity really defined only by default, brought about merely by a conspicuous lack of alternatives? These are demanding questions, and I doubt if they can ever be answered. What can be said, however, is that the bonds of togetherness, suggested by my respondents' national self-images, stand out as rudimentary and fragile indeed.

Moreover, while displaying the most common traits, the past dimension itself is certainly not devoid of problems. Doubtless, the proverbial elephant has at last been led out of the living room, and even though the reek of it to some extent remains, all categories of respondents have distanced themselves from the atrocities committed in the Stalin era. Even so, there is something amiss. If we visualise the Russian nation, however defined, as a family, there still is a yawning chasm dividing up the living room. The assessment of the Soviet period in its entirety is still a deeply divisive issue. From the point of view of trying to achieve a viable and solid civic national identity, the current situation is clearly not satisfactory. There is no way that a substantial fraction of the political elite can continue to regard the Soviet period as something to take pride in, while an equally large group views it as a deeply shameful aspect of the national past, without this having profoundly negative effects on cohesion and unity in Russia. So, it seems that, whereas the past dimension surely provides most of that precious affective glue needed to keep the state polity together, it also contains repellents, the effects of which will have to be dealt with somehow. Common sense has it that time is the only healer, but in the interim, deeply negative phenomena may come to the surface with potentially devastating consequences in their wake.

Clearly then, the present dimension does not offer much consolation to would-be architects of a Russian civic national identity. Indeed, this is where the bulk of the problems are encountered. Given the fact that Othering is so central an enterprise in the making of collective identities, it must be said that the interviewees excel in this regard. But even if they discern some formidable external adversaries, the Others are, to the largest extent, to be encountered in the internal arena. This could readily be seen from the response pattern concerning threat perceptions, where internal dangers to national security were deemed to be far more prolific than external ones.

On this score, it is striking how frequently it is the centre, Moscow, that is being Othered. It is the centre that is scapegoated and blamed for all ills that have befallen the country and the regions, and it is the centre that is seen as continuously scheming to worsen the situation even more. And if it is not thought of as scheming, then it is regarded as acting in such an inept and incompetent manner that it will make the crisis worse, even if its original intentions may have been good. Such an Othering of the centre might be the stuff that strong regional identities are made of, but it bodes ill for the future internal cohesion of the Russian Federation.

At the same time, it should be borne in mind that St. Petersburg is the only region where my respondents have displayed any kind of regional identity defined within positive parameters. Quite clearly, the heritage of Peter's city, the window on the west, is proudly held on to by these representatives of the political elite. They take note of the fact that their city is regarded as the cultural capital, and that it is considered to be a liberal city, as well as the home of the Russian intelligentsia. They steadfastly identify themselves with Western Europe and Scandinavia, and are so thoroughly European in these endeavours that they strive to distance themselves as far as possible from the United States, which is perceived to be so culturally alien to the Russian people. In these respects, St. Petersburg is unique among the four regions. In Volgograd, as well as in Khabarovsk, strong regional sentiments of identification and community seem to exist only due to the frustrations experienced in well-nigh all dealings with the federal centre.[1] In Perm, matters appear not to have proceeded that far, and the politicians there seem least dissatisfied with the federal powers.

If this strong Othering of the centre can be undone and neutralised, embryonic regional identities such as those in Volgograd and Khabarovsk will probably be stunted in their development, and I believe that there are fair prospects for President Putin and his administration to reverse the trend encountered under Yeltsin. Were the widespread dissatisfaction with the centre to continue to simmer, however, with persistent perceptions of ineptitude, ignorance and meanness, regional identities might well be consolidated in the other regions also. And here, I believe, the regions dealt with in my study could rather well typify sentiments in other Russian (*russkie*), territorially defined regions. Most probably, regional identifications are substantially stronger in the majority of the national republics. Unless the centre manages to restore or at least improve its legitimacy in the eyes of the regional elites, the centrifugal forces would seem to be potentially awesome.

To be sure, continued denigration of the centre would, in all likelihood, be harmful to a project geared at the construction of civic national identities in the Russian Federation. For even if the past is crucial for constructions of a civic national identity, the present tense is more important still. Sentiments of loyalty towards the centre are indispensable, since civic national identity certainly builds on what Ernest Renan (1882/1994) once called a 'daily plebiscite'. If that foundation displays visible cracks, the project is in trouble. National self-images represent national identities, and also inform them. Thus, if individuals who are part of regional elites feel and discern that they are being, if not cheated and double-crossed, then at least ignored by the centre, this is hardly bound to strengthen the affective glue, without which the bundle of national identifications will increasingly start to disintegrate. The idea of a civic national identity rests upon the notion that the state is the provider of desired goods and services and that it is a net provider of good actions. Otherwise, there would certainly be no rational grounds for keeping up such loyalty. If appeals are only made to affective sentiments, the civic components of national identity will probably not weigh heavily enough. For civic national identities there is no harking back to perceived times immemorial, and even though more recent elements of the past dimension of predominant national self-images are crucial, impressions of the present situation and the attainment of common goals tend to be of at least as much importance.

In their book about the complex relationship between the centre and the regions in post-Soviet Russia, Shlapentokh *et al* (1997:158) argue that the drastic amelioration of the international political climate started in the days when Gorbachev removed most of the pillars of support that had been propping up state patriotism in the Soviet Union and, subsequently, Russia. Patriotism had, in their interpretation, an emphasis on 'the might and well-being of the entire country'. In their argument the process of disarmament, the budding and growth of international contacts, and the disappearance of fear, all contributed to the erosion of sentiments undergirding the notion that the state polity itself was something to be proud of and to cater for. If one accepts this argument, one could claim that once the threat from the foreign Other was removed, it became decidedly more difficult to foster and sustain a viable civic national identity in Russia. Consequently, the gulf between the sets of questions on 'What are we? What are we not?' and 'What is our country? What is it not?' threatened to become ever wider. Sentiments of state patriotism lost their grip on the masses of the population and, Shlapentokh and his colleagues argue, among the political elites only the opposition, by way of communists and extreme nationalists, continued to peddle the idea of the need and desirability to nurture the might and well-being of the whole country.

This line of argument is rather familiar in the sense that it is deemed to be substantially easier to achieve in-group and intra-state cohesion in the face of clearly defined foreign threats. The crux of this matter is well-known in the discussion on intra-West solidarity after the demise of the Soviet Union. When referring to Russia, however, the question becomes even more portentous, as, in its logical continuation, it raises the problem of the very viability of the Russian Federation in the absence of international tension and conflict. The immensity of Russia would thus call for a powerful pressure from the outside to keep the state polity together, since the internal sources of friction and centrifugality are so legion, seeming so easily to rise to the surface.

This, of course, is an intriguing argument, but it is also somewhat irrelevant at the current point in time. Even though the Cold War is over, the world is not, unfortunately, such a happy and harmonious place that political elites of any country could claim to be totally devoid of outside threats. As has been discussed at some length in preceding chapters, there was, among my respondents, a markedly heightened proclivity over time to discern threats to Russian national security, notably from the United States and Nato. During the later part of 1998 and the first months of 1999, the political climate between Russia and the United States became strained, and there were numerous interviewees who gave admonitions to the effect that the only remaining superpower was hungry and on the move, stating that no country in the world was safe from its quest for increased power and influence.

This is not the main point I wish to make in this context, however. Rather, I would like to stress that the overwhelming tendency among my respondents to most of all dread perceived internal threats was consistent and unchallenged over time. Even if there was a clearly growing propensity to express concern over US assertiveness, these worries were almost dwarfed in comparison with the heated arguments made about looming dangers from within. Therefore, there are flaws in the simple logic of some kind of zero-sum, one-to-one relationship between internal and external threat perceptions, and their impingement on intra-state cohesion and basic modes of national identification. My findings would rather suggest that an increased sense of international crisis does not necessarily reduce the salience of exclusions and out-group categorisations being performed in the domestic arena. Certainly, history is replete with examples of this, not least Russia's own tragic experiences in the Stalin period.

The future prospects for sustaining positive national self-images in Russia that are related to a universal sense of commonality, as posited by theories on civic national identity, would thus seem to be bleak. More restrictive and excluding modes of identification appear to hold greater appeal. These might encompass most of the population, but those that are left out run the risk of rough times ahead. The concern often expressed by the Yeltsin administration, to the effect that there is no mobilising national idea in contemporary Russia, would, against this background, seem to be fully justified. Even when external enemy images do exist, all-encompassing bonds of togetherness appear to be missing in the internal arena.

Saying what we are also implies indicating what we are not. In the Russian case, it seems as if it is predominantly the latter operation that is being performed. In the external arena it is rather clear what Russia is not. It is not the United States, which is criticised and denigrated, even if it in certain respects clearly constitutes the benchmark against which several respondents would wish Russia to be measured. It is also not China which, although feared, is largely patronised and assessed as inferior, even by those who maintain that, like it or not, cooperation with this giant country is essential. Notably, this line of reasoning was also encountered among the inhabitants of the Far East. Moreover, the dwellers of the Russian (*russkie*) regions obviously do not hold Russia to be a part of the Islamic world, which above all is perceived as an internal threat to the fabric of the Russian state polity. And Russia is certainly not reducible to a former Soviet republic, in view of the fact that the other former republics are either perceived as younger brethren, or no longer constituting a part of the family at all.

These chiefly negative definitions evidently furnish certain bonds of commonality, but they do very little to identify answers to the accursed question of what Russia is. In all these cases, one can detect a tendency to believe that Russia is indeed supreme to the rest of the world. Maybe the crux of the matter is that the seasoned idea of Russian supremacy in moral, cultural and other fields still lingers, whereas it remains very unclear what the positively phrased characteristics of Russia actually are. The distinguishing features appear to a great extent to be identified, also by members of the political elite, by default.

There is an old saying, often referred to by my interviewees, that Russia essentially has but two problems, namely *duraki* (fools) and *dorogi* (roads). In other words, the root cause of Russia's incessant miseries is to be found in the unfortunate combination of the two. The first part of the quip refers to the fact that Russia, over and over again, seems to have been exceptionally unfortunate in her choice of political leaders, while the second part alludes to the traditionally appalling condition of a large part of the infrastructure in the vast state polity. Considering that *bezdorozh'e* (the impassability of roads in connection with the breaking of the frost in spring-time or due to mud-locking in the autumn), is still an overwhelming problem encountered not only in the countryside, but also in many Russian cities, the second part of the saying seems to have retained its topicality. And this is not a trivial statement, since in the vast Russian Federation, communications are all important. Quite simply, they need to function. Unless they do, an important precondition for the development of intra-state cohesion is eroded, and it will become even harder to establish a commonality approaching that of a civic national identity. The term communications in this context need not only refer to roads in the more traditional sense of the word. Any resident of or visitor to Russia can probably testify to the deplorable condition of telecommunications within the country. When making inter-urban phone-calls, and indeed even intra-urban or intra-block calls, the audibility is frequently very low, and one often finds oneself yelling, in the vain hope that some fragment of one's message will get across.

In the preceding pages, we have encountered the grievances of the city-dwellers of Khabarovsk in the Far East, and we have noted how neglected they felt by the centre. They felt out of sight and out of mind, and due to the sheer distances separating their region from the European parts of the Russian Federation, they experienced such extensive economic problems that they felt increasingly inclined to integrate with their Asian neighbours on the Pacific instead. So, roads remain indeed a major cause of concern in contemporary Russia. We may well live in an age of globalisation, where other means of communication will eventually supplant traditional modes of intercourse, like getting together in person, but it will presumably take quite some time before state-of-the-art technology is generally available all over Russia. Computerisation is still not the magic wand that can nullify the physical distances, and at times it would seem as though 'only national television remain[s] to link the provinces and the capital' (Shlapentokh et al 1997:152). In sum, although the belonging to the state polity of Russia would seem to be a legal fact of life, regional elites continue to feel cut off, disregarded and frustrated.

Judging by the damning statements made, primarily, by my respondents in Volgograd and Khabarovsk, the prevalence of *duraki* at the helm of Russian politics is still experienced as a problem among regional elites. We saw in the preceding pages that the trust expressed in Yeltsin and his presidential administration was extremely low in many quarters. Among the respondents representing the KPRF, the politics of the incumbent president were indicated as one of the most formidable threats to Russia's national security from within. Needless to say, if the figureheads of the centre are looked upon as fools and unworthy representatives, it will be very hard for them to attain the basic legitimacy needed for wielding power effectively, with the consent of the people. Again, this will certainly be detrimental to the attainment of the kind of togetherness and commonality associated with the concept of civic national identity.

As these concluding thoughts are being written, during the summer of 2000, President Putin has embarked on a course of action that strongly indicates an intention to try to knit the various parts of the state polity closer together. He has certainly seemed to be aware of the prevailing problems: 'Most people don't have any idea of what state they are living in. This is a time bomb that must be defused and destroyed', he diagnosed at one point in time (Japaridze 2000). While being characteristically harsh and forceful, his language on the matter did really not serve to reinforce hopes about the attainment of the ideals of civic national identity anytime soon. Identity cannot be requisitioned from above, it has to be constructed from below. Otherwise the result is not likely to be encouraging. In the best case, the authorities will, to borrow Dahrendorf's (1990:96) congenial phrase, 'produce a Brasilia rather than a Rio de Janeiro, an artificial construct which people yearn to escape for the nooks and crannies of the real thing'. In the worst case, if the strong hand tries to impose officially sanctioned identities, while thwarting those that constitutes the people's preferred choices, the outcomes might be downright appalling and very much removed from the ideals of democracy, to which official Russia tries to aspire.

Assessing the concrete course of action during the first six months of his presidency, one can see that Putin, in his drive to reduce the tendencies of centrifugality, has not only embarked on a roughshod policy of war towards the most intransigent region, Chechnya, but has also started to devise policies to rein in the executives of other regions. In May 2000, he announced the creation of 7 new administrative macro districts, to manage and oversee the work of federal agencies in the regions (*Russian Regional Report*, 24 May 2000). At the present point in time, it is unclear what exactly the net effect of the new structure will be, apart from adding a new bureaucratic echelon, replacing the old system of 89 presidential representatives overseeing the regions with 7 new presidential representatives of seemingly highly powerful stature. There seems to be little doubt, however, that Putin will endeavour to launch a course of action aimed at firmly entrenching the indisputable predominance of the federal centre. Most likely, he will attempt to do this by suggesting amendments to the constitutional structure of the Russian Federation. Today, in the summer of 2000, it is a widespread belief that the new macro districts are not only planned to serve as the bureaucratic mainstay of the 7 presidential representatives and overseers. Rather, Putin will probably try to slash the component parts of the Federation, the *sub'ekty*, from 89 down to that very same number of 7. Instead of having to deal with close to a hundred, more or less independent and unruly chiefs of regional executives, he will thus, in such a case, have 7 potentially close to omnipotent viceroys on his hands. Seen from the outsider's perspective, Putin might well thereby stand to find that the cure is even worse than the disease. And the question is, has he thereby solved the perennial problem of the *dorogi*? Will he be able to pull the parts of the state polity closer together? For obvious reasons, these questions have to remain open.

In a short-time perspective, at least, Vladimir Putin might not be able to do very much about the road conditions throughout Russia. What he can do, in such a perspective, is try to influence the perceptions of himself in the public mind. It is more or less a precondition for a successful first presidential tenure that he manages to continue to compare favourably with his immediate predecessor, Boris Yeltsin. From New Year's Eve 1999, when he became Acting President, to the presidential elections in March 2000, it was quite clear that Putin was determined to confer the image of himself as a man of few words, but all the more action. Instead of the ailing, faltering old President, here was now his youthful successor, the black-belted *judoka*. Indeed, instead of the old President with his concessions to the regions, here was the young Acting President, intent on bringing the recalcitrant Chechnya to heel. Instead of the old President, who was himself widely perceived to be one of the main roots to the problem, there was all of a sudden this young contender for the presidency, who appeared to suggest a host of quick fixes to tricky problems.

According to the line pursued by Putin ever since he was appointed Prime Minister in the late summer of 1999, the influence of the fundamentalist terrorism, allegedly typified by Chechnya, had not only to be restrained but weeded out. When the second Chechen War was launched by the centre in September 1999, this was partly a response to small-scale, armed Chechen incursions into the neighbouring national republic of Dagestan but, above all, it followed upon the bomb blasts which had left more than 300 casualties, mainly civilians, in Moscow and other Russian cities. The authorities claimed to see the hand of Chechen terrorists behind the misdeeds and, even if the connection was never proven, this served as the *casus belli* for the second post-Soviet war against Chechnya. The hard line advocated to deal with Chechnya soon became the most crucial, and some critics would say the only, policy line suggested by Vladimir Putin's political platform.

And indeed, Putin's hawkish policies on Chechnya revealed themselves to be a miracle recipe for successful campaigning for the presidential elections in March 2000. Through this war-making effort, several concerns were addressed all at once. As was mentioned earlier, the Republic of Chechnya was the perfect scapegoat, the perfect internal Other, on which to put the blame for domestic shortcomings. It epitomised several worries, such as nationalism and separatism, fundamentalist Islam, as well as terrorism and organised crime. In other words, it was ideal, and by making such a thorough emphasis on his Chechnya policies, Putin made his electorate forget about that other paramount cause of concern, namely the social and economic situation of the country.[2] This sleight of hand was most successfully pulled, and Putin was elected already in the first round, by a resounding majority of the vote. This was somewhat ironic, however, since the war-making effort in Chechnya was, if anything, a severe additional drain on the economic resources of the country. Therefore, this was quite clearly another instance of mortgaging the future. Nonetheless, it is far too early to say whether, in the final analysis, Putin will be seen as a political master magician or just another *durak* standing at the helm of Russian politics – with dire and harmful consequences pending for the state polity.

At any rate, the tendency to depict large or distinct groups within the Russian Federation as discernible threats is clearly not conducive to the establishment of the relatively harmonious domestic climate, thought to be a key characteristic of civic national identity. The finger-pointing towards the Northern Caucasus, and Chechnya in particular, rather serves to cement ethnic identifications within the Russian Federation. As one insightful respondent put it, 'ideological, ethnic, and religious bonds are rigid and brittle, and the friend can easily turn into an enemy' (P 20). And, one might add, by using such criteria to weld a sense of belonging and togetherness, there is always the risk of identifying new out-groups within the state that are not welcome to the community at large.

Unfortunately, however, there are factors that do seem to promote the reinforcement of ethnically based identification in Russia. The suspicion articulated towards peoples from the Caucasus, Chechens in particular, is certainly a case in point, as, to a lesser extent, are the tendencies towards depicting fundamentalist Islam as an internal enemy. And where these two factors, the ethnic and the religious, reinforce each other, as in Chechnya, the ground is more or less set for creating a clear-cut out-group within the Russian Federation itself. This is, of course, conducive to strong ethnic identifications and emotional attachments within the in-group, but it is certainly not instrumental to the process of constructing a more overarching civic national identity in Russia, encompassing all *rossiyane*. The creation of groups of outcasts within Russia might indeed stimulate joint actions for the attainment of joint objectives, and spur united efforts involving ethnic *russkie* and maybe other Slavic peoples as well. It has, however, substantial drawbacks that should be taken into account. The stakes are high, and I would maintain that the strategy is tantamount to playing with fire. If nothing else appears on which to construct togetherness, apart from the dislike of a common internal enemy, one cannot help but wonder who will be next in line, once the Chechen rebellion has been vanquished.

Notes

1. Concerning the Russian Far East, or more specifically Primorskii Krai with Vladivostok at its centre, Alexseev and Troyakova (1999:219) note that 'while embodying a distinct social and geographical identity, Far Eastern regionalism embodied, at best, a very weak political identity'. They also argue that one basic trait of the Far Eastern identity that after all can be discerned is the feeling of being 'disconnected from Moscow in time and space' (Alexseev and Troyakova 1999:216).
2. Shevtsova (1999:119) is, somewhat surprisingly in view of the unpopularity of the war, of the opinion that the first post-Soviet Chechen war served the same purpose for Yeltsin during the election campaign of 1996.

Bibliography

Abrams, A. (1999), 'Commemorative Holidays in Post-Soviet Russia', *Report of the Kennan Institute for Advanced Russian Studies*, vol. 16, p.1.
Alexseev, M. A. and Troyakova, T. (1999), 'A Mirage of the "Amur California": Regional Identity and Economic Incentives for Political Separatism in Primorskiy Kray', in M. A. Alexseev (ed.), *Center-Periphery Conflict in Post-Soviet Russia. A Federation Imperiled*, Macmillan, Houndmills, pp. 205-246.
Alvesson, M. and Deetz, S. (2000), *Kritisk samhällsvetenskaplig metod*, Studentlitteratur, Lund.
Anderson, B. (1983), *Imagined Communities*, Verso, London.
Avraamova, E. M. (1998), *Vremya peremen: sotsial'no-ekonomicheskaya adaptatsiya naseleniya*, Izdatel'estvo 'ISEPN', Moskva.
Barner-Barry, C. and Hody, C.A. (1995), *The Politics of Change. The Transformation of the Former Soviet Union*, St. Martin's Press, New York.
Barrington, L.W. (1997), '"Nation" and "Nationalism": The Misuse of Key Concepts in Political Science', *Political Science & Politics*, vol. 30, pp. 712-716.
Baucom, I. (1999), *Out of Place. Englishness, Empire, and the Locations of Identity*, Princeton University Press, Princeton.
Berglund, S., Hellén, T. and Aarebrot, F.H. (eds) (1998), *The Handbook of Political Change in Eastern Europe*, Edward Elgar, Cheltenham.
Bermeo, N. (1992) 'Democracy and the Lessons of Dictatorship', *Comparative Politics*, vol. 24, pp. 273-291.
Billig, M. (1995), *Banal Nationalism*, Sage Publications, London.
Blanton, S.L. (1996), 'Images in Conflict: The Case of Ronald Reagan and El Salvador', *International Studies Quarterly*, vol. 40, pp. 23-44.
Bloom, W. (1990), *Personal Identity, National Identity and International Relations*, Cambridge University Press, Cambridge.
Boynton, G.R. and Lodge, M. (1994), 'Voter's Image of Candidates', in A.H. Miller and B.E. Gronbeck (eds), *Presidential Campaigns & American Self Images*, Westview Press, Boulder, pp. 176-189.
Brown, D. (1999), 'Are there good and bad nationalisms?', *Nations and Nationalism*, vol. 5, pp. 281-302.
Brubaker, R. (1996), *Nationalism Reframed. Nationhood and the national question in the New Europe*, Cambridge University Press, Cambridge.
Buzan, B. (1983), *People, States, and Fear. The National Security Problem in International Relations*, Wheatsheaf Books, Brighton.

Buzan, B., Waever, O. and de Wilde, J. (1998), *Security. A New Framework for Analysis.* Lynne Rienner Publishers, Boulder.
Christie, C.J. (1998), *Race and Nation: A Reader*, I.B. Tauris Publishers, London.
Cohen, S. (1999), *Politics without a Past. The Absence of History in Postcommunist Nationalism*, Duke University Press, Durham.
Cottam, M.L. (1992), 'Recent Developments in Political Psychology', in M.L. Cottam and Chih-yu Shih (eds), *Contending Dramas. A Cognitive Approach to International Organizations*, Praeger, New York, pp. 1-18.
Dahrendorf, R (1990), *Reflections on the Revolution in Europe*, Chatto & Windus, London.
Depkat, V. (1997), 'The Enemy Image as Negation of the Ideal: Baron Dietrich Heinrich von Bülow (1763-1807)', in R. Fiebig-von Hase and U. Lehmkuhl (eds), *Enemy Images in American History*, Berghahn Books, Providence, pp. 110-133.
Dijkink, G. (1996), *National Identity & Geopolitical Visions. Maps of Pride & Pain*, Routledge, London.
'Election for the President of the Russian Federation' (1996), *Final Statement of the OSCE/ODIHR Observer Mission*, 5th July 1996.
Ertürk, K.A. (ed.) (1999), *Rethinking Central Asia. Non-Eurocentric Studies in History, Social Structure and Identity*, Ithaca Press, Reading.
Fiebig-von Hase, R. (1997), 'Introduction', in R. Fiebig-von Hase and U. Lehmkuhl (eds), *Enemy Images in American History*, Berghahn Books, Providence, pp. 1-40.
Fiebig-von Hase, R. and Lehmkuhl, U. (eds) (1997), *Enemy Images in American History*, Berghahn Books, Providence.
Geertz, C. (1988), *Works and Lives. The Anthropologist as Author*, Polity Press, Cambridge.
Gerndt, H. (1988), 'Zur kulturwissenschaftlichen Stereotypenforschung', in H. Gerndt (ed.), *Stereotypvorstellungen im Alltagsleben: Beiträge zum Themenkreis Fremdbilder - Selbstbilder - Identität: Festschrift für Georg R. Schroubek zum 65. Geburtstag*, Münchner Vereinigung für Volkskunde, München, pp. 9-12.
Greenfeld, L. (1992), *Nationalism. Five Roads to Modernity*, Harvard University Press, Cambridge, Ma.
Halbach, U. (1996), 'Der Islam in Russland', *Berichte des Bundesinstituts für ostwissenschaftliche und internationalen Studien*, Der Bundesinstitut für ostwissenschaftliche und internationale Studien, Köln.
Hall, R.B. (1999), *National Collective Identity. Social Constructs and International Systems*, Columbia University Press, New York.
Hedenskog, J. (1999), *Mellan självstyre och centralstyre. S:t Petersburg och dess förhållande till centralmakten under 1990-talet*, FOA, Stockholm.
Hedetoft, U. (1995), *Signs of Nations. Studies in the Political Semiotics of Self and*

Other in Contemporary European Nationalism, Aldershot, Dartmouth.
Hellberg Hirn, E. (1998), *Soil and Soul: The Symbolic World of Russianness*, Ashgate, Aldershot.
Heradstveit, D. (1979), *The Arab-Israeli Conflict: Psychological Obstacles to Peace*, Universitetsforlaget, Oslo.
Herb, G. H. (1999), 'National Identity and Territory', in G.H. Herb and D.H. Kaplan (eds), *Nested Identities. Nationalism, Territory, and Scale*, Rowman & Littlefield, Lanham.
Herb, G.H. and Kaplan, D.H. (eds) (1999), *Nested Identities. Nationalism, Territory, and Scale*, Rowman & Littlefield, Lanham.
Herrmann, R.K. and Fischerkeller, M.P. (1995), 'Beyond the enemy image and spiral model: cognitive strategic research after the cold war', *International Organization*, vol. 49, pp. 415-450.
Hirshberg, M.S. (1993), 'The Self-Perpetuating National Self-Image: Cognitive Biases in Perceptions of International Interventions', *Political Psychology*, vol. 14, pp. 77-98.
Hochschild, A. (1994), *The Unquiet Ghost. Russians Remember Stalin*, Penguin, Harmondsworth.
Holme, I.M. and Solvang, B.K. (1997), *Forskningsmetodik. Om kvalitativa och kvantitativa metoder*, Studentlitteratur, Lund.
Holmes, L. (1997), *Post-Communism. An Introduction*, Polity Press, Cambridge.
Hönicke, M. (1997), '"Know your enemy". American Wartime Images of Germany, 1942-1943', in R. Fiebig-von Hase and U. Lehmkuhl (eds), *Enemy Images in American History*, Berghahn Books, Providence, pp. 231-278.
Huntington, S.P. (1996), *The Clash of Civilizations and the Remaking of World Order*, Simon & Schuster, New York.
Hurd, I. (1999), 'Legitimacy and Authority in International Politics', *International Organization*, vol. 53, pp. 379-408.
Ivanov, V.N. (1999), *Rossiya federativnaya (krizis i puti ego preodoleinya)*, Institut sotsial'no-politicheskikh issledovanii, Moskva.
Japaridze, M. (2000), 'Putin Makes Regional Concession', *Infobeat*, 31 August http://www.infobeat.com/stories/cgi/story.cgi?id=256935940-f8.com.
Jepperson, R.J., Wendt, A. and Katzenstein, P.J. (1996), 'Norms, Identity, and Culture in National Security', P.J. Katzenstein (ed.), *The Culture of National Security: Norms and Identity in World Politics*, Columbia University Press, New York, pp. 33-75.
Jönsson, C. (1984), *Superpower. Comparing American and Soviet Foreign Policy*, Frances Pinter, London.
Kaplowitz, N. (1990), 'National Self-Images, Perception of Enemies, and Conflict Strategies: Psychopolitical Dimensions of International Relations', *Political Psychology*, vol. 11, pp. 39-82.

Karlsson, K-G. (1987), *Historieundervisning i klassisk ram. En didaktisk studie av historieämnets målfrågor i den ryska och sovjetiska skolan 1900 – 1940*, Dialogos, Lund.

Karlsson, K-G. (1995), 'Riket utan gränser', in B. Furuhagen (ed.), *Ryssland – ett annat Europa. Historia och samhälle under 1000 år*, Utbildningsradion, Stockholm, pp. 89-113.

Karlsson, K-G. (1999), *Historia som vapen. Historiebruk och Sovjetunionens upplösning 1985-1995*, Natur och Kultur, Stockholm.

Katzenstein, P.J. (ed.) (1996), *The Culture of National Security: Norms and Identity in World Politics*, Columbia University Press, New York.

Kellas, J.G. (1998), *The Politics of Nationalism and Ethnicity*, Macmillan, Houndmills, Basingstoke.

Kelman, H.C. (1965), 'Social-Psychological Approaches to the Study of International Relations: Definition of Scope', in H.C. Kelman (ed.), *International Behavior. A Social-Psychological Analysis*, Holt, Rinehart and Winston, New York, pp. 3-42.

Kingston-Mann, E. (1999), *In Search of the True West. Culture, Economics, and Problems of Russian Development*, Princeton University Press, Princeton.

Kochan, L. and Abraham, R. (1983), *The Making of Modern Russia*. Pelican Books, Harmondsworth.

Kolikov, N.P. (1997), 'World War II and National identity in the Soviet Union and Today's Russia', in S. Ekman and N. Edling (eds), *War Experience, Self Image and National Identity: The Second World War as Myth and History*, The Bank of Sweden Tercentenary Foundation and Gidlunds Förlag, Stockholm, pp. 58-64.

Kolstoe, P. (1995), *Russians in the Former Soviet Republics*, C. Hurst, London.

Kommers, J. (1991), 'Between Structure and Context: Sources, Source Criticism, and Alterity Studies', in R. Corbey and J. Leerssen (eds), *Alterity, Identity, Image. Selves and Others in Society and Scholarship*, Rodopi, Amsterdam, pp. 105-121.

Kommisrud, A. (1996), *Stat, nasjon, imperium: habsburgsmonarkiet, Tsar-Ryssland og Sovjetunionen: et historisk sosiologisk perspektiv*, Spartacus forlag, Oslo.

Konstitutsiya Rossiiskoi Federatsii (1995), Izvestiya, Moscow.

Kovalev, S. (2000), 'Putin's War', *New York Review of Books*, February 10.

Kowert, P. and Legro, J. (1996), 'Norms, Identity, and Their Limits: A Theoretical Reprise', in P. J. Katzenstein (ed.), *The Culture of National Security: Norms and Identity in World Politics*, Columbia University Press, New York, pp. 451-497.

Krause, J. and Renwick, N. (eds) (1996), *Identities in International Relations*, Macmillan Press, Oxford.

Kvale, S. (1997), *Den kvalitativa forskningsintervjun*, Studentlitteratur, Lund.

Kymlicka, W. (1995), *Multicultural Citizenship*, Clarendon Press, Oxford.
Lane, D. (1996), *The Rise and Fall of State Socialism. Industrial Society and the Socialist State*, Polity Press, Cambridge.
Langlands, R. (1999), 'Britishness or Englishness? The historical problem of national identity in Britain', *Nations and Nationalism*, vol. 5, pp. 53-69.
Lapid, Y. and Kratochwil, F. (eds) (1996), *The Return of Culture and Identity in IR Theory*, Lynne Rienner Publishers, Boulder, London.
Lapidus, G.W. (1999), 'The Dynamics of Secession in the Russian Federation: Why Chechnya?', in M.A. Alexseev (ed.), *Center-Periphery Conflict in Post-Soviet Russia. A Federation Imperiled*, Macmillan, Houndmills, pp. 47-93.
Lebed', A. (1995), *Za derzhavu obidno...*, Redaktsiya gazety 'Moskovskaya pravda', Moskva.
Lebow, R.N. (1981), *Between Peace and War. The Nature of International Crisis*, The Johns Hopkins University Press, Baltimore and London.
Macey, D.A.J (1987), *Government and Peasant in Russia, 1861-1906. The Prehistory of the Stolypin Reforms*, Northern Illinois University Press, DeKalb.
Magomedov, A. (1997), 'Lokal'nye elity i ideologiya regionalizma: sravnitel'nyi analiz v Rossii', in *Na putyakh politicheskoi transformatsii (politicheskie partii i politicheskie elity postsovetskogo perioda)*, Vypusk 8, Chast' II, Moskovskii Obshchestvennyi Nauchnyi Fond, Moskva, pp. 36-66.
Maier, C.S. (1988), *The Unmasterable Past. History, Holocaust, and German National Identity*, Harvard University Press, Cambridge, Ma.
Marcus, G.E. and Fischer, M.M.J. (1986), *Anthropology as Cultural Critique. An Experimental Moment in the Human Sciences*, Chicago University Press, Chicago.
Mavratsas, C.V. (1999), 'National identity and consciousness in everyday life: towards a sociology of knowledge of Greek-Cypriot nationalism', *Nations and Nationalism*, vol. 5, pp. 91-104.
McAuley, M. (1997), *Russia's Politics of Uncertainty*, Cambridge University Press, Cambridge.
Melnikova, O. and Shirkov,Y. (1990), 'Image of the enemy. A description of the existing image of the enemy among the Soviet people by an associative technique', *Educational and Psychological Interactions*, no. 102, School of Education, Malmö.
Melvin, N. (1995), *Russians beyond Russia. The Politics of National Identity*, Royal Institute of International Affairs, London.
Merton, R.K., Fiske, M. and Kendall, P.L. (1990), *The Focused Interview. A Manual of Problems and Procedures*, The Free Press, New York.
Miller, A.H. and Gronbeck, B.E. (1994), 'Presidential Campaign Politics at the Crossroads', in A.H. Miller and B.E. Gronbeck (eds), *Presidential Campaigns & American Self Images*, Westview Press, Boulder, pp. 253-270.
Miller, D. (1995), *On Nationality*, Clarendon Press, Oxford.

Milojkovic-Djuric, J. (1994), *Panslavism and National Identity in Russia and in the Balkans 1830-1880: Images of the Self and Others*, East European Monographs, New York.

Möller, P.U. (1999), 'Bokomtaler: Klas-Göran Karlsson, Bo Petersson and Barbara Törnquist-Plewa (eds), Collective Identities in an Era of Transformations. Analysing Developments in East and Central Europe and the former Soviet Union', *Nordisk Östforum*, vol. 13, pp. 74-76.

Möller, T. (1996), *Brukare och klienter i välfärdsstaten. Om missnöje och påverkansmöjligheter inom barn- och äldreomsorg*, Publica, Stockholm.

Moses, J. C. (1994), 'Saratov and Volgograd 1990-1992: A Tale of Two Russian Provinces', in T.H. Friedgut and J.W. Hahn (eds), *Local Power and Post-Soviet Politics*, M E Sharpe, Armonk, NY, pp. 96-137.

Nederveen Pieterse, J. (1991), 'Image and Power', in R. Corbey and J. Leerssen (eds), *Alterity, Identity, Image. Selves and Others in Society and Scholarship*, Rodopi, Amsterdam, pp. 191-203.

Neumann, I.B (1996), 'Self and Other in International Relations', *European Journal of International Relations*, vol. 2, pp. 139-174.

Neumann, I.B (1999), *Uses of the Other. 'The East' in European Identity Formation*, University of Minnesota Press, Minneapolis.

Nilsson, A-M. (1998), *Maktfördelningen i den ryska konstitutionen*, (mimeographed paper), Stockholm.

Oommen, T.K. (1997), *Citizenship, Nationality and Ethnicity. Reconciling Competing Identities*, Polity Press, Cambridge.

Orwell, G. (1986), *Animal Farm*, Secker & Warburg/Octopus, London.

Parekh, B. (1994), 'Discourses on National Identity', *Political Studies*, vol. 42, pp. 492-504.

Parekh, B. (1995), 'The Concept of National Identity', *New Community*, vol. 21, pp. 255-268.

Patton, M.Q. (1987), *How to Use Qualitative Methods in Evaluation*, Sage Publications, Newbury Park.

Pearson, D. (2000), 'The ties that unwind: civic and ethnic imaginings in New Zealand', *Nations and Nationalism*, vol. 6, pp. 91-110.

Pechenegina, T.A. (1996), 'Perm: Restructuring of the Industrial Potential', *Problems of Economic Transition*, vol. 38, pp. 51-58.

Petersson, B. (1990), *The Soviet Union and Peacetime Neutrality in Europe: A Study of Soviet Political Language*, MH Publishing, Gothenburg.

Petersson, B. (1997), 'Ryssland, Centralasien och den problematiska återintegreringen', *Nordisk Östforum*, vol. 11, pp. 47-58.

Petersson, B. (1998a), 'Russian Self-Images among Regional Politicians. Comparing a Pilot Study on Perm and the Case of St. Petersburg', *CFE Working paper series*, no. 1, Centre for European Studies, Lund.

Petersson, B. (1998b), 'Russian Self-Images in Perm — Findings from a Pilot Study', in K-G. Karlsson, B. Petersson and B. Törnquist-Plewa (eds), *Collective Identities in an Era of Transformations. Analysing Developments in East and Central Europe and the former Soviet Union*, Lund University Press, Lund, pp. 37-73.

Petersson, B. (1999), 'A Tale of Four Cities', *The Soviet and Post-Soviet Review* vol. 23, pp. 251-284.

Petersson, B. and Wagnsson, C. (1998), 'A State of War: Russian Leaders and Citizens Interpret the Chechen Conflict', *Statsvetenskaplig Tidskrift*, vol. 101, pp. 167-181.

Pipes, R. (1997), *Den ryska revolutionen*, Natur och Kultur, Stockholm.

Porter, T.E. (1991), *The zemstvo and the emergence of civil society in late Imperial Russia*, Mellen University Press, San Francisco.

Preston, P.W. (1997), *Political/Cultural Identity. Citizens and Nations in a Global Era*, Sage Publications, London.

Prizel, I. (1998), *National Identity and Foreign Policy. Nationalism and leadership in Poland, Russia and Ukraine*, Cambridge University Press, Cambridge.

Putnam, R. (1973), *The Beliefs of Politicians. Ideology, Conflict and Democracy in Britain and Italy*, Yale University Press, New Haven and London.

Renan, E. (1882/1994), 'Qu'est-ce qu'une nation?', in J. Hutchinson and A. Smith (eds), *Nationalism*, Oxford University Press, Oxford, pp. 17-18.

RFE/RL Newsline, vol. 4, Part I, 10 May 2000.

RFE/RL Newsline, vol. 4, Part I, 19 July 2000.

Riasanovsky, N.V. (1985), *The Image of Peter the Great in Russian History and Thought*, Oxford University Press, New York.

Ringmar, E. (1996), *Identity, Interest and Action. A cultural explanation of Sweden's intervention in the Thirty Years War*, Cambridge University Press, Cambridge.

Robertson, A. (1998), 'Through the Looking-Glass', in K-G. Karlsson, B. Petersson and B. Törnquist-Plewa (eds), *Collective Identities in an Era of Transformations. Analysing Developments in East and Central Europe and the former Soviet Union*, Lund University Press, Lund, pp. 74-78.

Rouhana, N.N. (1997), *Palestinian Citizens in an Ethnic Jewish State: Identities in Conflict*, Yale University Press, New Haven and London.

Russian Regional Report, vol. 5, 17 May 2000.

Russian Regional Report, vol. 5, 20, 24 May 2000.

Sakwa, R. (1996), *Russian Politics and Society*, Routledge, London.

Sautman, B. (1995), 'The Devil to Pay. The 1989 Debate and the Intellectual Origins of Yeltsin's Soft Authoritarianism', *Communist and Post-Communist Studies*, vol. 28, pp. 131-151.

Scheff, T. (1994), 'Emotions and Identity: A Theory of Ethnic Nationalism', in C. Calhoun (ed.), *Social Theory and the Politics of Identity*, Blackwell, Oxford.

Scholte, J.A. (1996), 'Globalisation and Collective Identities', in J. Krause and N. Renwick (eds), *Identities in International Relations*, Macmillan Press, Oxford, pp. 38-78.
Shaw, D.J.B. (1999), *Russia in the Modern World. A New Geography*, Blackwell, Oxford.
Shevtsova, L. (1999), *Yeltsin's Russia. Myths and Reality*, Carnegie Endowment for International Peace, Washington DC.
Shlapentokh, D.V. (1997), 'Eurasianism. Past and Present', *Communist and Post-Communist Studies*, vol. 30, pp. 129-151.
Shlapentokh, V., Levita, R. and Loiberg, M. (1997), *From Submission to Rebellion. The Provinces Versus the Center in Russia*, Westview Press, Boulder.
Sikevich, Z.V. (1996), *Russkie: 'obraz' naroda*, Izdatel'stvo S-Peterburgskogo universiteta, St. Peterburg.
Smith, A.D. (1991), *National Identity*, Penguin Books, London.
Smith, A.D. (1995), *Nations and Nationalism in a Global Era*, Polity Press, Cambridge.
Stenelo, L-G. (1984), *The International Critic. The Impact of Swedish Criticism of the U.S. Involvement in Vietnam*, Studentlitteratur/Westview Press, Lund/Boulder Colorado.
Stoner-Weiss, K. (1997), *Local Heroes. The Political Economy of Russian Regional Governance*, Princeton University Press, Princeton.
Sucharov, M. (1999), 'Types and Roles in International Relations: Beyond the Green Room', unpublished paper prepared for the Annual Meeting of the International Studies Association, Washington DC, February 1999.
Svedberg, E. (2000), *The 'Other' Recreated. A Relational Approach to East-West Negotiations*, Lund Political Studies 112, Lund.
Sydsvenska Dagbladet, 25 January 2000.
Sydsvenska Dagbladet, 14 June 2000.
Tempelman, S. (1999), 'Constructions of Cultural Identity: Multiculturalism and Exclusion', *Political Studies*, vol. 47, pp. 17-31.
Thibault, J-F. and Lévesque, J. (1997), 'The Soviet Union/Russia: Which Past for Which Future?', in P.G. Le Prestre (ed.), *Role Quests in the Post-Cold War Era. Foreign Policies in Transition*, McGill-Queen's University Press, Montreal, pp. 15-39.
Tishkov, V. (1997), *Ethnicity, Nationalism, and Conflict in and after the Soviet Union – The Mind Aflame*, Sage Publications, Beverly Hills.
Tumarkin, N. (1994), *The Living & The Dead. The Rise and Fall of the Cult of World War II in Russia*, Basic Books, New York.
Vainshtein, G. (1994), 'Totalitarian Public Consciousness in a Post-Totalitarian Society: The Russian Case in the General Context of Post-Communist Developments', *Communist and Post-Communist Studies*, vol. 27, pp. 247-259.

van Alphen, E. (1991), 'The Other Within', in R. Corbey and J. Leerssen (eds), *Alterity, Identity, Image. Selves and Others in Society and Scholarship*, Rodopi, Amsterdam, pp. 1-16.

van Evera, S. (1996), 'Hypotheses on Nationalism and War', *International Security*, vol. 18, pp. 5-39.

Vendil, C. (2000), *The Belovezha Accords and Beyond: Delineating the Russian State*, Defence Research Establishment, Stockholm.

Vertzberger, Y.I (1990), *The World in Their Minds. Information Processing, Cognition, and Perception in Foreign Policy Decisionmaking*, Stanford University Press, Stanford.

Waever, O. and Kelstrup, M. (1993), 'Europe and its nations: political and cultural identities', in O. Waever, B. Buzan, M. Kelstrup and P. Lemaitre (eds), *Identity, Migration and the New Security Agenda in Europe*, Centre for Peace and Conflict Research, Copenhagen, pp. 61-92.

Waever, O., Buzan, B., Kelstrup, M. and Lemaitre, P. (eds) (1993), *Identity, Migration and the New Security Agenda in Europe*, Centre for Peace and Conflict Research, Copenhagen.

Wagnsson, C. (2000), *Russian political language and public opinion on the West NATO and Chechnya. Securitisation theory reconsidered*, University of Stockholm, Stockholm.

Walker, R.B.J. (1993), *Inside/outside: International Relations as Political Theory*, Cambridge University Press, Cambridge.

Webber, M. (1996), *The international politics of Russia and the successor states*, Manchester University Press, Manchester.

Yin, R.K. (1984), *Case Study Research. Design and Methods*, Sage Publications, Beverly Hills/London/New Delhi.

Zdravomyslov, A. G. (1996), 'Etnopoliticheskie protsessy i dinamika natsional'nogo samosoznaniya rossiyan', *Sotsiologicheskie issledovaniya*, vol. 12, pp. 23-32.

Interviewee Profiles

State Duma

SD 1: non-resident of Moscow, KPRF, b. 1941, Male, Russian. March 1998.
SD 2: non-resident of Moscow, NDR, b. 1958. Male, Russian. April 1998.
SD 3: non-resident of Moscow, RR, b. 1960. Male, Russian. April 1998.
SD 4: non-resident of Moscow, KPRF, b. 1945. Male. Russian. April 1998.
SD 5: non-resident of Moscow, KPRF, b. 1952. Male. Buryat. April 1998.
SD 6: non-resident of Moscow, KPRF, b. 1951. Female. Tatar. April 1998.
SD 7: resident of Moscow, KPRF, b. 1945. Male. Russian. April 1998.
SD 8: non-resident of Moscow, NDR, b. 1961. Male. Bashkir. May 1998.
SD 9: non-resident of Moscow, NDR, b. 1947. Male. Russian. May 1998.
SD 10: non-resident of Moscow, Yabloko, b. 1941. Male. Russian. May 1998.
SD 11: non-resident of Moscow, Yabloko, b. 1942, Male. Russian. May 1998.
SD 12: non-resident of Moscow, LDPR, b. 1963. Male. Russian. May 1998.
SD 13: resident of Moscow, NDR, b. 1937. Male. Russian. May 1998.
SD 14: non-resident of Moscow, NDR, b. 1967. Male. Russian. June 1998.
SD 15: non-resident of Moscow, NDR, b. 1963. Male. Russian. June 1998.
SD 16: non-resident of Moscow, Yabloko, b. 1953. Male. Russian. June 1998.
SD 17: non-resident of Moscow, NDR, b. 1951. Male. Russian. June 1998.
SD 18: non-resident of Moscow, NDR, b. 1944. Male. Russian. June 1998.
SD 19: resident of Moscow, LDPR, b. 1970. Male. Russian. March 1999.
SD 20: resident of Moscow, LDPR, b. 1931. Male. Russian. March 1999.
SD 21: resident of Moscow, Yabloko, b. 1953. Female. Russian. March 1999.
SD 22: resident of Moscow, KPRF, b. 1945. Male. Russian. March 1999.
SD 23: resident of Moscow, Yabloko, b. 1950. Male. Russian. April 1999.
SD 24: resident of Moscow, Yabloko, b. 1946. Male. Russian. April 1999.
SD 25: resident of Moscow, KPRF, b. 1929. Male. Russian. April 1999.
SD 26: resident of Moscow, KPRF, b. 1956. Male. Russian. April 1999.
SD 27: resident of Moscow, KPRF, b. 1951. Male. Russian. April 1999.
SD 28: non-resident of Moscow, LDPR, b. 1964. Male. Russian. November 1997.
SD 29: non-resident of Moscow, NDR, b. 1954. Male. Russian. November 1997.
SD 30: non-resident of Moscow, Yabloko, b. 1960. Male. Armenian. November 1997.
SD 31: non-resident of Moscow, KPRF, b. 1956. Male. Russian. November 1997.
SD 32: non-resident of Moscow, NDR, b. 1960. Male. Chukchi. November 1997.
SD 33: non-resident of Moscow, KPRF, b. 1955. Female. Russian. November 1997.

Perm
P 1: Yabloko, b. 1959. Male. Russian. September 1997.
P 2: KPRF, b. 1928. Male. Russian. September 1997.
P 3: KPRF, b. 1941. Male. Russian. September 1997.
P 4: KPRF, b. 1962. Female. Russian. September 1997.
P 5: Independent, b. 1947. Male. Russian. September 1997.
P 6: RKPR, b. 1937. Male. Ukrainian. September 1997.
P 7: Independent, b. 1954. Male. Russian. September 1997.
P 8: DVR, b. 1950. Male. Russian. September 1997.
P 9: Social Democrat, b. 1963. Male. Russian. September 1997.
P 10: Independent, b. 1945. Male. Ukrainian. September 1997.
P 11: Independent, b. 1962, Male. Russian. September 1997.
P 12: NDR, b. 1941. Male. Russian. September 1997.
P 13: Independent, b. 1943. Female. Russian. September 1997.
P 14: NDR, b. 1939. Male. Russian. September 1997.
P 15: NDR, b. 1941. Male. Russian. September 1997.
P 16: Social Democrat, b. 1954. Male. Russian. September 1997.
P 17: DVR, b. 1949. Male. Jew. September 1997.
P 18: DVR, b. 1961. Male. Tatar. September 1997.
P 19: Honour and Motherland, b. 1945. Male. Russian. September 1997.
P 20: Movement 'Region', b. 1944. Male. Russian. September 1997.

St. Petersburg
Spb 1: Independent, b. 1951. Male. Russian. November 1997.
Spb 2: Independent, b. 1938. Male. Tatar. November 1997.
Spb 3: Independent, b. 1953. Male. Russian. November 1997.
Spb 4: RKPR, b. 1945. Male. Russian. November 1997.
Spb 5: DVR, b. 1947. Male. Russian. November 1997.
Spb 6: Independent, b. 1944. Male. Russian. November 1997.
Spb 7: Independent, b. 1947. Male. Uzbek. January 1998.
Spb 8: Independent, b. 1939. Male. Russian. January 1998.
Spb 9: KPRF, b. 1937. Male. Russian. January 1998.
Spb 10: Independent, b. 1948. Female. Russian. January 1998.
Spb 11: Independent, b. 1966. Male. Russian. January 1998.
Spb 12: DVR, b. 1949. Male. Russian. January 1998.
Spb 13: Independent, b. 1948. Male. Russian. January 1998.
Spb 14: Independent, b. 1953. Male. Russian. January 1998.
Spb 15: DVR, b. 1952. Male. Russian. January 1998.
Spb 16: Independent, b. 1962. Male. Russian. January 1998.
Spb 17: Independent, b. 1941. Male. Russian. January 1998.
Spb 18: Yabloko, b. 1959. Male. Russian. January 1998.
Spb 19: Independent, b. 1962. Male. Russian. January 1998.
Spb 20: Independent, b. 1939. Male. Russian. January 1998.

Volgograd
V 1: Independent, b. 1947. Female. Russian. May 1998.
V 2: KPRF, b. 1945. Male. Russian. May 1998.
V 3: KPRF, b. 1941. Male. Russian. May 1998.
V 4+5: KPRF, b. 1950. Female. Russian. May 1998 & KPRF, b. 1951. Female. Russian. May 1998.
V 6: Independent, b. 1950. Male. Russian. May 1998.
V 7: Independent, b. 1939. Female. Ukrainian. May 1998.
V 8: KPRF, b. 1951. Male. Russian. May 1998.
V 9: KPRF, b. 1956. Male. Russian. May 1998.
V 10: KPRF, b. 1940. Female. Russian. May 1998.
V 11: Independent, b. 1964. Male. Russian. May 1998.
V 12: Independent, b. 1960. Male. Russian. May 1998.
V 13: KPRF, b. 1962. Male. Russian. May 1998.
V 14: Independent, b. 1950. Male. Russian. May 1998.
V 15: Independent, b. 1953. Male. Russian. May 1998.
V 16: KPRF, b. 1930. Male. Russian. May 1998.
V 17: Independent, b. 1944. Male. Russian. May 1998.
V 18: Independent, b. 1943. Male. Russian. May 1998.
V 19: KPRF, b. 1944. Female. Russian. May 1998.
V 20: KPRF, b. 1946. Male. Russian. May/June 1998.
V 21: KPRF, b. 1949. Male. Russian. May 1998.

Khabarovsk
Kh 1: KPRF, b. 1950. Male. Russian. November 1998.
Kh 2: KPRF, b. 1933. Female. Ukrainian. November 1998.
Kh 3: KPRF, b. 1949. Male. Russian. November 1998.
Kh 4: Independent, b. 1945. Male. Russian. November 1998.
Kh 5: Independent, b. 1940. Male. Russian. November 1998.
Kh 6: Independent, b. 1956. Male. Russian. November 1998.
Kh 7: Independent, b. 1951. Male. Russian. November 1998.
Kh 8: KPRF, b. 1947. Male. Belorusian. November 1998.
Kh 9: KPRF, b. 1970. Male. Russian. November 1998.
Kh 10: Independent, b. 1950. Male. Russian. November 1998.
Kh 11: KPRF, b. 1951. Male. Russian. November 1998.
Kh 12: Independent, b. 1954. Female. Russian. November 1998.
Kh 13: Independent, b. 1948. Female. Russian. November 1998.
Kh 14: JAO. Independent, b. 1948. Male. Russian. November 1998.
Kh 15: JAO. Independent, b. 1946. Male. Jew. November 1998.
Kh 16: JAO. Independent, b. 1950. Male. Russian. November 1998.

Appendix A: List of Questions
(English Translation)

Past dimension:
1. Looking back on Russian history, are there any periods that make you feel particularly proud? If so, what periods? Could these period serve as models or sources of inspiration in today's period of transformation? Are there any periods that make you feel ashamed? If so, what periods?

External dimension:
1. Would you say that Russia has an international mission to fulfil? If so, what? Is there anything in Russian foreign policy today that makes you feel proud?. Is there anything in Russian foreign policy today that makes you feel ashamed? Is Russia a great power today? What are the bases of that power?. Would you say that there are any geographical areas outside the borders of Russia where Russia has a right to influence political developments? Which countries should be the main international partners of Russia today? Are there any external threats to Russian national security today? Do any countries pose threats to Russia?

External/internal dimension:
1. Are there any foreign countries that, in their entirety or partly, could serve as models for the future development of Russia?. What should be Russia's policy towards the Russian diaspora in the Near Abroad? How do you assess the ongoing projects aiming at re-integration within the CIS frame? How would you assess Russia's relations to Islam and the Islamic countries? Is there an internal Islamic factor in Russian politics? If so, what consequences might this entail? Is Russia, according to your view, the same thing as the Russian Federation in a geographical sense? If not, what is the difference?

Internal dimension:
1. Are there any internal threats to Russian national security? Do you see any risk of the future disintegration of Russia? Would you characterise Russia as a democracy today? What is the most important problem characterising the relations between the centre and the regions? Are there any particular problems affecting the relations between the centre and your region?

Index

1917 64-66, 75, 82, 89, 134, 152, 158, 167
1989 census 49, 53

Abkhazia 27
Aeroflot 139n
affective glue 10, 60, 71, 186-7, 189
Afghan scenario 171
Afghanistan 82-83, 86, 88, 95
Africa 101
age groups 1, 32, 56-57, 66, 71, 87-88, 97, 147-8, 163
agriculture 72, 76, 181
Albania 118n
Alexander II 62, 65-67, 70, 76-77
Alexseev, M.A. 196n
alienation 172-3
all-Russian identity 88
Amur 49
Animal Farm 24
anti-Semitism 175-6, 184n
apparatchiks 156
Asia 60, 101, 137, 192
Astrachan 181
attributes of statehood 164
August coup 2-3, 66, 147
Avraamova, E. 18, 111

Balkans 97, 106, 117
Baltic Sea 49
Baltic states 119
bandy effect 118n
Bardot, B. 41
Basayev, S. 172
Bashkir 48
Bashkortostan 47-48, 175
Belarus 129-33, 143
Belovezha accords 2
Berezovskii, B. 152
bezdorozh'e 191
Big Brother 181

bilateral treaties 46-47, 165
bipolarity 98
Birobidzhan 50, 54
Black Sea 49
Blagovezhensk 102
blockade 117
bomb scare 175, 195
bonds of togetherness 9, 16, 59, 186, 191, 195
Boyars 74
brain scanner 41
Brasilia 193
Brezhnev, L. 24, 53, 113
bridge 137
Britishness 26
Brown, D. 15, 26
Buddha 174
buffer 137-8
Buinyaksk 175
Bukharin, N. 24
Burkina Faso 123

Cadillac 41
camouflage 152, 156
can of pickles 42, 145, 186
Caspian region 172
casus belli 195
Catalonia 27
Catherine II (the Great) 62, 67-68, 185n
Caucasus 34, 109, 120, 131, 161, 163, 165, 169-70, 173-4, 185n, 195-6
Central Asia 12, 99
  and Russian diaspora 122
  attitude to 134-5
  internal borders 27
  states 27, 128, 134
Central Eastern Europe 71, 75
centrifugal forces 16, 165, 188-90, 193
Chechnya 30, 91, 109, 116, 171-3
  and bomb scare in Russia 175, 194
  as internal threat 34, 161, 169-74,

194-5
as Other 34, 169-70, 195-6
peace agreement with 48
people 14, 34, 174-5, 185n, 196
separatism 3, 16, 45, 48, 165-6, 172-3, 196
sharia laws 171-2
war 1994-96 3, 34, 48, 82, 85-86, 88, 90-1, 99, 145, 170-3, 196n
war 1999- 14, 34, 44n, 48, 77, 193-5
Chernomyrdin, V. 57
China
as model 109-11
as threat 95-96, 101-3
attitude to 101, 112, 114, 191
border 49, 102-3
cooperation with 101-6, 112
population growth 101
Christianity 137
Chuvashia 166
CIS 33, 104, 127-31, 133, 139n
citizenship 9, 121
civic culture 9-10
civic national identity 1, 9-16, 18, 26, 59, 72, 81, 87-89, 140, 145, 159, 171, 176, 187-90, 192-3, 195-6
civil society 76, 155
Civil War 160
civil war, risks of 167
clan-based societies 28, 134
Clash of Civilizations 100
clay 145
cleavages 32, 86-87, 89-91, 169
Clinton, B. 98
Cohen, S. 43n
Cold War 94-95, 190
collective amnesia 25
collective identity 6, 11, 13, 21, 37, 144
and action 8, 33
construction 7, 18, 23, 26-27, 87, 187
non-spatial 28
spatial 27-28
study of 32, 37-38, 41
collective remembrance 25
collectivisation 83
common heritage 21
Commonwealth of Independent States,
see CIS
Communist Party of the Russian Federation, see KPRF
Communist Party of the Soviet Union (KPSS) 2, 56, 80, 153, 156
computerisation 192
Congress of People's Deputies 46, 147
control group 31
conversion 51-53
corruption 154, 163
Cottam, M. 7
Crimean Tatars 14
crude oil 49, 51, 53, 182
cudgel 77, 159
customs union 129, 134
Czechoslovakia 83, 88

Dagestan 195
Dahrendorf, R. 193
daily plebiscite 188
default 60, 92n, 186, 191
Democratic Choice of Russia (DVR) 55, 57
democracy 2, 75, 77, 146-8, 152, 154-9, 193
as smoke screen 151, 155, 158
consolidation of 147, 150
economic 154
extent of in Russia 146-55, 159
in Soviet period 146
negative connotations 149, 156-8
progress towards 154, 180
democratisation 66, 155, 158
determinism 75, 159
dialectics 90
diamonds 51
diaries 35
diffusion 68
Dijkink, G. 118n
diplomatic means 117, 122
direct naming 42
disintegration 1, 16, 142, 159, 163-4, 166, 172, 178
Dnepropetrovsk 72
donor 51-52, 58n
dorogi 191, 194
Dostoyevskii, F. 124-5

Dudayev, D. 170
duraki 191-2, 195

economic threats 95
education 63, 76, 147, 154, 174
elections 19, 55-56, 147, 150, 154
    duma 1993 3, 56-57
    duma 1995 54, 56-57
    duma 1999 3, 54, 56-57, 184n
    presidential 1996 54, 152-3, 184n, 196n
    presidential 2000 4, 54, 194-5
electronic media 151-2
elephant in living room 25, 186
emotional bonds 9-10, 12, 16, 26, 196
enemy image 9, 14, 93-94, 100, 112, 160-2, 173-5, 185n, 191, 196
England 97
Estonia 13, 30, 115-6, 121-2, 128, 139n, 144
ethnic national identity 1, 9-11, 15, 26, 72, 195-6
Eurasianism 73
Europe 60, 101, 104-6, 113-5, 128, 137, 157
European Union (EU) 104-5, 130
executive branch 3, 47-48, 149, 153-4, 169, 180, 193-4

false Dmitriis 78
family metaphor 133, 191
Far Abroad 30
Far East 31, 49, 102-3, 144, 150, 152, 166-7, 182-3, 191-2, 196n
Far Eastern identity 196n
Far Eastern Republic 166
fata morgana 125
February revolution 75, 160
Federation Council 45, 48
Federation Treaty 45, 47
Finland 13, 104-6, 118n, 144
Finnish Winter War 88
flags 164
focus groups 35
foreign advisors 153
Former Soviet Union 30, 104-5, 120, 128
    and Russian diaspora 120-1
    assessment of 105, 127-8, 133
    cooperation with 104
    reintegration 121, 129-30
France 12, 104-6

Gaidar, Y. 57, 111
Garden Ring 179
Gazprom 154, 182
genetic pool 83
geopolitics 137
Germany
    business interests 105
    cooperation with 104-6
    as model 110
    Nazi past 53, 80, 92n, 105
    post-war experience 80
Gerndt, H. 43n
globalisation 192
glorified past 7
glory 26, 61, 81, 118, 173
Godot 184
golden age 10, 21, 23, 26
Gorbachev, M. 2, 24, 107, 123, 189
Grachev, P. 90
Great Patriotic War 67, 70, 72-73
    as centrepiece of identity 59-60, 65-67, 72, 89, 186
    as model 63, 70-71
    cult of 22, 92n
    pride in 59-63, 65-68, 71, 73
    reconstruction efforts 72
    Victory 73
Great reformers 62, 68-70, 75
Greenfeld, L. 89
Groznyi 172
Gulag archipelago 25, 50
Gulf of Finland 51
Gusinskii, V. 152

health care 147
Hedetoft, U. 10, 71
Hellberg Hirn, E. 18
Heradstveit, D. 35
Herb, G.H. 28
Hirshberg, M. S. 8

history
   and identity 21, 27
   different readings 22-23
   distortion 22, 83
   existential use 23
   legitimating use 24
   non-use 24-25, 71, 80, 90
   revisionism 84
Holocaust 84
Honour and Motherland 55, 57
Hoxha, E. 118n
human rights 154-5, 184n
Huntington, S. 100

ideal types 11
images 6-7
   of Others 8-9, 15, 93, 112
   partners 8
Imperial Russia 13
independent fiefdoms 164, 166
independents 55, 66, 86, 96, 127, 131-2, 148
India 101, 104-6, 117
Indian Ocean 117
indoctrination 10
in-group 8, 12-13, 17, 23, 34, 189, 196
Ingushetia 173
inside/outside divide 175
insider/outsider problem 40
instrumentality 23-24, 37-39
integration 129-34
intellectual resources 125
inter-city competition 179
internal cohesion 1-2, 5, 8, 17-18, 27, 32, 71, 162, 169, 176, 187, 189-90, 192
internal enemies 159-62, 165
International Relations theory 16
inter-religious relations 174
interviewee profiles 43n, 206-8
interviewer effect 104, 106, 119n
interviews 18
   and identity 35, 39, 41-43
   closed-ended questions 35-36
   open-ended questions 35-36
   questionnaire 42, 209
   respondent categories 31-33, 54-57
   semi-structured 36, 41-42
   taping 38, 42
   transcripts 36
intra-state tension 179
intra-West solidarity 189
Iran 95
Iraq 97
Islam 99-100, 137, 174, 191
   as external threat 95, 100
   as internal threat 100, 163, 165, 169, 171, 173, 175
   as threat 95-96, 99-100, 173-5
Islamic fundamentalism 34, 99-100, 163, 169, 173, 175, 179, 195-6
Islamic states 95, 166, 170, 175
   cooperation with 100
Ivan IV (the Terrible) 79, 153, 160
Ivanov, V.N. 43n

Japan 50, 95. 104-5
Jesus 174
Jewish Autonomous Oblast (JAO) 50, 54, 182
Jewry 50, 175
Joint Chiefs of Staff 98
judiciary 155, 185n
judoka 194
junior partner 134

Kampuchea 118n
Kaplowitz, N. 19-20
Karlsson, K-G. 23
Kazakhstan 116, 129, 134, 143
Kazaks 135
KGB 41
Khabarovsk 1, 31, 38, 52, 54, 58n, 60-64, 70, 73, 82, 84-85, 91, 95, 102-3, 105-6, 109, 112, 116, 118n, 122, 130, 139n, 142, 146, 149-50, 153-4, 164, 172-3, 175, 184
   background information 49-50
   energy costs 49, 184
   regional identity 188
   relations with centre 179, 182-4, 192
   transportation costs 49, 183
Khabarovsk Krai 50, 54, 173, 183-4
Khasavyurt agreement 48

Khasbulatov, R. 46
Khmer Rouge 118n
Khrushchev, N. 24, 66
Kiev 29, 133
Kingston-Mann, E. 185n
Kolikov, N.V. 43n
Komi-Permyak Autonomous Okrug 109
Korea 50
Kosovo 97-98, 106
KPRF 54-57, 61, 65-66, 70, 78, 85-87,
    92n, 96, 110, 112, 120, 130-3, 146,
    157-8, 163, 168-9, 173-5, 184n, 192
    background information 55-56
Krasnodar 109
Krasnoyarsk 166-7, 183
krai 45, 50, 166
Krasnyi Oktyabr' 167, 182
Krutov, A.N. 31
kulaks 160
Kurile Islands 167
Kymlicka, W. 10, 15, 44n
Kyrgyzstan 129, 134

Lane, D. 107, 119n
Latvia 13, 30, 115, 121-2, 128, 139n,
    144
Lebed, A. 48, 57, 167
legislative branch 3, 153, 155
legitimacy 3, 17, 24, 47, 154, 188, 193
Lenin, V. 24, 92n
Leningrad 51-52, 114
lesson-drawing 68
Levitan 176
Liberal Democratic Party (LDPR) 55,
    57, 65, 124
    background information 55-57
linguistic practice 86, 151
Lithuania 13, 30, 128, 139n
Little Russia 143
locale 27
local self-government 76, 155
loyalty 9, 12, 60, 162, 188
Lukashenka, A. 129, 132
Luzhkov, Y. 177, 180-1

Maastricht Treaty 27
Magomedov, A. 36

mantra 120
Maskhadov, A. 48
mass media 44n, 147, 150-2
McAuley, M. 44n
media barons 152
Mediterranean 117
Merton, R.K. 36
metaphor 42, 151, 156, 163, 186
Middle East 117
migration 102, 184
military-industrial complex 50-53, 184
military production 182
miners' blockade 168
Minin, K. 78
mission 8, 25-26, 136
mixed marriages 174
models 109
    Chinese 101, 109-11
    domestic 68-70, 71, 74, 77, 118n
    foreign 39, 107-9, 111, 119n
    German 110
    liberal 111
    paternalistic 111
    Scandinavian 119n
    social democratic 111
    Swedish 109-11, 119n
    United States 110-1, 113-4, 117
    Western 74
Moldova 139n
Molotov 50
Mongol yoke 12, 138
monocultured economy 49
mortgaging the future 125, 135, 195
Moscow 1, 30-31, 38-39, 44n, 45, 47,
    54, 78, 139n, 175, 178, 181, 195
    850th anniversary 178
    and regional identity 178
    and Russian identity 30, 51
    as capital 51, 177-8
    as federal centre 57, 103, 172, 177-9,
        182, 184, 196
    as Other 178, 187
    City Duma 31, 180
    competition with St. Petersburg 52,
        179-81
    living standards 177
    relations with regions 31, 177-8

Moses, J.C. 53
mosque 174
multi-polar world 106
Murmansk 109
Muslim card 163
myth 8, 10, 26, 68, 71, 92n, 186
Möller, P.U. 41-42

Narva 75
nation 28, 44n, 81, 92n
  civic 9-11, 15
  conflation with state 9
  ethnic 9-11, 15
national idea 160
national identity 1, 6, 12, 29, 81, 135
  and national self-images 1, 6-8, 188
  and war experience 70-71
  as challenged paradigm 27
  construction 12, 26, 28, 59, 72, 79, 160, 173
  development 12-13
  in Russia 13, 22, 32, 141
  study of 6, 40-41, 43
national interest 128, 144
national mobiliser 59, 66
national security 93-96, 99, 112, 118, 144, 161, 167-9, 173, 175, 187, 190, 193
national self-image 1-2, 5, 6-8, 15-16, 32-33, 43n, 55, 88, 91, 135, 140, 143, 186, 190
  and the future tense 135-6
  adjectival use 9
  affective aspects 7, 21, 80-81
  and collective action 8, 16-17, 162
  and images of Others 8, 93, 161, 176
  and national identity 1, 6, 10, 41, 43n, 140, 188
  and regional challenges 18
  cognitive aspects 7, 21
  construction 86, 102
  contending versions 17-18, 31-32, 89
  core 140
  definition 6-7
  external dimension 93-119
  external/internal dimension 120-39
  functions and effects 8-9, 17
  internal dimension 140-85
  main dimensions 5, 21-30, 133
  operational elements 19-20, 25
  outsider's view 40
  past dimension 7-8, 20-21, 59-92, 189
  study of 20, 34, 37-38, 41-43, 140
  unifying elements 186
nationalism 142, 163, 169, 173, 195
nationalist card 163
Nato 33-34
  and Ukraine 133
  as threat 95-96
  extension to the east 33
  Kosovo campaign 97, 106
Near Abroad 30, 116, 120-2, 127-8, 139n
near past 81
  assessment of 59, 86, 90
neighbouring countries 112, 128
networks 27, 104
Neumann, I.B. 14
New Russians 185n
Neva 51
Nikolaevsk-na-Amure 49
Nizhnii Novgorod 54, 78
nomenklatura 54
non-identity 111
Nordic countries 106
Northern Caucasus 161, 163, 169-70, 173-4, 195
North Ossetia 44n
nostalgia 55-56, 84, 120
Not-Abroad 30
Novgorod 30, 114
nuclear parity 113
nuclear weapons 16, 95-97
Nuremberg process 91

objective causes 89
objective reality 40, 42
oblast 45, 50, 166
October 1993 3, 147, 153, 156
October coup 82, 89
October revolution 61, 64-66, 85, 88, 160
official nationalism 10, 12, 16, 18
  in Imperial Russia 13

Soviet 13
official nationhood, see official nationalism
oil companies 177, 182
okrugi 45
Olympics 124-5
opportunists 156
organised crime 162-3, 169
Orwell, G. 24
Ossetia 173
Other 15, 87, 103, 171
   external 189
   images of 8-9, 15, 29, 93, 103, 107
   internal 95, 170-1, 179, 195
   non-physical 87
Othering 13-14, 28-29, 34, 87, 135, 176, 178, 187-8
Our Home is Russia (NDR) 55, 57, 149
out-group 8-9, 12, 34, 87, 93, 134, 162, 190, 196
outsider's view 40, 77
overextension 134

Pacific Ocean 49
Pakistan 95
Palestine 50
partocrats 156
passports 164
path metaphors 151
patriotism 126, 189
Patton, M.Q. 35
peacekeeping 128, 138
Pearson, D. 43n
pensions 147, 154
perestroika 2, 24, 66, 75
Perm 1, 31, 38-39, 52, 54, 61, 70, 82, 85, 92n, 95-96, 105-6, 109, 112, 116, 120, 122-3, 130-1, 133, 136, 139, 150, 157, 161
   background information 47, 50-51
   pilot study 44n
   relations with centre 179, 188
Perm Oblast 50, 172
Persian Gulf 117
Peter I (the Great) 30, 51, 59, 62-70, 73-75, 77-78, 89, 107, 160, 186-7
Peter Paul fortress 51

Petersson, B. 43n
Petrograd 51
pilot study 31, 41, 44n, 61
Pipes, R. 52
Poland 13, 78
politeness effect 39
political parties (in general) 55, 155
pollution 53
Poltava 75
poltora 108
population growth 101
power ministries 170
Pozharskii, Prince D. 78
presidential representatives 193
pride 7, 10, 12, 23, 56, 59, 62-64, 66, 73-74, 81, 88, 114-5, 180, 187, 189
pride/shame balance 70, 79-80
Primorskii Krai 196n
prostitution 157
Pskov 114
Pushkin, A. 124-5
Putin, V. 4-5, 34, 47-48, 54, 77, 92n, 169, 188, 193-5
Putnam, R. 35

Quebec 27
question-begging 41, 175
questionnaire 44n

racism 101
Real Abroad 128
Red Belt 31, 53, 61, 85, 149, 179, 181
referendum
   on Constitution 3, 19, 46-47, 140, 165
regional identity 27, 33, 178-9, 187-8, 196n
Renan, E. 25, 188
respondents
   age groups 57
   categories 31-33, 54-57
   non-Russian 57
   political affiliations 55
   regional mix 54
   women 57
Ringmar, E. 18
Rio de Janeiro 193

Rodina 29
role model 103, 107
Romanovs 78
rossiyane 11, 13, 15, 176, 196
rule of law 140
Russia
  and Chechnya 34
  and China 101-3, 112, 191
  and democracy 75, 77
  and foreign role models 107, 109
  and Germany 105
  and Islam 173-5, 191
  and loss of Union 30
  and national identity 11-15, 22, 26, 28-30, 41, 43, 59, 87, 173, 187-91, 196
  and Othering 160-1, 171, 174, 190, 195-6
  and the West 13
  and Ukraine 133
  and United States 98, 106, 112-5, 118, 190-1
  as balancer 137
  as bridge 137-8
  as example 138
  as symbol 143
  attitude to 140-1, 145
  cultural heritage 13, 62, 66, 123-5
  diaspora 33, 115-7, 120-2, 126, 128, 143
  Empire 12-13, 24, 49, 60, 62, 141
  European 144
  extent of 30, 124, 135, 141-4
  external threats 93-103, 106, 118, 158-9, 165, 190
  geographical extension 124
  great power status 4, 16, 21, 26, 74, 84, 98, 101, 117-8, 120-6, 128, 135-7, 139
  history 1, 22-23, 59-92, 107, 138, 143, 153, 160
  in Soviet period 134, 141
  industrialisation 63
  internal threats 94-95, 100, 107, 144, 159-61, 165, 167-8, 175, 191, 193
  international orientation 73
  international partners 100, 104-6
  Jewry 175
  land mass 101, 108, 165
  lands 144
  language 13, 45, 124, 139n, 143
  loss of superpower status 98, 117, 123-4, 136
  mentality 114, 159
  mission 122, 135-9
  multiculturalism 137
  natural resources 124
  near past 1, 59
  people 62, 66, 71, 83, 90, 123, 143, 167-8
  Petrine 73-75, 77, 141
  political leaders 191
  pre-revolutionary 141
  resurrection of Empire 140
  spheres of influence 117-8, 126-8
  uniqueness 108-9, 137-8
  vastness 16, 123-4, 138, 190, 192
Russia's Choice (VR) 58n
Russian Communist Workers' Party (RKPR) 55
Russian Federation
  and Caucasus 165
  and Chechnya 48, 91, 99, 166, 170-3, 190, 195
  and Nato 97
  and Tatarstan 47, 165
  and the CIS 128
  and the customs union 134
  and the former Soviet Union 104, 121-2, 133-5, 191
  attitude to 126, 140, 145
  borders 102, 121, 127, 141-4
  budget 47, 49, 51-52, 58n
  centre-region relations 1, 14, 44n, 47-48, 86, 146, 166, 177-9, 181-3, 189, 192
  Constitution 45-48, 140, 142, 146, 153, 178, 184n
  democracy 75, 146-51, 155-9, 193
  denomination 126, 140-2
  internal cohesion 15, 32, 34, 87, 162, 176, 178, 187, 189-91, 196
  national republics 31, 44n, 45-47, 142, 164, 166, 177, 188

negative connotations 145
North-South divide 54
nuclear weapons 16, 123
political crisis 75, 78, 139, 156, 159, 176
political leadership 91
political parties 55-56
population 11, 15, 29, 123, 143
president 2-4, 28, 46, 48, 129, 151-4, 162, 167, 169, 177, 188, 193-4
regions 3-4. 17, 32, 45, 58n, 177-84
regional identities 178
risks of disintegration 163-4, 166-7, 171-2
separatism 163
socio-economic crisis 14, 17, 43n, 68, 134, 154-6, 168-9, 176
under Putin 194-5
union with Belarus 129-33
Russian Federative Republic 2
Russian Regions (political bloc) 55, 57
Russian-Orthodox faith 13
Russian-speaking population 116
russkie 11, 13-15, 32, 43n, 45, 57, 91, 120, 133, 143, 176, 188, 191, 196

Sakhalin 109
Sakwa, R. 139n
salted pickle 41-42
Saratov 181
Scandinavia 104, 119n
scapegoating 2, 134, 161, 170, 176, 187, 195
secret police 160
semi-democracy 149
Semipalatinsk 102
separation of powers 154
separatism 161-2, 169, 195
Serbia 97, 106
shame 7, 22, 38, 64, 70, 80-90, 170, 173, 187
shame avoidance 88
sharia 171-2
Shevtsova, L. 196n
Shlapentokh, V. 189
shock therapy 111
Siberia 144, 168

Slavophiles 12-13, 73
Slavs 13, 143
Slovakia 43n
Smith, A. 43n
Smith, K. 92n
smuta 78
Snickers 124
social construction 8-9, 12, 18, 26, 43, 59, 70, 72, 87, 89, 103, 159-60, 188
social control 159
Social Darwinism 65
Social Democratic Party 55
South Africa 121
South Korea 105
sovereignty 166, 177
Sovetskaya Gavan' 49
Soviet man 14
Soviet Union 24, 28, 39, 103
  achievements 63
  and Central Asia 134
  and democracy 146-7
  and national identity 13
  and the Great Patriotic War 22, 60-61
  and United States 113
  as undisputed great power 122
  assessment 60, 64, 86-87, 89, 187
  colonialism 49
  continued mental existence 4, 128
  dissolution 1-2, 19, 23, 30, 34, 49, 52, 66-67, 75, 79, 84, 86, 88, 134, 158, 167, 189
  education 22, 174
  global role 136-7
  history distortion 22, 24
  industrial structure 50, 52, 183-4
  internal enemies 160
  inter-religious relations 174-5
  Jewry 49
  migration 184
  models for contemporary Russia 69-70, 77-78, 107
  national identity 14
  nostalgia 55-56, 84, 128, 131
  patriotism 189
  political legitimation 24-25
  political system 78
  pride in 59, 61-64, 66-69, 88, 187

reestablishment 78, 120, 128-9, 132, 140
shame of 80-83, 85-86, 88-89, 187
socio-economic safety net 67
space programme 59, 62, 65-67
superpower status 62, 109, 113, 117, 120-1, 123-4
territorial subdivisions 45
spheres of influence 126-7
stabiliser 137
St. Petersburg 1, 22, 30-31, 39, 45, 47, 54-55, 57, 61-63, 69-70, 73-74, 76, 82-83, 85, 89-90, 95, 99-100, 102-3, 105-6, 109, 116, 122, 126, 130-1, 145-7, 150, 154, 163-4, 166, 171
and Russian identity 51
as capital 51
as cultural capital 180
background information 49, 51-53
competition with Moscow 51-52, 179-81
liberal sentiments 149
regional identity 180, 187-8
relations with centre 179-81
Stalin, Y. 14, 24-25, 28, 38, 50, 52-53, 70, 81-89, 92n, 104, 146, 153, 160, 186, 190
Stalingrad 53, 58n
State Duma 30-31, 44n, 45, 54, 56, 59, 61-62, 65, 78-79, 82, 96-98, 100, 105-6, 108, 110, 124-5, 127-31, 136, 139, 146, 149-50, 157, 159, 163-4, 173, 178, 184n
state-centred paradigm 16, 28
Stepashin, S. 90-91, 92n
Stockholm 30
Stolypin, P. 59, 62, 65-67, 69-70, 75-77
strategic goods 94
strong hand 74, 77, 79, 158-9, 193
sub'ekt 45, 58n, 179
subgroups 60-61, 65-66, 70, 85, 90, 92n, 96, 104, 110, 127, 131, 136, 138, 147-8, 163
subsistence, minimal level of 43n
Sucharov, M. 43n
superpower 98, 112, 115
Sweden 30, 39, 75, 77, 97, 104-6, 111, 114, 119n, 176
as model 109-10, 119n

Tajikistan 28, 99, 128-9, 134
Tajiks 135
Tataro-Mongols 114
Tatarstan 45-47, 163, 165-6, 175, 177
taxes 46-47, 164, 177, 182
technology 114
telecommunications 192
telephone law 155
television 151-2, 157, 192
threats 9, 93, 173, 187, 190
economic 95-96
external 93-103, 112, 114, 118, 161, 189-90
internal 34, 93-95, 144, 159-71, 173, 175-6, 190-1, 193, 195
military 93
non-material 97
non-military 93
time factor 96-97, 131
Time of Troubles 78-79
totalitarianism 159
Tower of London 52
Tractor plant 53, 167
traitors 84, 86, 104
Transcaucasus 170
Transdnistriya 119, 139n
Trans-Siberian railway 49
Trotsky, L. 25
Troyakova, T. 196n
Tsaritsyn 53
Tumarkin, N. 22, 60, 71, 73, 92n
Turkey 166
turncoats 156

Ukraine 2, 72, 132, 143
and Russian identity 30, 133
assessment of 133
cooperation with 133
unemployment 158, 182, 184
United Nations 98, 185n
United States 4, 106, 113, 118n, 123, 125, 137
admiration of 115-117
as model 94, 108, 110-1, 113, 117,

122, 126
  as superpower 120
  as threat 95-101, 106, 111-2, 114, 137, 190
  as world policeman 117
  as yardstick 113, 116-8, 121
  assessment of 106, 114
  cooperation with 104-6, 113-5
  denigration of 113-5, 117
  Kosovo campaign 97
  mixed feelings against 112-3, 191
Unity/The Bear 4, 54, 56
Ural mountains 50, 144
usable past 23, 79
Ussuri 49
Uzbekistan 134
Uzbeks 135

van Alphen, E. 43n
Vanino 49
Vergangenheitsbewältigung 25, 88
Victory Day 92n
Vladivostok 196n
Volga Germans 14
Volgodonsk 175
Volgograd 1, 22, 31, 39, 53-55, 58n, 61-64, 68, 70, 73, 76, 82-86, 89-90, 94-95, 98, 102, 105-6, 109, 122-3, 130, 133, 136, 143, 145-6, 150, 152-3, 157-9, 163-4, 167-8, 175-6
  background information 53-54, 58n
  oppositional sentiments 83
  Red Belt location 149, 179, 181
  regional identity 188
  relations with centre 177, 179-82, 192
Volgograd Oblast 53, 167, 181-2

wage arrears 72, 154
Wagnsson, C. 33-35, 43n
Walker, R.B.J. 28-29
Washington 98
War of the Laws 48
weak centre, strong regions 177
Westernisers 12-13, 73
White House 3, 153
window on the west 52, 74, 77, 187
Witte, S. 62, 70, 77
women
  political representation 57
World War I 69
World War II 14, 52-53, 59-60, 113

xenophobia 160

Yabloko 55-56, 65
Yakovlev, V. 181
Yakutia 163
Yaroslavl 114
Yavlinskii, G. 56
Yeltsin, B. 1-4, 45-48, 54, 57, 60, 78-79, 82, 84-86, 88, 104, 122, 129, 147, 153, 166-71, 177, 184n, 188, 190, 192, 194, 196n
younger brethren 191
Yugoslavia 97-98

zemstvo 76-77
Zhirinovskii Bloc 58n
Zhirinovskii, V. 56-57, 140, 144
Zionism 176
Ziuganov, G. 56, 129, 153